This book is published with the consent and cooperation of POPULAR MECHANICS Magazine.

POPULAR MECHANICS Staff:
Editor-in-Chief: Joe Oldham
Managing Editor Production: Deborah Frank
Graphics Director: Bryan Canniff
Automotive Editor: Tony Swan
Home Improvement Editor: Steven Willson
Electronics/Photography Editor: Frank Vizard
Boating/Outdoors Editor: Joe Skorupa
Science Editor: Abe Dane
Editorial Production: John Bostonian Jr.

**POPULAR MECHANICS
1992 YEARBOOK**
Editor:
  C. Edward Cavert
Manufacturing:
  Ron Schoenfeld
Book Design and Production:
  The Bookmaker
  Fairfax, Virginia
Editorial Assistance:
  Wilma Cavert
  Nancy Coggins
Cover Photography:
  Brian Kosoff
Cover Design:
  Alan Andresen

ISBN 0–87851–119–9
Library of Congress Catalog Card Number: 85–81760
GST Hearst Registration No. R105218291.

10 9 8 7 6 5 4 3 2 1
Printed in the United States of America

Although every effort has been made to ensure the accuracy and completeness of the information in this book, Hearst Direct Books and Popular Mechanics Magazine make no guarantees, stated or implied, nor will they be liable in the event of misinterpretation or human error made by the reader or for any typographical errors that may appear. Plans for projects illustrated in this book may not meet all local zoning and building code requirements for construction. Before beginning any major project, consult with local authorities or see a structural architect. WORK SAFELY WITH HAND AND POWER TOOLS. WEAR EYE PROTECTION. READ MANUFACTURER'S INSTRUCTIONS AND WARNINGS FOR PRODUCTS.

PIPE FITTINGS

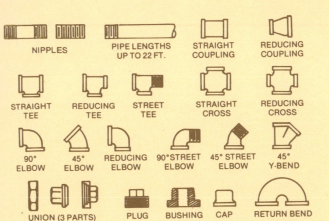

Here are the common steel pipe fittings. Nipples are simply short lengths of pipe threaded on both ends. Reducing fittings join two different sizes of pipe.

Compression fittings of the flared-tube type are the easiest for the novice to handle when working with copper tubing.

STANDARD STEEL PIPE (All Dimensions in Inches)					
Nominal Size	Outside Diameter	Inside Diameter	Nominal Size	Outside Diameter	Inside Diameter
1/8	0.405	0.269	1	1.315	1.049
1/4	0.540	0.364	1 1/4	1.660	1.380
3/8	0.675	0.493	1 1/2	1.900	1.610
1/2	0.840	0.622	2	2.375	2.067
3/4	1.050	0.824	2 1/2	2.875	2.469

SQUARE MEASURE
144 sq in = 1 sq ft
9 sq ft = 1 sq yd
272.25 sq ft = 1 sq rod
160 sq rods = 1 acre

VOLUME MEASURE
1728 cu in = 1 cu ft
27 cu ft = 1 cu yd

MEASURES OF CAPACITY
1 cup = 8 fl oz
2 cups = 1 pint
2 pints = 1 quart
4 quarts = 1 gallon
2 gallons = 1 peck
4 pecks = 1 bushel

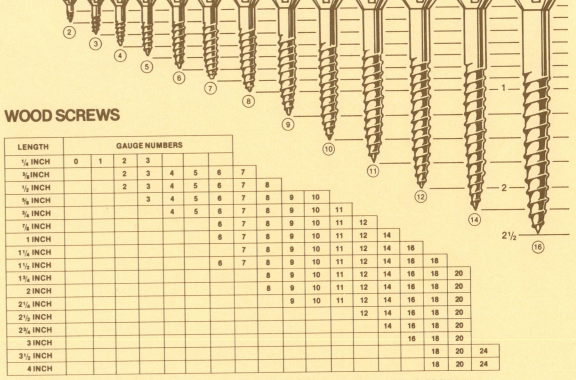

WOOD SCREWS

LENGTH	GAUGE NUMBERS														
1/4 INCH	0	1	2	3											
3/8 INCH			2	3	4	5	6	7							
1/2 INCH			2	3	4	5	6	7	8						
5/8 INCH				3	4	5	6	7	8	9	10				
3/4 INCH					4	5	6	7	8	9	10	11			
7/8 INCH							6	7	8	9	10	11	12		
1 INCH							6	7	8	9	10	11	12	14	
1 1/4 INCH								7	8	9	10	11	12	14	16
1 1/2 INCH						6	7	8	9	10	11	12	14	16	18
1 3/4 INCH								8	9	10	11	12	14	16	18	20
2 INCH								8	9	10	11	12	14	16	18	20
2 1/4 INCH									9	10	11	12	14	16	18	20
2 1/2 INCH												12	14	16	18	20
2 3/4 INCH													14	16	18	20
3 INCH													14	16	18	20
3 1/2 INCH														16	18	20	24
4 INCH															18	20	24

WHEN YOU BUY SCREWS, SPECIFY (1) LENGTH, (2) GAUGE NUMBER, (3) TYPE OF HEAD—FLAT, ROUND, OR OVAL, (4) MATERIAL—STEEL, BRASS, BRONZE, ETC., (5) FINISH—BRIGHT, STEEL BLUED, CADMIUM, NICKEL, OR CHROMIUM PLATED.

Popular Mechanics

do-it-yourself yearbook

The best illustrated home reference guide from the world's most authoritative source for today's how-to-do-it information.

1992

HEARST DIRECT BOOKS

NEW YORK

Contents

Basic masonry toolkit

■ Of the jobs that homeowners are likely to take on themselves, concrete and masonry improvements are among the most frequently avoided. To most of us, these jobs seem just too heavy and unforgiving to tackle alone. The skills required to get the work done right the first time are often specialized and unfamiliar.

While these reservations may be justified on large projects, most smaller concrete and masonry chores are within just about everyone's reach. With some preparation and the right equipment, jobs like repair-ing loose brickwork, pouring a walkway slab and even building a concrete-block wall are well within the range of the average do-it-yourselfer's abilities. Starting off with the right tools can make all the difference between a job done well and a call to a pro to make things right.

The 17 tools featured here will help you handle any masonry or concrete project—large or small. The collection is made up of professional-grade tools. While the complete toolkit isn't cheap (the one shown totaled about $225), buying better quality tools is generally an economical move if you expect to use them often. With the exception of the trowels, however, you could substitute less expensive equipment. Cheap trowels, by contrast, will leave their signatures on every job. A few years from now you'll have forgotten the extra dollars paid for a better tool, but the results of an unsatisfactory, inexpensive tool will be around for some time.

Text and photos for *Basic Masonry Toolkit* by Merle Henkenius.

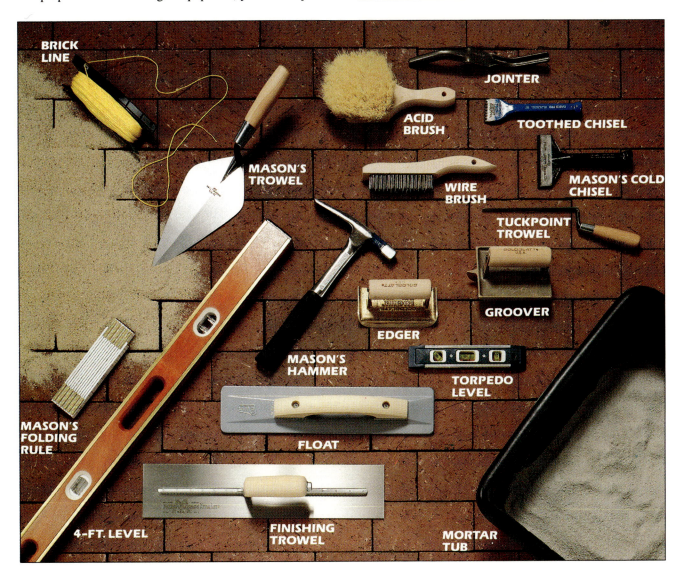

BRICK LINE

JOINTER

ACID BRUSH

TOOTHED CHISEL

MASON'S TROWEL

WIRE BRUSH

MASON'S COLD CHISEL

TUCKPOINT TROWEL

EDGER

GROOVER

MASON'S HAMMER

TORPEDO LEVEL

MASON'S FOLDING RULE

FLOAT

4-FT. LEVEL

FINISHING TROWEL

MORTAR TUB

1 After screeding the concrete level with the form, use a hand float to smooth the slab and pull cement to the surface.

2 When the surface has been floated, compact and round slab perimeter with an edger. Follow the inside of the form.

3 Use a groover to cut control joints in sidewalks, drives and outdoor slabs. It should penetrate one-quarter of thickness.

4 Finish by sweeping a trowel in half circles across slab. Hold trowel nearly level. Use two passes for smooth surface.

Along with describing each tool shown, there is also some basic information on how and when the tools are used. Most of the tools are designed for concrete work—slabs, walks and driveways. Some are for masonry projects—laying brick or concrete block or repairing mortar joints. Depending on the kind of projects you're going to handle, you may need all the tools or you may get by with a selection that suits the job at hand.

Mortar Mixing Tub

When mixing small quantities of mortar or cement with a garden hoe or shovel, a plastic mortar box is a handy piece of equipment. Made of tough, flexible ABS plastic, these seamless tubs are easy to clean—even when the mortar has been allowed to set for too long. The usual size will handle roughly 2-cu.-ft. batches at a time (two bags of premixed concrete).

Larger projects, of course, require a rotating-drum-type mixer or curbside truck delivery. Electric- or gas-powered rotating-drum mixers can be rented when they're required.

Concrete Finishing Float

When constructing concrete slabs, the concrete is first poured into wooden forms, and then screeded (trimmed level to the top of the form with a 2×4 or 2×6 board). The next step, after the water settles, is to float the surface with a magnesium or wood hand float. Sweeping the float across the surface will smooth and compact the concrete. It will also draw cement up to the surface for a harder finish. A floated slab of concrete should have an even, but gritty appearance.

When floating, start with a small area. If the surface puddles and appears too smooth, you've started too soon—wait for the slab to dry slightly before trying again. Floating too early will cause crazing or dusting at the surface. *Crazing* is a condition where the surface develops tiny hairline cracks. *Dusting* is evidenced by a chalky appearance on the cured surface. Both conditions are avoidable if you float the slab at the correct time.

5 Use mason's trowel to first spread mortar along preceding course. Then butter end of the next brick and set in place.

6 With the new brick in place, tap it down with the trowel handle and slice away the excess mortar with the edge of the trowel.

7 Once the mortar in the joint begins to set, strike each joint with a jointer to form a smooth, compressed seam.

8 To cut a concrete block, tap the chisel lightly in a line completely around the block until the two halves fall apart.

Edger and Groover

After floating and before the final troweling, edgers and groovers are used to trim the slab perimeter and form control joints. When the concrete begins to set, run an edger around the slab using the inside of the form as a guide. Ideally, the edger should round and compact the slab's edge without puddling or lining the concrete. If the concrete appears too wet, wait awhile and then try again.

Cutting control joints with a groover should be done at the same point in the process. Keep in mind that control joints are not merely decorative. By cutting a groove across a slab of concrete, the slab is deliberately weakened along that line. Stresses that might ordinarily create a crack along the slab surface will, instead, cause the slab to crack precisely and invisibly in the groove.

It's best to use a deep-blade groover to make control joints. If you have a shallow groover, use a trowel to cut the groove deeper. A control cut should penetrate one-quarter of the slab thickness. Control joints should be cut about every 40 in. in sidewalks and every 10 ft. in driveways.

Concrete Finishing Trowel

After the edges are trimmed, control joints are added and the concrete begins to set, the surface should be troweled with a good, long finishing trowel. Extra-smooth surfaces require two trowelings, while coarse surfaces may be troweled once and then broomed (drawing a broom across the surface to create a uniform texture). The trowel should glide over the surface in crescent-shaped sweeps and be held in a nearly flat position. As with floating, try a small area first. If you see water puddling behind the trowel, or the trowel leaves distinct edge lines or chatter marks (tiny ripples), then wait a bit longer.

Troweling at the right time is critical, so test the surface often. Ideally, the trowel will smooth the floated surface with two or three passes under medium pressure. Keep in mind that when troweling a large slab, you'll have to average out the entire job around the ideal troweling time. In other words, if it takes 30 minutes to trowel the slab, start when the surface is on the wet side of ideal. Otherwise, the concrete will be too dry to trowel properly when you reach the end of the job.

Avoid adding extra water to the mix in anticipation of the concrete setting before you've finished troweling. Although it may seem like this will provide added time to work, a wetter mix is always weaker than a dryer pour. Instead, you can extend the slab's setting time by wetting the soil bed before pouring the concrete.

If you're going to pour from a truck delivery, it's a good idea to have the driver come prepared with a small bottle of superplasticizer. When added to the mix before pouring, this additive will cause the concrete to work and feel wetter for about an hour without actually being wetter.

Masonry Trowel

The masonry trowel is the workhorse of the mason's trade. With it, you'll butter the ends of bricks and blocks, tap them into place, and even break bricks in two (by striking the brick several times with the trowel edge). For these reasons, a bargain-basement trowel just isn't good enough.

Masonry trowels are available in different sizes. Use a small one for brickwork and a large one for concrete blocks. If you're only going to buy one, an 8- to 10-in. model is a reasonable compromise. This size may feel a little hefty for the smaller jobs, but it will stand the test of time.

Jointer

A jointer is a narrow tool designed to fit between blocks or bricks for smoothing and sealing the mortar joints. It's used after the mortar has begun to set, and the most common type leaves a recessed, concave mortar line. Other styles are available for forming V joints or weather joints, where the mortar is flush with the lower course, but angled back so it's recessed under the upper course.

The mortar joint in brickwork is often finished with a related tool called a *rake*. Performing the same job as a jointer, this tool has two wheels and a protruding blade. When run along the joint, the blade trims the mortar to a uniform depth.

Masonry Levels

Because a perfectly level and plumb wall is the ultimate goal, you'll need to own a level—and use it often. A short torpedo level is useful for leveling individual bricks or blocks, while a 4- to 6-ft. level will keep the wall plumb and true. You won't need to check every block, or even every course of blocks, but you should check regularly to catch any accumulating error in level or plumb.

Mason's Rule

The mason's rule is a folding ruler that has a variety of spacing marks on its side. These are designed to help determine the number of courses in a wall and the mortar width. When bricking a wall that extends from a foundation to a soffit, for example, the first thing to determine is how many courses of brick will be needed to fill the space. You'll also need to know about any adjustment in mortar thickness so that the last course ends at the correct height. The spacing indicators printed on a mason's rule make these calculations quick and easy. You can, however, do the job with an ordinary tape measure, pencil and note pad.

Brick Line

The best way to keep each course from pitching up or down is to stretch a taught string horizontally along the wall. This string, or brick line, is tied at reach end to story poles, usually made on site from 2×4s. Each story pole has a mark every 8 in. so that a level line can be stretched across the wall at 1-block intervals.

Mason's Hammer and Chisels

A mason's hammer serves two purposes. It can be used conventionally to drive chisels and nails, or it can be turned over and used as a chisel to break blocks and bricks. The break that a hammer makes is fairly crude. To produce a more exact cut, a chisel is used. You'll find a variety of chisels available on the market from 4-in. cold chisels to tooth-edged mortar chisels.

When cutting blocks or bricks, use a cold chisel with a 3- or 4-in.-long edge. Don't try to do the job in one stroke. Instead, tap lightly in a line all around the block until it breaks evenly. The aim is to create a series of stress cracks that follow the line made by the chisel.

Tooth-edged chisels are used to remove old mortar and clean mortar joints in preparation for tuckpointing.

Tuckpoint Trowel

Tuckpointing is a method of packing mortar neatly between bricks or building stones. The method is frequently used to restore old masonry walls whose mortar is soft and crumbling.

In a typical situation, the joints are first cut deeper and cleaned with a tooth-edged chisel. Mortar is then placed on a mason's trowel, and the trowel is held against the brick next to the cleaned joint. The tuckpoint trowel is then used to slice off small amounts of mortar and squeeze it into the gap between the bricks or stones.

Cleanup Brushes

If you do much concrete or masonry work, you'll need at least two cleanup brushes. A soft-bristle acid brush and water will help rinse away mortar and concrete from tools and walls. If brick walls show too much mortar residue, they'll need to be brushed with muriatic acid or a special masonry detergent. Really stubborn bits of mortar and concrete can be brushed from tools and work with a wire-bristle brush.

Plate joiner users guide

■ Most woodworkers would agree that the bulk of woodworking is simply a matter of joining pieces of wood together in a neat, strong and efficient manner. There is a new tool that's catching on with pros and amateurs alike—the plate joiner.

The plate joiner is essentially a small, plunge-cutting circular saw. It's designed to quickly and accurately cut matching slots in pieces that are to be joined. Oval-shaped wooden plates (often called *biscuits*) are glued into the slots to join the pieces.

The plates are made of die-cut beech, with the grain oriented diagonally to resist breaking in the completed joint. The plates are compressed so they're slightly thinner than the slot.

When they come in contact with water-based glue, they quickly swell, locking the joint together. This means that you usually can remove your clamps sooner than with conventional joints so that they're free for the next assembly.

Plate Joiner Users Guide was written by Rosario Capotosto. Photos by Rosario Capotosto. Technical art by Eugene Thompson. For information on Lamello products, contact Colonial Saw, 100 Pennbroke St., Kingston, MA 02364.

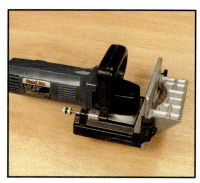

1 The Freud JS100 tool shows standard plate joiner configuration. Blade is gear-driven and motor has slide switch.

2 The upright handle and trigger-type ON/OFF switch makes the belt-driven Porter Cable 555 plate joiner unique.

3 Adjustable depth-of-cut stop has three positions to suit the three plate sizes. Knurled knob permits fine-tuning.

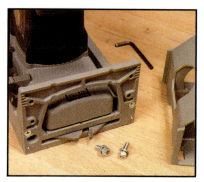

4 With fence removed, faceplate and blade are visible. Spring-loaded spurs on faceplate grip stock and prevent shifting.

Unlike dowel joinery, which requires precisely aligned holes, plate joinery permits as much as 3/32-in. lateral alignment of the parts immediately after assembly. Any slight misalignment of the slots is then easily compensated for.

Although relatively new to most small workshops, plate joinery was developed in the mid-'50s by Swiss cabinetmaker Herman Steiner, who subsequently marketed the Steiner Lamello plate-joiner system throughout Europe. Low-cost plate joiners have recently made this method affordable for all small shops and home woodworkers.

About The Tool

Several manufacturers offer plate joiners including Elu, Freud, Kaiser, Lamello, Porter-Cable and Vitruex. Although these machines have some design differences, the basic components are similar and they're all designed to accommodate standard plate sizes. Two popular models are the Freud JS 100 (Fig. 1) and the Porter-Cable 555 (Fig. 2). Both have a spring-loaded base that keeps the blade safely retracted until it's plunged into the work. An adjustable stop sets the depth of cut to match one of three plate

sizes: Small, No.0; Medium, No.10 and Large, No.20 (Fig. 3).

The faceplate of the typical plate joiner, the part that is held up against the workpiece, contains a pair of spurs to prevent the tool from shifting as the cut is made (Fig. 4). Joiners also have a fence for registering the tool against the surface of the work. The Lamello Top plate joiner, for example, has a completely adjustable fence that can be pivoted to suit any bevel angle from 0° to 90°. Other tools, such as the P-C and Freud tools shown, have nonpivoting fences that handle only the more common 45° and 90° operations.

Basic Plate Joinery

The speed and effectiveness of the plate joiner are due to the ease by which it can accurately register the plate slots so the mating pieces will align properly. The basic procedure for using a plate joiner involves referencing both the base of the tool and the work against a flat surface, such as your worktable. Here, the joiner fence is not used and the worktable top must be flat and clean for best results. Aligning the tool horizontally is done with the index mark on the faceplate.

5 The first step in making a plate joint is to align mating pieces and mark the center of the plate joint slot on both pieces.

6 Align index mark on joiner faceplate with centerline of joint. Turn on power and push forward to make the slot.

7 Apply glue to the slots and to the surfaces to be butted. Insert plate in one slot, join the second piece and clamp.

First, align both pieces as they are to be joined and mark the center of the plate joint slot on each piece (Fig. 5). Then, with both the plate joiner and the workpiece resting on the worktable, align the index marks of the plate joiner with the mark on the first piece. Turn on the motor and quickly advance and retract the blade to make the cut (Fig. 6). Then, repeat the process on the other piece and apply glue to the slots. Insert the plate in one slot (Fig. 7), and join the pieces. Before clamping, check that the registration marks on the pieces are aligned and shift the components, if necessary.

Note that the index mark on the faceplate aids in aligning the slot with the end or edge of the stock, while the actual surface of the worktable registers the slot across the thickness of the stock. When using the joiner in this manner, be sure the worktable is clean and flat, and place the finish side of the wood down for the best alignment.

While the most direct way to apply glue is simply to squirt a little along the slot and push it in with a thin stick, this method isn't very efficient. With fast-setting glue and many slots to fill, it can be frustrating. The best tool for this job is the specifically designed Lamello glue bottle. This has a narrow nozzle with holes on the sides for distributing glue in the slot. You can, however, improvise a simpler and even cheaper substitute by using a slim-nozzle hair-coloring applicator available at cosmetic counters. Simply increase the hole size to $3/32$ in. to handle the thicker glue, and use a wax-coated toothpick as a stopper.

Because the plate joiner blade is centered $7/16$ in. from the plane of its base, it registers a slot that's centered $7/16$ in. from one face of the stock. Although this puts the slot slightly off center in $3/4$- or $13/16$-in.-thick lumber, the asymmetrical slot has little effect on the joint. Just be sure that the working face of each component to be joined is placed down on the worktable before the cut is made. When the stock is especially thick or extra strength is required, you can simply cut two parallel slots, each $7/16$ in. from the stock faces.

8 To position slot at center of thin stock, such as $1/2$-in. plywood panel, install fence at correct distance from blade.

9 This mitered edgebanding uses two plate sizes: No.10 plate for the narrow miter and No.20 along the panel edges.

10 Edge mitering is done by setting the fence for 45°. Most tools register against the inside of the joint as shown here.

11 To join shelf to case side, first clamp shelf to side panel at shelf location. Then mark joint centers on both panels.

12 With base of tool held flat against cabinet side, align index mark with slot centers and cut all slots in shelf edge.

13 To cut corresponding slots in cabinet side, hold tool upright against shelf edge and align index mark with centers.

14 After all slots have been made, apply glue, insert plates and assemble. Check for accurate alignment before clamping.

For precisely centering the slot in thin stock, or when the size of the work prohibits using a worktable as a reference surface, you can use the adjustable joiner fence. To use the fence for basic edge-to-edge operations, such as applying a solid-wood banding around a plywood panel, first adjust the fence so the slot will be positioned appropriately across the stock thickness. Then, mark the slot positions on the mating pieces. Hold the fence firmly against the face of the work with the faceplate against the stock edge. Align the index mark and make the plunge cut (Fig. 8). When making the corresponding slots in the adjoining stock, make sure that the fence is held against the same working face to ensure good alignment.

Always use the largest plate permissible for the joint being made and adjust the depth slightly deeper than one-half the plate width. Bear in mind that the actual slot is longer than the plate that's suited for it. This places limitations on the width of the stock used for both regular face frames and mitered frames. A No.20 plate, for example, will require at least a 3-in.-wide surface for the slot to be completely contained. The small No.0 plate needs only about 2¼ in. Using mitered frame joints allows slightly narrower stock, as the angled joint face is longer than the stock width. Often, two size plates are necessary in one assembly (Fig. 9).

To cut slots for an edge-miter joint, set the fence in the 45° miter position and make the cuts. Most joiners, such as the Freud unit shown, register the cut against the inside work surface (Fig. 10). The Porter-Cable fence (visible in Fig. 8) registers against the outside surface. This system ensures that the outside of the joint will be aligned regardless of variation in stock thickness.

Besides joining stock edge to edge, the plate joiner excels at edge-to-face joints typical in shelf and cabinet construction. Because there's no traditional joinery involved, each component can be cut to its exact size for assembly.

To join the edge of a shelf to a case side, first mark the shelf location on the side component. Position the shelf edge at this mark, align the side edges of both pieces, and secure the components with a clamp so

15 When edge gluing lumber, reference slots from best side of stock. Place slots 2 in. from end and 4 to 12 in. between.

16 Offset joints can be made by supporting the tool on a spacer block to locate the slot. L-block holds the work in place.

17 Here, two plates are installed at each corner of mitered frame for extra strength. Band clamp holds pieces until glue sets.

they don't shift. Then, mark the slot locations on the panels (Fig. 11). With the fence removed, rest the joiner on the side component and cut the slots in the end of the shelf (Fig. 12). To cut the corresponding slots in the side component, place the base of the joiner against the shelf edge, align the centered index mark with the slot locations and cut the slots in the side (Fig. 13). After all the cuts have been made, apply glue to the slots, install the plates and assemble the components (Fig. 14).

Like doweling, plate joinery is an excellent way to align and strengthen glued-up panels (Fig. 15). For good alignment, determine the best side of each board and make these the reference faces for all slots. In this way, any variation in thickness from one board to the next will be apparent only on the poorer side of the

18 Lamello K20 plastic plate holds components securely with or without glue. Use it where clamping is impossible.

19 For aligning and stabilizing solid-surfacing materials, the plastic, translucent Lamello C20 plate is available.

20 The Lamello aluminum KD fitting is inserted into No.20 size slots. Panel is cut away from fitting at top to show fitting.

21 Lamello hinges are flush mounted in recesses milled with plate joiner. Hinge halves are detachable for installation.

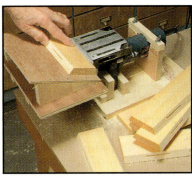

22 Bench-mounted joiner is ideal for small parts and repetitive jobs. Here, guideblock uniformly registers stock for miter joint.

23 With appropriate shopmade bevel platform in place on joiner stand table, slots are cut for miter joints of any angle.

24 Bevel platform can also be used with handheld plate joiner for bevels other than 45°. Clamp stock to prevent shifting.

25 Platform jig consistently positions joiner and stock. A pair of projecting nail points in the base anchor workpiece.

assembled panel. Place slots 2 in. from the ends of the boards and 4 to 12 in. apart.

Offset joints, such as the leg-to-apron joint of a table, are easily made by using a spacer block under the joiner base, and resting the stock directly on the worktable (Fig. 16). An L-shaped block clamped behind the workpiece takes the thrust of the plunge cut and allows you to use both hands on the joiner.

Plate-joined mitered frames are easier to assemble than dowel-joined frames because the components can be shifted for the best alignment. Use a band clamp wrapped around the perimeter of the frame until the glue sets (Fig. 17).

Special Plates

While most joiner manufacturers offer only the standard wooden plates, the Lamello system increases the versatility of any joining machine with several special-purpose products.

When it's impossible to apply clamping pressure, the K20 adhesive plate may solve the problem. It's made of plastic and has barbed cross ribs that grip the sides of the slot (Fig. 18). Although no glue is necessary, ordinary wood glue can be used.

The C20 joining plate is made of translucent polypropylene and is used to join solid-surfacing materials, such as Corian and Avonite (Fig. 19). This plate is primarily used to align and stabilize the joint, and glue is not normally required.

For knockdown (KD) shelving and similar applications, Lamello offers a 2-part aluminum plate that fits into No.20 slots. It's glued in place with a 2-part adhesive (Fig. 20).

The Lamello Duplex is a sleek, detachable cabinet hinge that's available in left- or right-handed versions in brass, nickled-steel or black finish (Fig. 21).

Jigs and Fixtures

Although the portability of the plate joiner is a desirable feature, handling small stock or performing repetitive work is better done on a stationary machine. The shopmade joiner stand shown is designed to convert the Freud joiner into a versatile stationary tool. With a few modifications, the idea can be adapted to any joiner.

The stand has a wood base with blocks that support the tool upside down. Shape the rear support block to fit the motor housing and hold the tool level. The small

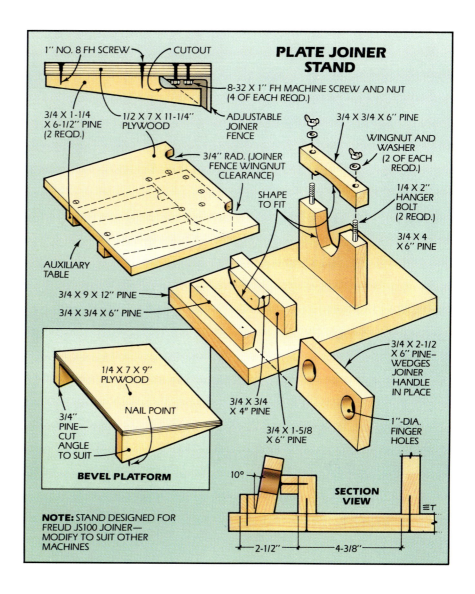

PLATE JOINER STAND

1" NO. 8 FH SCREW

CUTOUT

8-32 X 1" FH MACHINE SCREW AND NUT (4 OF EACH REQD.)

3/4 X 1-1/4 X 6-1/2" PINE (2 REQD.)

1/2 X 7 X 11-1/4" PLYWOOD

ADJUSTABLE JOINER FENCE

3/4 X 3/4 X 6" PINE

WINGNUT AND WASHER (2 OF EACH REQD.)

3/4" RAD. (JOINER FENCE WINGNUT CLEARANCE)

SHAPE TO FIT

1/4 X 2" HANGER BOLT (2 REQD.)

3/4 X 4 X 6" PINE

AUXILIARY TABLE

3/4 X 9 X 12" PINE

3/4 X 3/4 X 6" PINE

3/4 X 2-1/2 X 6" PINE— WEDGES JOINER HANDLE IN PLACE

1/4 X 7 X 9" PLYWOOD

NAIL POINT

3/4" PINE— CUT ANGLE TO SUIT

3/4 X 3/4 X 4" PINE

3/4 X 1-5/8 X 6" PINE

1"-DIA. FINGER HOLES

BEVEL PLATFORM

NOTE: STAND DESIGNED FOR FREUD JS100 JOINER— MODIFY TO SUIT OTHER MACHINES

10°

SECTION VIEW

2-1/2"   4-3/8"

curved piece on the front support block fits inside the joiner handle. To lock the tool to the stand, a cross-piece is tightened over the motor section with two wingnuts. A slide-in block with finger holes tightly wedges the handle in place. To attach the plywood table with flathead screws as shown, you'll need to drill four holes through the joiner fence. Two cleats under the plywood reinforce the table. Note that the Freud joiner requires two ¾-in.-rad. cutouts, as shown, to provide clearance for the fence-height adjustment knobs.

To use the stand, blocks can be clamped to the platform to align the stock and ensure accurate repet-itive cuts (Fig. 22). The joiner can handle edges beveled to any angle with the addition of a simple bevel platform shown in the drawing. Just construct the platform at the desired angle and use protruding nail points, as shown, to hold it in position on the joiner stand auxiliary table (Fig. 23).

When the joiner isn't in the stand, a similar bevel platform makes joining edge miters other than 45° easy (Fig. 24). Holding narrow pieces is made easier by using a joiner platform that has blocks to position the tool and the stock. Two nail points protruding about ³⁄₃₂ in. from the platform base serve to hold the work while the cut is being made (Fig. 25).

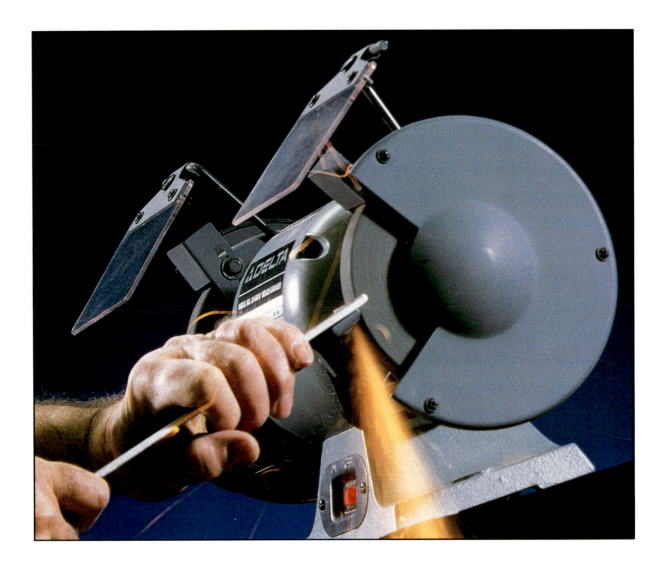

Bench grinder users guide

■ If your metalworking tools are limited to a hacksaw and a few files, you're missing out on one of the most useful tools around—the bench grinder. Once you've had one in your workshop for a while, you'll probably find it indispensable for performing a variety of jobs around the home and shop.

Woodworkers have long recognized the grinder as a fast and efficient machine for shaping bevels prior to honing. It's also an excellent tool for putting the finished edge on cold chisels, shears, axes and other cutting tools.

Besides keeping your tools sharp, the grinder is *the* tool for removing burrs from castings, dressing rough-sawn metal and handling general metal shaping. A variety of interchangeable abrasive wheels is available in different grades and types to suit specific applications.

This versatile tool, however, isn't limited to ordinary grinding operations. Substitute the grinding wheel with a wire wheel, and you're ready to remove rust, scale and paint; switch to a buffing wheel for polishing metals and plastics.

As with any other power tool, it pays to familiarize yourself with both the principles of operation and the various accessories available so you can safely achieve the intended results. Once you know how the tool works and which wheels you should use on specific jobs, all that's necessary is a little practice to refine the techniques of grinding, shaping, cleaning and polishing.

Text and photos for *Bench Grinder Users Guide* by Rosario Capotosto. Bench grinders and accessories are available from mail-order suppliers as well as local hardware and tool dealers. Following are sources for more hard-to-find items: Woodcraft, 210 Wood County Industrial Park, Parkersburg, WV 26102; Garrett Wade, 161 Avenue of the Americas, New York, NY 10013; Sears Tool Catalog, Sears Tower, Chicago, IL 60684.

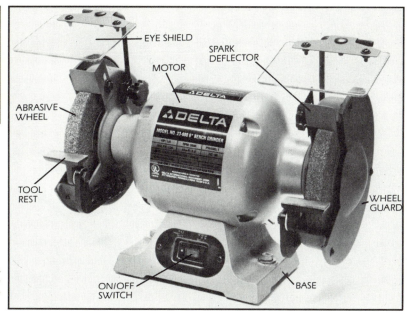

Typical grinder has two wheels driven by a central motor. Safety features include wheel guards, spark deflectors and eye shields. Toolrests are adjustable.

The Grinder

Compared to most other machines, a grinder is the essence of simplicity. It is an electric motor with shafts on each end where the wheels are mounted. Each wheel is secured by a nut, and the nut pressure is distributed on the wheel by large washers (Fig. 1). To keep the nuts from loosening, the direction of each shaft thread is opposite to the wheel rotation—the lefthand shaft has a lefthand thread and the righthand shaft has a righthand thread.

The size of the grinder is designated by the diameter of the wheel that can be used. Grinders are generally available in 5-, 6-, 7- and 8-in. sizes. Motors range from ¼ to 1 hp with no-load speeds from 3400 to 3800 rpm. Unless you plan to use your grinder for extra heavy-duty work, a 6-in. model will be satisfactory.

When selecting a grinder, first check to see that the motor housing doesn't protrude beyond the circumference of the wheel. If it does, the length of straight work passed across the wheel will be severely limited. Make sure the toolrests are adjustable both in terms of angle and distance from the wheel. Toolrests should be kept about ⅛ in. from the wheel (Fig. 2). Turn the grinder on and let it run for a minute or so. A well-balanced motor with true shafts will run quietly and smoothly.

Safety standards require wrap-around wheel guards that cover all but a 90° segment of each wheel. The outer covers of the wheel guards should be easily removable for changing wheels. On top of the wheel guards you'll find adjustable spark deflectors (Fig. 3) and each wheel will have a shatterproof eye shield. Don't, however, rely on the eye shield alone for eye protection—always wear safety goggles when using the grinder.

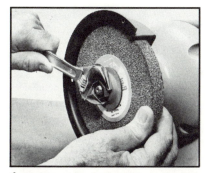

1 Tighten wheel mounting nuts with hand pressure on wheel—never over-tighten. Keep washer and wheel face free of debris.

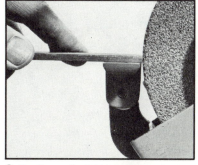

2 Position adjustable toolrest no more than ⅛ in. from wheel. Right-angle position shown produces a square ground edge.

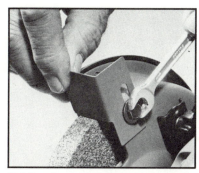

3 Adjust the spark deflectors to within ⅛ in. of the wheel to prevent sparks from flying out over the top of the wheel.

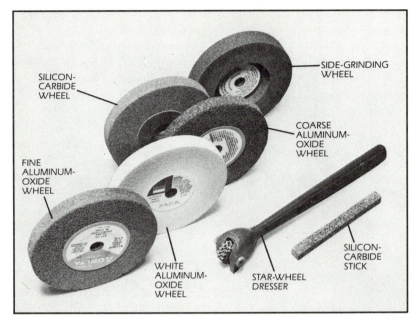

Most wheels are made of aluminum oxide or silicon carbide. Side-grinding wheel permits flat grinding, and star-wheel dresser and silicon-carbide stick keep wheels in shape.

Wheels

There are two synthetic materials commonly used in grinding wheels: aluminum oxide and silicon carbide. Aluminum oxide is the choice for grinding high-speed steel, carbon steel, malleable iron and wrought iron. Silicon carbide is best suited for cast iron, tungsten carbide, brass, bronze, aluminum and glass.

Wheels are available in grain sizes from 10 to 1000 grit, and this range is divided into four categories: coarse, medium, fine and very fine. When selecting a grain size, remember that a coarse wheel will cut faster than a fine wheel, but will leave a rougher surface.

The *grade* of the wheel refers to the hardness or strength of the bonding agent that holds the grains together and is indicated in a range from A to Z. Grades A to H are called soft, I to P medium and Q to Z are rated hard.

As a rule, soft wheels are used on hard materials and harder wheels are used on soft materials. Softer wheels are especially useful for grinding cutting tools because the dulled grains readily fall away exposing fresh, sharp grains. This reduces heat buildup. A medium-grade wheel (**K**) is suitable for general-purpose grinding.

The *structure* of a wheel refers to the grain spacing or density and ranges from 1 to 15. A low number indicates dense spacing and is appropriate for hard, brittle material. Soft metals, however, tend to clog a dense wheel and are better worked with a more open-grained wheel. Wide grain spacing also results in a coarser finish than close spacing. Tool grinding is best done in the 5 to 8 range.

The material that holds the grains together in most wheels is a vitrified glass-like bonding agent. Industrial wheels and cutoff wheels may have a different bonding agent.

These characteristics are encoded on the side of most wheels such as **9A 60 J8 V5**. The **A** stands for aluminum oxide (the **9A** here stands for one manufacturer's white aluminum-oxide wheel). If the letter was **C**, the wheel would be silicon carbide. The **60** refers to the grain size, **J** indicates a medium hardness grade,

4 This wheel is partially clogged and needs to be dressed. If wheel clogs often, it may be too hard for the material being ground.

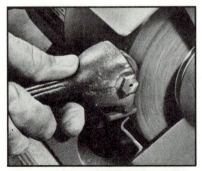

5 Use a star-wheel dresser to true face of wheel that has worn unevenly. Heavy sparking indicates more pressure is needed.

6 To clean and restore the sharpness to a dull or clogged wheel, pass a silicon-carbide stick over the rotating wheel.

and **8** stands for medium density. The **V** indicates vitrified bonding and the **5** is a manufacturer's symbol.

A new grinder usually comes with a pair of general-purpose, aluminum-oxide wheels—a 36 grit for rough work and rapid stock removal, and a 60 grit for fine work and sharpening. You might add a 100-grit wheel for finish grinding and a silicon-carbide wheel for touching up carbide-tipped tools. Side-grinding wheels permit safe use of the wheel side when a flat-ground surface is required. For trouble-free sharpening of chisels and plane irons, choose a white aluminum-oxide wheel for fast, cool cutting.

When a grinding wheel is worn out of shape or becomes dull, loaded or glazed, it must be trued and dressed (Fig. 4). *Truing* is done with a star-wheel dresser which removes material from the wheel until it runs true (Fig. 5). *Dressing* is done to clean and restore the sharpness of the wheel face and is accomplished with a silicon-carbide stick (Fig. 6).

Always check a wheel for cracks before mounting it—a damaged wheel can fly apart and cause serious injury. After a visual inspection, lightly tap the wheel side at four points near the circumference with a screwdriver handle. A good wheel will produce a clear metallic ring. If the sound is dull, discard the wheel.

Techniques

To shape the bevel on chisels and plane irons, first set the toolrest so the tool contacts the wheel at the appropriate angle. Then, with the blade firmly on the toolrest, grind the bevel with a continuous, smooth side-to-side motion and light pressure (Fig. 7). If a discoloration appears on the edge, excessive heat has drawn the temper and the tool won't stay sharp for long (Fig. 8). The solution is to grind away the affected area and regrind the bevel (Fig. 9). Always keep a bowl of water on hand to cool the edge as the grinding proceeds.

Drill bits and lathe skew chisels are best sharpened on the side of a side-grinding wheel. Special grinding jobs like these benefit from shopmade jigs secured to the toolrest bracket (Figs. 10 and 11).

Both jigs are based on a ½-in.-thick plywood platform that replaces the toolrest. Shape this piece to suit your grinder and cut a 1¼-in.-deep notch for the wheel. The platform is secured to the toolrest bracket with 1×4 right-angle stock.

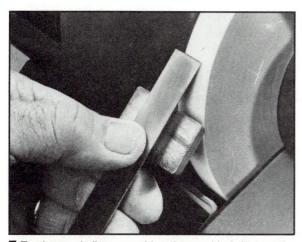

7 To shape a hollow-ground bevel on a chisel, first set the toolrest angle. Index finger under toolrest guides chisel across wheel.

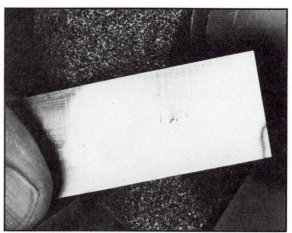

8 Discoloration on this chisel indicates overheating that has drawn the temper from the steel. Edge won't stay sharp during use.

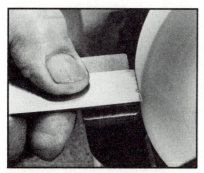

9 To regrind an overheated tool edge, set toolrest to 90°. Grind beyond discoloration. Reset toolrest and reshape bevel.

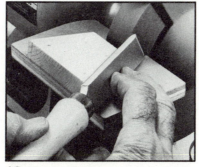

10 Sharpen flat-ground bevel of lathe skew chisel on side-grinding wheel. Jig keeps blade positioned for uniform bevel.

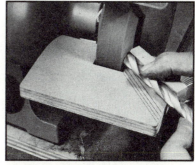

11 Use jig attached to toolrest bracket to sharpen drill bits. Guide block, set at 59° to wheel side, properly aligns edge of bit.

To flat grind the bevels on a skew chisel, first make the guide block to attach to the platform. Cut compound angles on each side so the chisel will meet the wheel side at the correct angle. You can use a 78° bevel angle (as shown) with the tool tilted 10° from the vertical. Center the block on the plywood platform and secure with nails and glue.

To make the drill bit sharpening jig, attach a ½-in.-sq. guide block to the right side of the wheel notch so it's positioned 59° to the wheel. Then, lay out guidelines at 47° to the wheel, spaced about ⅛ in. apart. Place the bit against the guide block so the cutting edge is horizontal. Let the edge contact the wheel and immediately rotate the bit 1/6 of a turn while shifting it to align with the guidelines. Then, sharpen the other edge in the same way (Figs. 11 and 12).

Smoothing rough-sawn metal is another common job for the grinder. Set the toolrest at right angles to the wheel and pass the stock gently across the wheel edge (Fig. 13). Smooth edges on round stock by grinding a bevel on the edge. Set the toolrest at 90°, hold the stock at an angle and rotate it clockwise (Fig. 14).

To smooth the edges of glass, remove the toolrest and hold the glass below the center of a silicon-carbide wheel and shape the edge freehand (Fig. 15). The grinder is an excellent tool for duburring iron castings and removing rivets when disassembling garden tools (Figs. 16 and 17).

Cleaning and Polishing

To clean rusty, corroded metal or remove paint, simply remove one of the wheels and install a wire brush wheel. These come in coarse or fine grades. Use the coarse wheel for heavy cleaning jobs and the fine one for delicate work where a satin finish is required (Fig. 18). Fiber wheels are available for light-duty tarnish removal. When cleaning edged garden tools such as shears, hold the edge away from the rotating wheel, not directed into it (Fig. 19).

To polish metal and plastics, you'll need a cloth wheel and buffing compound. Cloth wheels are either tightly sewn or loose, where the layers of fabric are secured only at the hub. The tightly sewn wheel provides a stiffer edge, but the loose wheels allow you to polish tight curves.

Buffing compounds are very fine abrasives that come in a range of grades. Jewelers rouge is the finest grade and should be used on precious metals and when the highest gloss is desired. For chrome, use slightly coarser white pumice compound. Tripoli is a medium grade compound and, for the coarsest buffing, choose emery buffing compound.

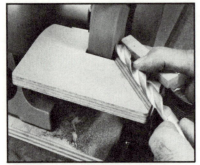

12 Finish sharpening bit by rotating bit clockwise 1/6 turn while shifting it to guidelines positioned at 47° to wheel side.

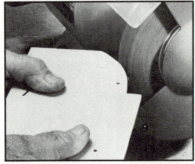

13 To smooth hacksaw marks in metal-working, first set toolrest to 90°. Support work on toolrest and feed against the wheel.

14 Bevel round stock by supporting it on a level toolrest and rotating the stock clockwise while moving across wheel face.

15 Use a silicon-carbide wheel to smooth glass. Remove toolrest and guide work freehand below wheel center-line.

16 Silicon carbide is also recommended for grinding cast iron. Avoid heavy pressure that may overheat and damage wheel.

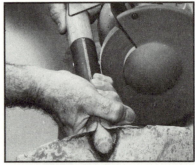

17 Riveted tools like this garden shovel can be disassembled for repair by grinding away the rivet heads with a coarse wheel.

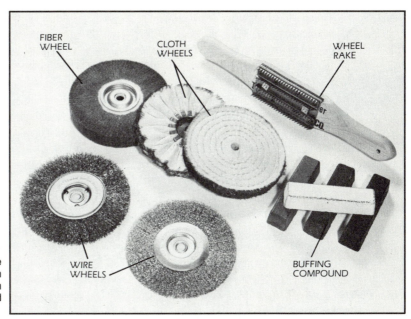

Wheels for cleaning and polishing include wire wheels, fiber wheels and cloth wheels. Cloth wheels are impregnated with buffing compound before use and cleaned with a wheel rake.

To polish, first install a buffing wheel and, with the grinder turned on, hold the buffing compound against the wheel to impregnate the cloth with abrasive (Fig. 20). Then, bring the workpiece up to the lower area of the wheel and apply gentle pressure (Figs. 21 and 22).

To keep your cloth wheels in shape, have a wheel rake on hand for removing caked compound (See Fig. 23).

18 Use a coarse wire wheel to remove rust and scaling paint. Fine wire wheels mar less and produce a satin-like finish.

19 To remove tarnish on garden shears and other tools, use a fiber wheel. Always hold tool cutting edge away from wheel rotation.

20 Prepare cloth wheel for buffing by pressing compound to wheel edge while grinder is running. Avoid heavy application.

21 Use a cloth wheel loaded with white compound (pumice) to polish chrome. Hold work to lower section of wheel.

22 Use a loose cloth buffing wheel for reaching into confined areas. Jewelers rouge is appropriate for precious metals.

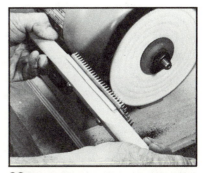

23 Wheel rake is used to dress the edge of cloth buffing wheels. It removes caked compound and trims frayed edges flush.

Chain saw maintenance

There was a time when chain saws were the province of professional loggers, tree surgeons and landscape architects. But over the past 10 to 15 years, millions have been sold to average consumers who quickly appreciated the usefulness of these tools. Not only are they indispensable for cutting firewood, but they are also the tool of choice for routine tree pruning and cleaning up storm-damaged limbs. Like any piece of power equipment, however, these saws must be well-maintained to work properly and safely.

Chain Saw Maintenance was written by Steven Willson with illustrations by George Retseck.

Chain Saw Features

All chain saws are basically the same. They have a small 2-cycle engine with a long, round-nose bar attached to the side. The cutting chain slides along a groove in the bar and is driven by a sprocket that comes off the engine crankshaft. Depending on the particular saw, the tool may come equipped with a chain brake, automatic chain oiler and other features.

Because of these differences, your first task is to read your owner's manual carefully. This booklet will explain your saw's special features and will give you a concise troubleshooting guide that will help you diagnose poor performance. Also keep in mind that even though the material here deals with chain saws, most of the techniques apply to any small 2-cycle engine, including those found on string trimmers, leaf blowers, garden sprayers and even some lawnmowers and snowblowers.

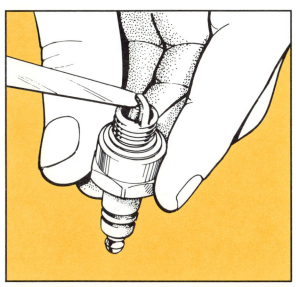

1 Remove spark plug and clean thoroughly. Check for correct gap with gauge and adjust if necessary. Replace plug yearly.

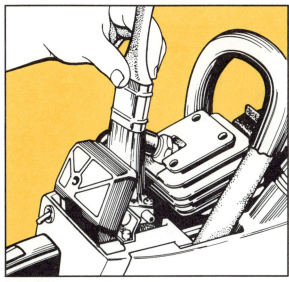

2 Remove dust and dirt from around the carburetor and air filter. Use either a stiff paint brush or a shop vacuum to do the job.

Spark Plug

Begin by draining the oil and gas fuel mixture from the fuel tank or by running the engine until the tank is dry. If your saw has been sitting for a couple of months, it's a good idea to flush the empty tank with a little fresh gas to remove any oil sediment.

Remove the spark plug and check its electrodes for dirt, oil and corrosion. A fouled plug indicates several possible problems: improper carburetor adjustments, the wrong gas-to-oil fuel mixture and, in some cases, excessive flooding when starting the engine.

If your plug is fouled, clean it thoroughly with emery paper and shake or blow away any debris. It's also a good idea to wash the plug in gas, using an old tooth-brush. After the plug is dry, closely inspect the center and curved electrode for pitting. If either is pitted or rounded over, file both until they are smooth and flat, then gap the plug to match manufacturer's specifications (Fig. 1). Frequent users should install a new plug every 100 hours of engine use. A ballpark figure for occasional users is to replace the plug every year.

Air Filter

Your engine will run well only if the proper amount of fuel and air are mixed in the carburetor. Because of this, it's essential that you keep the air filter clean at all times.

To check your air filter, begin by brushing away dirt and debris from around the filter cover (Fig. 2). Then press the CHOKE button to close off the carburetor port. This will prevent any debris from falling into the carburetor when you remove the filter. (*Note:* On some saws, the choke is simply a flapper built into the carburetor cover. Once the cover is removed, the carburetor port is exposed. On these saws, be extremely careful when removing the cover to keep debris from falling into the port.) Remove the filter cover, take it out and brush clean (Fig. 3).

Wash the filter according to manufacturer's recommendations. You can use soap and water and blow dry the filter with compressed air.

Some manufacturers, however, suggest other solvents. No matter what your situation, replace the filter if it is torn or still dirty after several attempts to clean it.

Fuel Filter

The fuel filter is designed to keep debris from entering the fuel line and fouling the carburetor. On most saws it's at the end of the fuel line, inside the fuel tank. To inspect this filter, fish it out of the tank using a wire

3 Remove the air filter and, again, brush off the debris. Then wash the filter with soap and water, rinse clean and let it dry.

coat hanger with a loop bent in the end (Fig. 4). Guide the wire into the fuel tank using a flashlight and hook it over the plastic fuel line. Gently pull the line until the filter pops out of the hole. If you pull too hard, you run the risk of tearing the fuel line.

Once the filter is out, check to see if it is clogged with any debris. If it is, pull the filter off the end of the line and wash it with gas and a toothbrush, or blow it out with compressed air. If neither cleans the filter completely, get a new one.

Reinstall the filter on the end of the line and then push everything back into the fuel tank.

Make sure the filter goes to the bottom of the tank, otherwise you won't use the complete fuel capacity.

Muffler and Spark Arrestor

The muffler has two basic purposes: to quiet the engine *and* to direct harmful exhaust gases away from the user. If it is loose or corroded, it will fail to do both jobs. It's a good idea to inspect it periodically.

To do this, you first have to remove the covering panel that prevents you from touching the very hot muffler during operation. This is usually part of the chain sprocket housing. Wiggle the muffler to make sure it's tight (Fig. 6). If it isn't, tighten the bolts to the torque specifications given in your owner's manual. If the muffler is corroded, replace it.

Depending on the age and make of your saw, it may or may not come with a spark arrestor. This device is simply a fine metal screen that prevents red-hot ex-

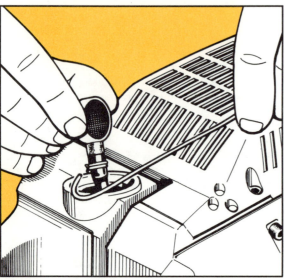

4 Remove the fuel tank cap and fish out fuel pickup line with a bent coat hanger. Make sure line's filter is clean. If not, replace it.

5 Remove the starter housing assembly and brush debris from entire unit, particularly air vents. Inspect all parts for wear.

Pull Cord Starter

At least once a year it's a good idea to remove the starter housing assembly, even if the pull cord has been working well (Fig. 5). This gives you the chance to clean the vent slots thoroughly and check for worn parts that may need replacement. If your pull cord is broken, then follow the manufacturer's directions on how to replace it—different saws require different techniques and tools. If the starter itself is broken, take the saw to your dealer for repair.

haust particles from leaving the muffler and possibly causing a fire. These days you can't cut on most public lands unless your saw has a spark arrestor.

On the saw shown, this screen is located just below the exhaust deflector fins. By unscrewing the fin plate (Fig. 7), the arrestor can be lifted out and washed with soapy water and a tooth brush. Compressed air also works well to clean this screen. Because the arrestor is exposed to such intense heat, holes are frequently burned in the screen. When this happens, the arrestor

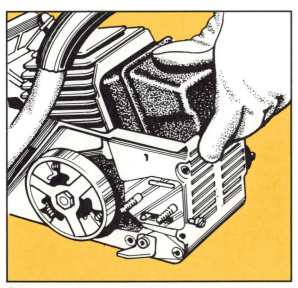

6 Grasp the muffler assembly and wiggle to make sure it's not loose. Also, check for rust. If muffler is damaged, replace it.

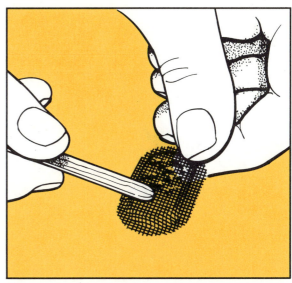

7 Remove spark plug arrestor screen and remove debris with a brush. For stubborn spots, scrape with small wood stick.

should be replaced. In any case, you should inspect the arrestor every time you use the saw to make sure it's in good shape.

On some saws, particularly older ones, this arrestor can be screwed to the inside of the muffler. In these cases, the muffler has to be disassembled to reach it. Consult your owner's manual for the more involved procedure.

When the muffler and engine fins are exposed, brush away and vacuum up any debris (Fig. 8). Be especially careful to remove the debris from around the engine cooling fins. Because these saws are air cooled, such debris reduces the airflow around the engine and can cause overheating and damage.

Chain Bar

To free up the chain bar—and the chain for that matter—first loosen the chain tensioning screw at the front of the saw. Then remove the sprocket housing on the side of the saw using either a socket wrench or the combination tool usually sold with the saw (Fig. 9). Once the chain is loose and the cover is off, lift the chain from the bar groove, and set it to one side. Then remove the bar (Fig. 10).

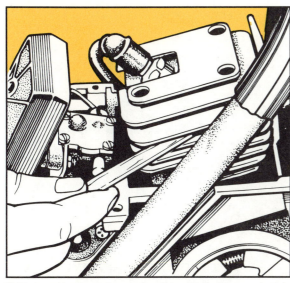

8 Thoroughly clean the engine fins with a thin wood stick, followed by a stiff paint brush. Be sure to vacuum all debris.

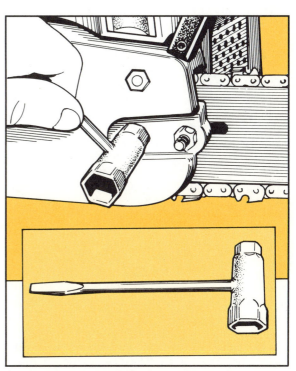

9 Remove the nuts that hold the chain bar and sprocket housing using socket wrench or tool (inset) supplied with saw.

10 Once the sprocket housing is off, remove the outer bar plate. Then lift chain off sprocket and remove chain bar.

Chain

After giving the chain a thorough cleaning with solvent and a toothbrush, reinstall the bar, chain and sprocket housing. Then tighten the chain tensioning screw until the chain is nearly tight. This will keep the chain stable as you sharpen it.

The sharpening techniques required will depend on the type of chain that's on your saw. Consult your owner's manual for specific directions. Most saws, however, are sold with what is called a *standard chain*. This has cutting teeth joined by drive links that run in the bar groove. The cutting teeth have a top plate, side plate and depth gauge (sometimes called a *raker*). You must sharpen all three of these surfaces whenever the chain is dull.

11 Using a thin wood stick, clean the oil-soaked debris from chain groove on the bar. Use a small nail for stubborn spots.

Thoroughly clean the debris from around the drive sprocket and clutch assembly. Compressed air works well for this, but if the wood chips and dust are caked on, a liberal dose of cleaner/lubricant—like WD-40—and a stiff toothbrush will do the trick. Wipe the saw dry with a rag and complete a visual check of the sprocket assembly. If you detect any worn parts, have them replaced.

Next, clamp the chain bar in a vise—preferably one with protected jaws—and remove any dirt and debris from the bar groove. You can use a piece of scrap wood for this job, shaving the end until it slides easily in the groove (Fig. 11). Remember that the bar does wear unevenly—more stress is exerted on the cutting side. Because of this, manufacturers suggest that you turn the bar over before every heavy work session to equalize the wear.

Once the groove is free of debris, clean the oil holes on the side of the bar. These holes allow the chain oil to flow along the chain groove. If they are clogged, the oil won't be able to do its job and both the chain and bar will be short lived.

Next, inspect the groove rails for wear. Over time, the movement of the chain will create small, metal burrs along these rails. File these surfaces flat and smooth. If the bar groove is distorted or bent, it's time to replace the bar.

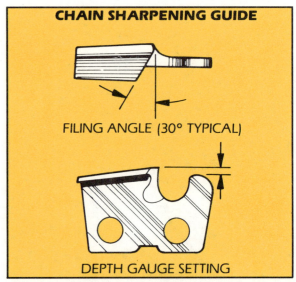

CHAIN SHARPENING GUIDE

FILING ANGLE (30° TYPICAL)

DEPTH GAUGE SETTING

12 Sharpening angles vary depending on type of chain and manufacturer. The filing angle above is a general guideline.

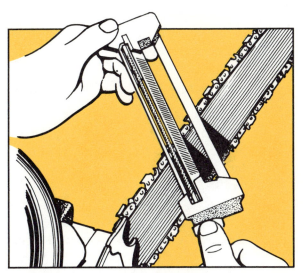

13 Reinstall the bar, chain, plate and housing, then tighten chain. Sharpen teeth with a combination file guide.

14 Once the chain is sharpened, adjust tensioning screw with saw tool to match manufacturer's recommended tolerance.

Many people use a special round file for the top and side plates and a separate flat file for the depth gauge. (The manufacturer stipulates which files to use.) But a better idea—especially for the novice sharpener—is to use a combination filing guide like the one shown in Fig. 12. This tool files all three surfaces at once, maintaining the proper angle and the proper distance between the top of the teeth and the top of the depth gauge (Fig. 13).

The trick in sharpening is to file all the teeth the same way. Start by finding any tooth that has a chip or nick and file until that fault is removed. Keep track of the number of file strokes required. Then, file all the remaining teeth, using the same stroke and the same number of strokes. If your chain is in particularly rough shape, have it sharpened professionally or buy a new one.

Once the chain is sharp, readjust the chain tension to manufacturer's specifications (Figs. 14 and 15), lubricate the front chain sprocket on the guide bar (Fig. 16), and reinstall the spark plug. Fill the chain oil reservoir, add the proper fuel mixture to the fuel tank, and give the cord a pull. Your saw should start right up.

If it doesn't, or if it runs rough or the chain moves even when the saw is idling, then you'll have to adjust the carburetor. Because carburetor adjustments vary depending on the saw, be sure to read your owner's manual carefully. Generally, you'll have to adjust both the low- and high-speed mixture needles first. Then adjust the idle screw once the saw is running.

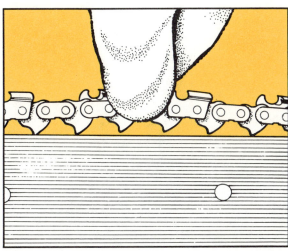

15 The bottom of a properly adjusted chain should just clear the top edge of the bar. Always adjust chain when it is cool.

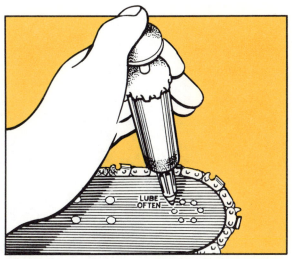

16 Using a grease gun—available from your dealer—lubricate roller at nose of chain bar with automotive grease.

Hollow-wall anchors

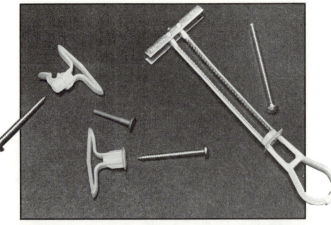

The Toggler anchoring system can cut down on your hardware clutter because these clever devices were designed with versatility in mind. The basic Toggler is the screw anchor which can work in both solid-wall *and* hollow-wall applications. It has a poly-

Toggler anchor system offers three options: simple picture hook with screw *(left)*, wall anchor with screw *(middle)* and toggle-type anchor with bolt *(right)*. Plastic setting key *(arrow)* is used to snap open wings on picture hook and wall anchor.

Hollow-Wall Anchors was written and photographed by Rosario Capotosto. Togglers are available at hardware stores and home centers and are usually sold in packages of eight for about $1.70. For more information, contact Toggler Anchor System, Div. of Mechanical Plastics Corp., P.O. Box 328, Castleton St., Pleasantville, NY 10570.

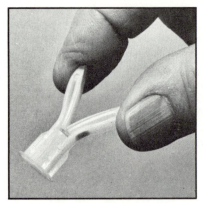

1 To install anchor, first bore hole in wall then squeeze anchor wings together.

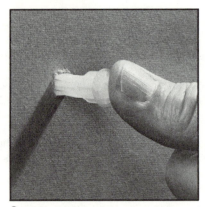

2 Insert folded anchor into hole and press until flush with surrounding surface.

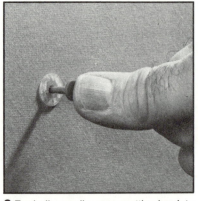

3 For hollow walls, press setting key into anchor to push out wings on inside of wall.

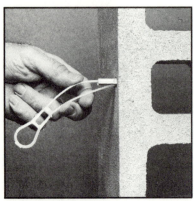

4 To install toggle-type anchor, fold wing against strap and push into hole.

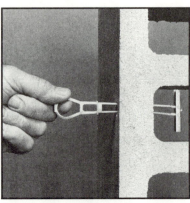

5 Once through hole, pull out until wing hits inside surface of wall.

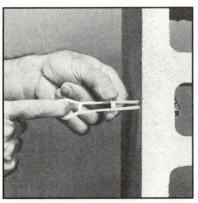

6 Secure anchor by pushing cap into hole until flush with surrounding surface.

propylene anchor and a small plastic setting key (Fig. 1). All you do is drill a hole in your wall and slide the anchor in place (Fig. 2). For solid walls, the anchor is just wedged into the hole, like a normal plastic anchor. If the wall is hollow, you simply slide the key setting pin into the anchor and push (Fig. 3). This action forces the wings on the anchor to pop out and bear against the inside surface of the wall. Once you remove the setting pin, all you do to attach something is drive a self-tapping machine screw through the object and into the anchor.

If you have to support heavier loads—up to 150 pounds per anchor when installed in concrete block—the Toggler toggle bolt fills the bill in ways that a standard toggle bolt can't. This version is installed in the wall *independent* of any bolt (Figs. 4–6). Because the support wing on the inside of the wall is secured by the fixture, instead of the bolt, the bolt that holds the object can be removed and replaced at any time without the wing falling down inside the wall.

The basic anchor is complemented with other models for specific purposes: a picture hook, an anchor for mounting perforated hardboard with the correct spacing from the wall, and ones designed for mounting wire rack storage systems, adjustable metal shelf standards and all sorts of electric cables.

The basic anchors come in different sizes, depending on the thickness of the wall material. The smallest one works in panels—like those found on hollow-core doors—that are ⅛ to ¼ in. thick. The next size handles material that is ⅜ to ½ in. thick, and the largest is designed for surfaces that are ⅝ to ¾ in. thick. These dimensions indicate the thicknesses that allow the anchor to expand fully on the back side of the surface covering. Of course, in solid-wall applications they'll all work. Each anchor will hold at least 40 pounds of weight and is designed to accept screws ranging from sizes No.6 to No.14.

Another virtue of these toggle bolts is that they require a smaller wall hole. Most ¼-in. toggle bolts require a ¾-in. hole but the Togglers need only a ½-in. hole. The anchor is designed with a flange around its plastic cap that covers the edges of the hole and leaves a presentable finished appearance when exposed.

7 Once cap is firmly seated, bend straps from side to side until they break off.

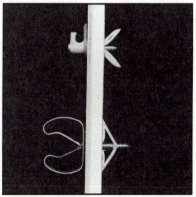

8 Attach object to wall using bolt of proper length. Bolt threads into wings.

9 Attach desired hardware to wall anchor using self-tapping machine screw.

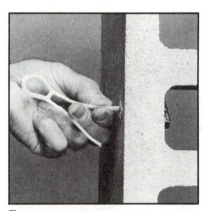

10 Anchor *(back side view)* can hold screws from size No.6 *(left)* to No.14 *(right)*.

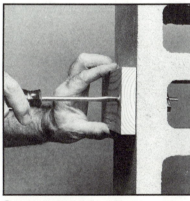

11 Fully spread anchor *(bottom)* grips best, but also holds weight when partially spread *(top)*.

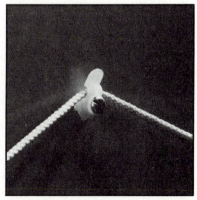

12 Picture hook is great for hanging frames and supporting small cable wires.

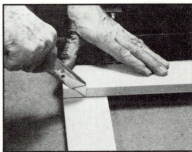

1 Rip and crosscut the stiles and rails. Lay the pieces on one another, then mark the half-lap joint with a razor knife.

2 Cut the half-laps using a miter gauge and a dado head on a table saw. Blade height equals half the board thickness.

Country pine mirror

■ Build this hall mirror and add a touch of charm to your home's decor. An experienced woodworker can build this piece in a weekend, and an inexperienced woodworker will find it an ideal project from which to gain experience.

To reduce the materials cost, you can use No.2 pine instead of C-select (clear). To get the necessary clear stock, simply rip and crosscut between the knots. If you have to use a piece with a knot in it, face the knot toward the mirror's back.

The project shown uses a 1/16-in.-thick by 16-in.-wide by 24-in.-long mirror. You can buy the mirror at your local glass shop or buy an inexpensive one at the local home center and remove the frame. Check the mirror's actual size before you begin this project. Adjust the project dimensions to suit the mirror, if necessary. When assembled, there should be a 1/16-in. space around the mirror (1/8-in. total clearance).

Rails and Stiles

Rip and crosscut the stock for the rails and stiles. To mark the ends for the half-lap joints, lay a rail across a stile and scribe a line along the rail using a razor knife or sharp pencil (Fig. 1). Install a dado head in a table saw and adjust the blade so 3/8 in., or half the stock thickness, is above the saw table. Cut the notches by making multiple crosscut passes, pushing the workpiece over the blade using a miter gauge (Fig. 2).

Install a 3-bead molding cutter on the table saw, and position the fence 1/4 in. away from the edge of the blade.

Note that the bead cuts in the stiles are stopped 3½ in. from the end of each board. This operation is easily controlled with a long auxiliary fence—simply a board temporarily attached to the rip fence. A pair of stop-blocks are clamped in place on the board to limit the length of the bead cuts.

To locate the stopblocks, raise the molding head cutter so it just clears the saw table (about the height of one bead). Turning the molding head by hand, make cross marks on the saw table where the molding head emerges and where it descends. If necessary, stick some tape on the saw table and mark on the tape. Marking is easier if you butt a piece of scrap wood against the fence and cutter head and draw a line

Country Pine Mirror was written by Rosario Capotosto. Photos by Rosario Capotosto and J.R. Rost. Technical art by Eugene Thompson.

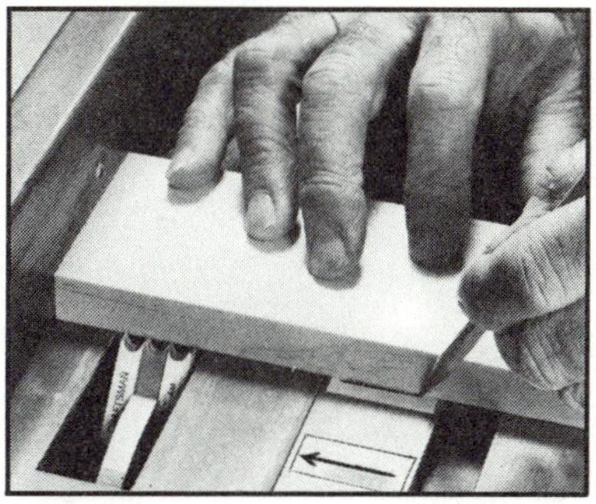

3 Apply tape to table saw bed to set up for beading cuts. Marks on tape indicate where beading cutter engages the workpiece.

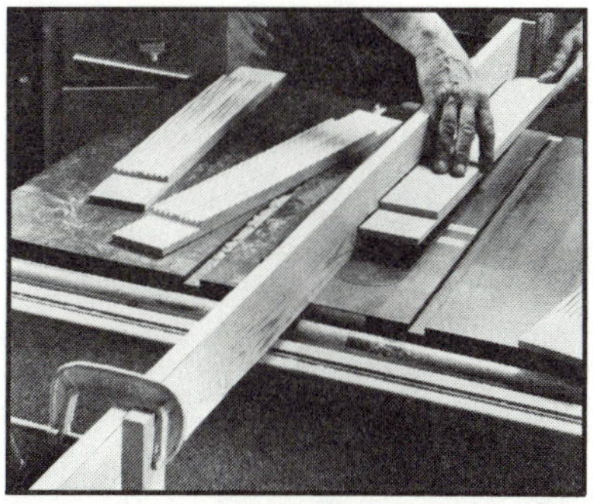

4 To start beading, butt stile against stopblock clamped to auxiliary fence. Lower stile into blade and push forward.

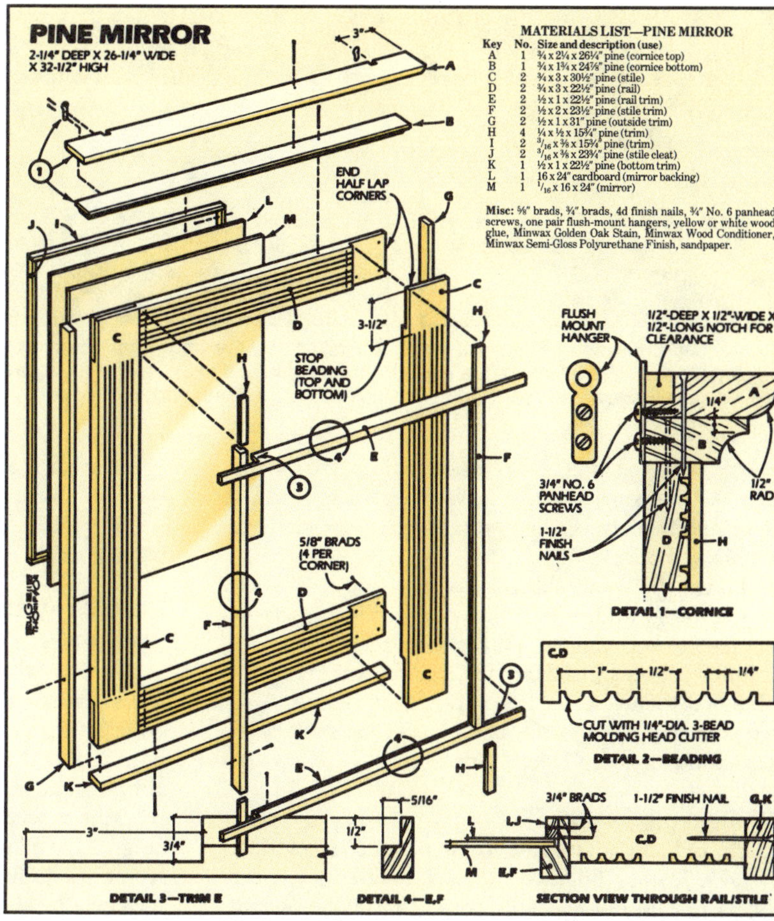
PINE MIRROR
2-1/4" DEEP X 26-1/4" WIDE X 32-1/2" HIGH
3"
A
B
1
END HALF LAP CORNERS
G
J
I
L
M
C
D
3-1/2"
H
STOP BEADING (TOP AND BOTTOM)
E
4
3
F
5/8" BRADS (4 PER CORNER)
K
FLUSH MOUNT HANGER
1/2"-DEEP X 1/2"-WIDE X 1/2"-LONG NOTCH FOR CLEARANCE
1/4"
1/2" RAD.
3/4" NO. 6 PANHEAD SCREWS
1-1/2" FINISH NAILS
DETAIL 1—CORNICE
C,D
1"
1/2"
1/4"
CUT WITH 1/4"-DIA. 3-BEAD MOLDING HEAD CUTTER
DETAIL 2—BEADING
5/16"
3/4"
1/2"
DETAIL 3—TRIM E
DETAIL 4—E,F
3/4" BRADS
1-1/2" FINISH NAIL
I,J
E,F
SECTION VIEW THROUGH RAIL/STILE

MATERIALS LIST—PINE MIRROR

Key	No.	Size and description (use)
A	1	¾ x 2¼ x 26¼" pine (cornice top)
B	1	¾ x 1¾ x 24⅞" pine (cornice bottom)
C	2	¾ x 3 x 30½" pine (stile)
D	2	¾ x 3 x 22½" pine (rail)
E	2	½ x 1 x 22½" pine (rail trim)
F	2	½ x 2 x 23½" pine (stile trim)
G	2	½ x 1 x 31" pine (outside trim)
H	4	¼ x ½ x 15¾" pine (trim)
I	2	3/16 x ⅜ x 15¾" pine (trim)
J	2	3/16 x ⅜ x 23¾" pine (stile cleat)
K	1	½ x 1 x 22½" pine (bottom trim)
L	1	16 x 24" cardboard (mirror backing)
M	1	1/16 x 16 x 24" (mirror)

Misc: ⅝" brads, ¾" brads, 4d finish nails, ¾" No. 6 panhead screws, one pair flush-mount hangers, yellow or white wood glue, Minwax Golden Oak Stain, Minwax Wood Conditioner, Minwax Semi-Gloss Polyurethane Finish, sandpaper.

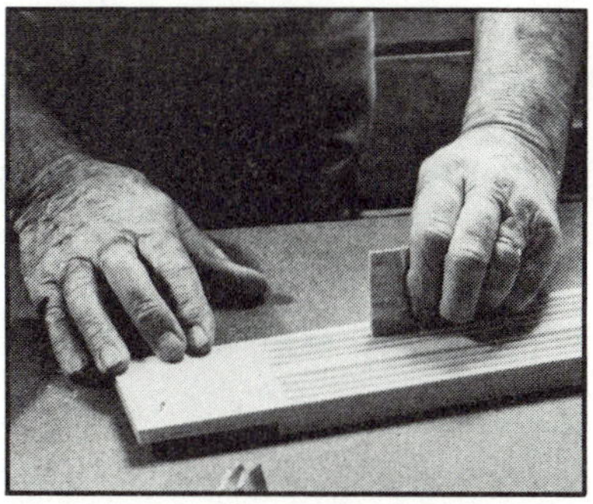

5 Lightly hand sand the beading with folded fine-grit sandpaper. Avoid rounding over the beading's crisp corners.

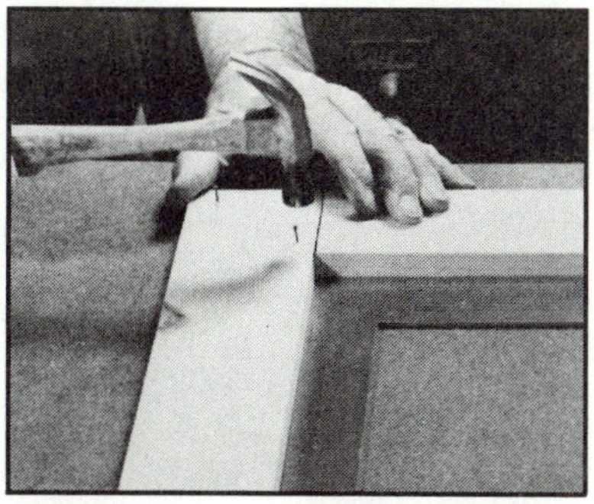

6 Butt a framing square into the frame corners. Apply glue to the joints and drive in ⅝-in. nails from back of joints.

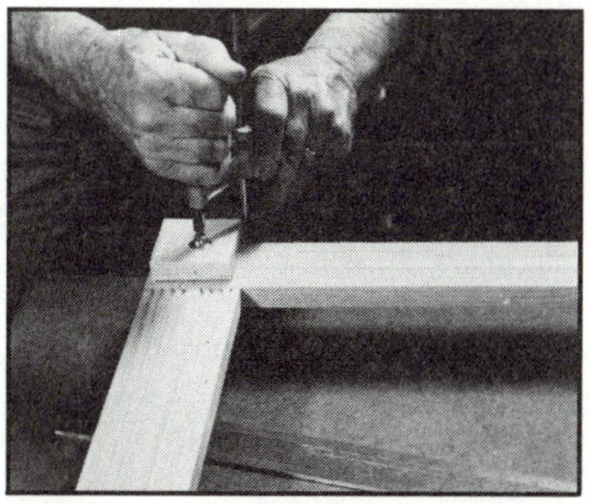

7 After nails are driven, clamp corners tight and let glue set. Use scrap blocks under the clamp heads to avoid marring.

against its edge (Fig. 3). Lower the beading cutter head after you've made the two marks on the saw table.

Mark 3½ in. from each end, on the edge of each stile. Lay stile on the saw table so the mark on its edge farthest from you aligns with the mark on the saw table farthest from you (the stile should extend back from the aligned marks toward you). Butt a block against the stile's end closest to you and clamp the block to the auxiliary fence. Or make a mark on the auxiliary fence and clamp a block on the mark.

Slide the stile forward until the mark on the stile closest to you aligns with the mark on the saw table closest to you. The stile should extend from the aligned marks away from you. Butt a block against the end of the stile farthest from you and clamp it to the auxiliary fence.

To make the stopped-bead cuts on the stiles, simply butt the stile against the block closest to you and lower it onto the blade (Fig. 4). Push the stile forward until it hits the second block. Shut off the saw, and when the blade has stopped spinning, pivot up the workpiece.

To make the beading cut on the rails, simply push them over the beading cutter. There's no need to use stopblocks. With both rails and stiles, make one pass

8 Cut rabbet in rail and stile trim with two cuts on table saw. Use a feather board to keep workpiece against the saw fence.

9 First attach the upper and lower rail trim with glue and nails. Apply glue sparingly to notched end of the trim pieces.

10 The stile trim pieces go on next. Hold frame upright in a vise. Glue and nail the trim. Set and fill nailheads.

over the beading cutter, swap the workpiece end for end and make a second pass to cut the other three beads.

Use folded pieces of fine grit sandpaper to sand the grooves and beads (Fig. 5).

Sand the rails and stiles and apply glue to the lap joints sparingly. Use four ⅝-in. nails driven in from the back at each joint. Align the parts for nailing with a framing square butted into the inside corner (Fig. 6). These nails only keep the parts from sliding. Use clamps to close the joints, and protect the surface of the joints with scrap blocks (Fig. 7).

Making Trim Strips

Rip the rail and stile trim and the outside trim strips. Set up a feather board on the table saw to cut the rabbets on the rail and stile trim. The feather board keeps the strips securely against the fence. Make a cut along one edge. Readjust the feather board, tip the strip 90°, and make the second cut to complete the rabbet (Fig. 8). Cut the end notches on the rail trim strips with the dado head on the table saw.

Test fit the trim pieces. Measure from the edge of one rabbet to the edge of the other rabbet to determine if the mirror will fit with clearance. Apply a thin bead of glue, and nail in the rail trim strips with ¾-in. brads (Fig. 9).

Crosscut the stile trim strips to fit, check for mirror clearance, and glue and nail them in place (Fig. 10). Glue and nail the small trim pieces in place.

Crosscut the outside trim pieces to fit, glue and nail them in place. Crosscut the bottom trim piece. Attach it with glue and nails. Then, fill any exposed nailheads with wood filler, and sand the filler flush.

Cornice And Finish

The cornice is made in two parts, each edge molded separately with a router using a ½-in.-rad. corner round bit for the top cornice piece and a ½-in.-rad. cove bit for the bottom piece. To avoid tearout when cutting the shape on the ends of each cornice piece, simply clamp scrap backup strips on the edges of the workpiece when cutting the molding on the end grain (Fig. 11). To assemble, glue and nail the lower section to the frame first, then add the second (Fig. 12).

When the glue is dry, cut the mortises for the hanger screws or nails and attach the flush-mount hangers.

Finish is optional. Here is how you can obtain the warm-toned finish on the mirror shown. First, sand the piece with 220-grit sandpaper and then wipe down the piece with a tack cloth to remove dust.

Apply a coat of wood conditioner to prevent uneven stain absorption. Follow with golden oak stain and two coats of semi-gloss polyurethane.

Install the mirror. Back it with cardboard, then nail in the cleats, sliding the hammer along the cardboard (Fig. 13).

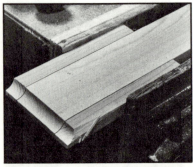

11 Clamp scrap strips to edges of cornice moldings when routing end grain. Scrap edge splinters, workpiece doesn't.

12 Glue and nail lower cornice molding to rail, then glue and nail on upper molding. Divide the cornice overhang equally.

13 Place cardboard behind mirror. Nail cleats to rails and stiles. Lay hammer on cardboard and swing into the brads.

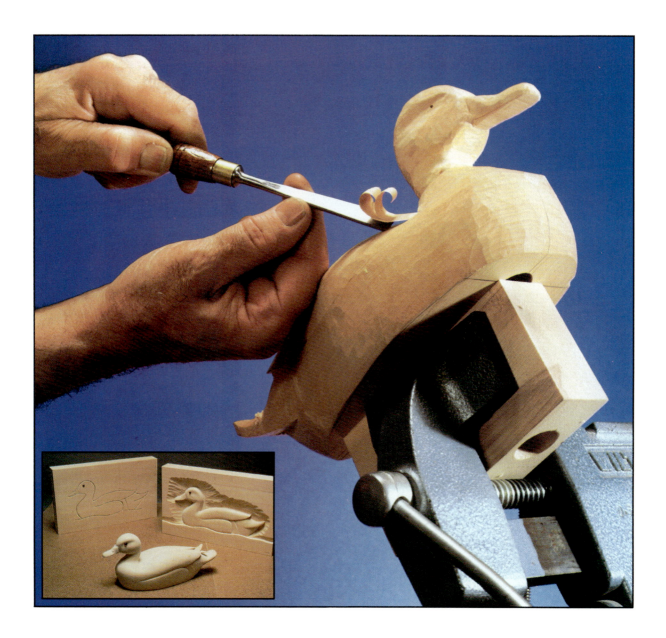

Woodcarving techniques

■ If your carving experience is limited to things like shaping the legs of Queen Anne furniture or adding simple carved details to a chair back—or if you haven't even tried carving yet, then you're missing out on one of the most enjoyable, relaxing and rewarding areas of woodworking.

The three types of carving presented here are chip carving, relief carving and carving in the round. A duck motif has been chosen to illustrate the techniques because its graceful contours and simple details are not too difficult to reproduce. If you've never carved before, practice the carving techniques in the order they are presented, so that each exercise acts as a foundation for the next.

Carving tools are available in a variety of shapes and sizes, but you'll need only a few basic tools for the projects described here (Fig. 1). The toolkit has straight and bent gouges, straight and skew chisels, a veiner, a V-tool, chip carving knives and a mallet. A standard carpenter's chisel is also handy and can be used in place of the straight carving chisel, if necessary. For smoothing, the kit includes a round file, half-round file, 4-in-hand rasp/file and a set of rifflers to shape delicate details.

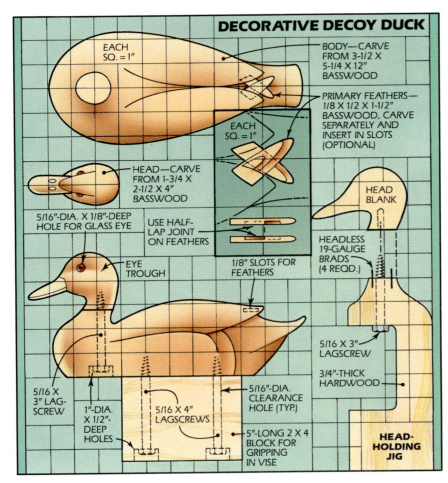

DECORATIVE DECOY DUCK

EACH SQ. = 1"

BODY—CARVE FROM 3-1/2 X 5-1/4 X 12" BASSWOOD

PRIMARY FEATHERS—1/8 X 1/2 X 1-1/2" BASSWOOD, CARVE SEPARATELY AND INSERT IN SLOTS (OPTIONAL)

EACH SQ. = 1"

HEAD—CARVE FROM 1-3/4 X 2-1/2 X 4" BASSWOOD

HEAD BLANK

5/16"-DIA. X 1/8"-DEEP HOLE FOR GLASS EYE

USE HALF-LAP JOINT ON FEATHERS

HEADLESS 19-GAUGE BRADS (4 REQD.)

EYE TROUGH

1/8" SLOTS FOR FEATHERS

5/16 X 3" LAGSCREW

3/4"-THICK HARDWOOD

5/16 X 3" LAG-SCREW

1"-DIA. X 1/2"-DEEP HOLES

5/16 X 4" LAGSCREWS

5/16"-DIA. CLEARANCE HOLE (TYP.)

5"-LONG 2 X 4 BLOCK FOR GRIPPING IN VISE

HEAD-HOLDING JIG

Text and photographs for *Woodcarving Techniques* by Rosario Capotosto. Carving tools, equipment and the 8mm glass eye used for the duck decoy shown are available from Constantine, 2050 Eastchester Rd., Bronx, NY 10461.

The most important requisite for carving is a razor-sharp cutting edge. If a tool bevel needs to be re-shaped, do this on a coarse bench stone. Then shift to a medium stone to smooth the bevel until a wire edge or burr is formed. Remove the wire edge on a fine stone. Use a fine slipstone of the proper shape to hone the inside of a gouge or V-tool. Polish the bevel on an extra-fine stone and then strop on a strip of leather charged with jeweler's rouge.

Although there are many woods suitable for carving, basswood is one of the easiest to work with and it has a tight, straight-grained structure that holds detail well. White or sugar pine will also work for these projects.

1 A simple carving kit includes straight and bent gouges, straight and skew chisels, a veiner, a V-tool and a mallet. Chip carving knives (*bottom left*) are used for decorative surface carving. Files and rasps smooth carved surfaces and rifflers shape and smooth details.

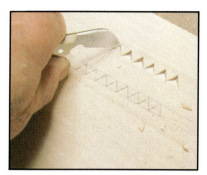

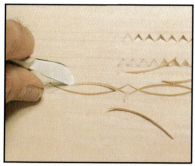

2 Begin the 3-cut triangle by making two cuts from the triangle apex. Then, make a low-angle cut from the triangle base.

3 Six-cut triangle begins with three stop cuts made from the center of the triangle. Remove waste by cutting in from sides.

4 Make sweeping chip cut by holding the knife blade at 45°. Then, steadily and slowly pull the blade across the surface.

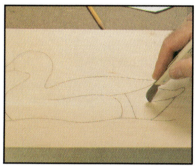

5 After laying out the duck profile, begin carving by holding the knife at 90° to make stop cuts that follow the outline.

6 Use a French curve to lay out lines parallel to and about 1/8 in. from the original lines. Use 1/16-in. spacing around the beak.

7 Hold the knife at 45° to the surface and cut along the second set of lines to remove wood and delineate the shape.

Chip Carving

In chip carving, small knives are used to make shallow incisions in the surface of the wood. The designs produced are traditionally decorative patterns made up of repetitive geometric elements. Basic chip carving cuts include 3-cut and 6-cut triangles and the sweeping curved cut.

To chip carve the 3-cut triangle motif, first lay out a row of triangles along the grain. Then, make stop cuts on the two sides of each triangle that go across the grain. These cuts meet at the apex, where they should be about 1/8 in. deep. The cuts taper to zero depth at the triangle baseline. Remove the chip by holding the knife at a low angle and cutting in at the baseline to meet the stop cuts (Fig. 2).

To make the 6-cut triangle, basically an inverted-pyramid shape, lay out another row of triangles and draw three lines from the center to the corners of each triangle. Make three vertical stop cuts along these centerlines, inclining each cut so it's deepest at the center and at zero depth at the corners. Then, make a slanting cut from each triangle side to remove the three chips (Fig. 3).

To produce a sweeping cut, first draw the outline on the wood and then make a vertical stop cut along the center of the line. Then, hold the knife at 45° to the surface at the far end of the line and draw the knife

toward you while making a slicing cut. Make a similar cut on the other side of the line to complete the V-cut (Fig. 4).

When you feel comfortable using the chip carving knife, you can tackle the duck panel. Begin by making a paper pattern of the duck shape as shown in the drawing (page 34) and then transferring the outline to the stock. To emphasize the outline, create deeper shadow areas and increase contrast, using a cut that isn't a true V, but one that has a slanted side while the other is vertical.

Make a vertical stop cut along the entire outline (Fig. 5). Using a French curve, draw a parallel line about 1/8 in. outside the original cutline, except at the beak where the spacing should be about 1/16 inch. Add parallel lines on the lower side of the wings, and a water line at the bottom of the duck (Fig. 6). Vertical stop cuts must be made where lines intersect to prevent the wood from splitting beyond that point.

To form the grooves, hold the knife at a 45° angle and make slow slicing cuts on the secondary lines (Fig. 7). Cut with the grain. Where the grain direction changes in the middle of a cut, it may be necessary to stop the cut and finish it from the opposite direction. To finish the panel, lightly sand with 220-grit sandpaper. Then bore the hole for the glass eye and attach it with glue.

Relief Carving

A relief carving is a carved design that projects from a recessed background. The background may be level and smooth or trench-carved, as in the example shown. To begin, select a block of wood at least 1 in. thick and transfer the duck outline from a pattern. Screw a 2×4 block to the back of the work so that it can be held in a vise. Position the screws under the thickest part of a carving.

Use a small V-tool to make an outlining cut around the figure. Keep the cut about 1/8 in. outside the line, and change the direction of the cut when necessary to avoid working against the grain (Fig. 8).

Setting-in is the next step. Using the V-groove as a guide, make shallow vertical cuts along the outline using the chisels and gouges that most closely match the curves. Use a mallet to drive the tools, but avoid deep cuts which crush the wood fibers. Next, use a gouge to make short passes up to the vertical cuts to create walls around the outline. Repeat the process to deepen the walls gradually (Figs. 9 and 10).

To deepen the background to its finished depth of about 5/8 in., use a bent gouge and make scalloped cuts radiating from the outline.

Next, begin molding the duck shape by drawing a pencil guideline about 1/2 in. from the body perimeter. Use gouges to roughly contour the body, taking off small chips around the head and chest areas. Use wide chisels to make the long sweeping cuts that define the wing and tail sections (Fig. 11). Shape the wing indents with the V-tool (Fig. 12) and then make paring cuts to fine trim the contours.

Bore the 5/16-in. eye socket before the final head rounding. Pare down the beak with a shallow gouge and use the V-tool to incise the lower jaw. Use a razor knife to form the nostril. Smooth the beak details with rifflers, sand all but the background with 220 paper (Fig. 13), and glue in the eye.

8 Begin relief carving by using the V-tool to outline the duck profile. Keep the cut in the waste area—about 1/8 in. from the line.

9 After making vertical cuts around the outline using straight gouges and chisels, remove waste with a gouge.

10 As work progresses, continue alternating between grounding cuts made with bent gouge and cuts that follow outline.

11 Shape convex curves of duck with a straight carving chisel. Change cut direction when necessary to follow grain.

12 Use the V-tool to incise the separation between the wings. To see contours of carving clearly, light the work from a low angle.

13 Sand the figure—not the background. Start with 150-grit and work through to 220-grit paper for a smooth finish.

Carving in the Round

Carving a decorative decoy duck in three dimensions is a little more challenging than the relief-carved version. Not only is there more carving involved, but the work must be symmetrical and sensitively done to appear realistic. The tools and techniques are similar to those used in relief carving.

If you can't find a large enough block of basswood for this project, you can make the block by gluing together smaller pieces. For the carving shown, two pieces of 1¾×5¼×12-in. basswood were used. Be sure to orient the grain direction of the pieces in the same way to avoid grain reversal problems when carving across glue joints. The head is carved from a separate block for ease of handling and better control.

Use paper patterns to transfer the top and side profiles to the block (Fig. 14). Band saw the side profile, and tack the waste back on to the block to replace the top profile outline (Fig. 15). Then, band saw the top profile. Before sawing the head roughly to shape, bore a ¹⁄₁₆-in.-dia. hole through the head at the eye location. This will serve as a pilot for the final eye socket hole to be bored later. Then, cut the side and top profiles of the head in the same way as the body.

Bore and counterbore the holes for the lagscrew that holds the head to the body as shown in the drawing. Make the head-holding jig, also shown in the drawing, and secure the head blank to it with a lagscrew. Use four brads with the heads nipped off to keep the head from rotating on the holding jig.

Begin shaping the head by whittling with a knife (Fig. 16). For more careful shaping and detailing, secure the holding jig in a vise. Use a knife, V-tool and skew chisel to finish detailing the bill (Fig. 17), and use a fine razor knife to form the nostrils. After the head is roughed out, use a gouge to shape the characteristic eye trough along each side of the head (Fig. 18).

Next, remove the head-holding jig and temporarily secure the head to the body. Check the mating surfaces

14 Mark top and side view of decoy body on the stock. Make sure both views are accurately aligned. Repeat for head blank.

15 Band saw the side profile first. Replace the waste to reinstall the top view layout. Then, band saw to the top outline.

16 Fit the head blank to the head-holding jig and shape head by whittling. Note how thumbs are placed to help control cut.

17 After preliminary shaping, install head-holding jig in vise and begin shaping bill details with small skew chisel.

18 Use a gouge to shape the eye trough recess, as shown in drawing. This is an important feature of the duck's head.

19 Begin rounding the body by making a series of chamfer cuts around the bottom. Use the mallet for heavy work only.

for a good fit. Trace the neck outline on the body block and remove the head. Then, screw a 2×4 block to the bottom of the body blank for securing the blank in a vise.

Begin carving the duck body to rough shape with a large straight chisel and gouge. Use a mallet to drive the tools for initial heavy stock removal and resort to hand power only for final shaping. Generally, use the hand that you have on the tool handle to apply the cutting power and allow the hand on the blade to guide the cut. For sweeping, modeling cuts, allow both hands to guide and power the tool (Figs. 19 through 25).

After the body is carved, attach the head permanently with glue and the lagscrew. Then, blend the neck to the body with a gouge (Fig. 26). Use a combination of rasps and files to remove the carving marks and smooth the work (Figs. 27 and 28). Some ducks, such as the Mallard that this carving is modeled after, have primary feathers that project well out of the body. Because it's difficult to carve them out of a solid block, they're carved separately and inserted in slots cut below the large feathers carved at the rear. Sand the entire carving, finishing off with 220-grit sandpaper. Then use a ⁵⁄₁₆-in. drill bit to bore the eye sockets and secure the glass eyes with glue.

20 Use chisel with bevel up on convex curve. Pressure is applied with hand on handle. Hand on blade controls the cut.

21 Use gouge in pivoting motion to form the concave shoulder curvature. Always follow grain direction of block.

22 Use a skew chisel for cleaning out tight areas. Work is firmly secured in vise by a 2×4 block screwed to the work.

23 Use a straight gouge to shape the depression on decoy back. The neck joint has been shaped to match head.

24 After preliminary body shaping, use a paper pattern to lay out wing-pocket shape symmetrically on sides of decoy.

25 Use the V-tool to cut the wing-pocket divisions on the decoy sides. Screwed-on block permits gripping work in vise.

26 Install decoy head with glue and lagscrew. Use a gouge to blend the head with the body so the surfaces are continuous.

27 After shaping nostrils with razor knife, smooth and refine the beak details with riffler rasps or files before sanding.

28 Use a flat file for smoothing convex areas, a half-round file for large concave surfaces and a round file for small curves.

Bowl making

If you're interested in woodworking projects that can be completed in a few evenings or over a weekend—and are more than just a set of plans and instructions—then bowl making may be the answer. You can make bowls that are traditional or contemporary, useful or decorative, and in an infinite variety of shapes and sizes.

Of course, the most typical wooden bowl is lathe turned from a single, solid piece of wood that's mounted on the lathe faceplate. Lathe turning need only be one component in your repertoire of bowl-making techniques. There are many ways to shape a bowl—by hand or by machine—and each way lends itself to certain forms and surface patterns. In fact, experimenting with different construction techniques is a great way to come up with new and different designs.

Bowls that you'll use to hold food should be finished with a nontoxic finish such as Behlen's Salad Bowl Finish or mineral oil, rubbed in well and buffed. Decorative bowls can be finished with any wood finish.

1 Hold carving blank in vise using a 2×4 screwed to waste area. Bent gouge shapes inside bowl wall near edge.

Carved Bowl

The most basic way to shape a bowl is to carve it by hand. To shape the inside of the butternut bowl shown, use a 25mm, No. 8 bent gouge. For heavy waste removal, use a router and band saw.

Begin by screwing a gripping block to the workpiece so the stock can be held in your vise. Place the screws in the waste area of the blank. After marking the inside and outside wall outlines, start shaping the interior walls with the bent gouge, leaving the waste in the center (Fig. 1). Secure an oversize base to your router so that it can span the bowl edges. Then, rout away most of the center waste with a ¾-in. corebox bit (Fig. 2). Finish shaping the inside with the gouge, and follow with sanding (Figs. 3 and 4). Although the outside of the bowl can be carved as well, you can also cut it on the band saw. Set the band saw bevel angle so it conforms to the angle of the carved inside wall, and then cut to the line.

2 Use a router and ¾-in. corebox bit to remove waste quickly at center. Oversize base supports router on bowl perimeter.

3 After most of the waste has been removed with the router, resume with bent gouge until desired shape is achieved.

4 Rub carbon paper in bowl to mark high spots for trimming. Shape outside by carving or band sawing at bevel, then sand.

Band-Sawn Bowl

This large bowl is easy to make because all the waste is sawn away quickly with a band saw. While the shape shown is an ellipse, the method is suitable for a variety of other regular or irregular shapes. The depth of the bowl is limited by the capacity of the band saw.

Start with a 3-in.-thick oak blank, roughly 10 in. wide and 18 in. long. If solid stock of this size isn't available, or you want a larger bowl, simply make a laminated blank from smaller pieces. To lay out the bowl's elliptical outline, first center two nails on the long axis of the bowl blank so they're about three-quarters of the bowl length apart and mark the bowl ends. Place a string loop around the pins and adjust its length so that when it's held taut along the bowl axis, it reaches an end mark. Then run a pencil around the inside of the taut string to produce the ellipse (Fig. 5). You may have to adjust the string length or move the nails to get the proportions correct. After

the inside and outside lines are marked, cut the blank in half on the band saw.

Next, adjust the band saw for a 30° bevel and saw to the inside wall lines on each half (Fig. 6). Then, glue the halves back together to form a single block with the interior walls shaped (Fig. 7). Note that the waste stock needn't be thrown away—you can use it to make a smaller band-sawn bowl of the same shape. This smaller bowl will nest in the larger one.

Smooth the inside with a drum sander mounted in a drill. Then, glue a ⅜-in.-thick bottom board to the bottom of the blank. When the glue has dried, use your band saw set to 30° to cut the outside wall (Fig. 8). Carefully smooth the rough-sawn surface with a belt sander equipped with 100- then 120-grit belts. Then finish smoothing with 180- and 220-grit paper and orbital sander (Fig. 9).

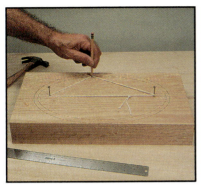

5 Lay out ellipse with two nails and string loop. Ellipse size and proportion are controlled by nail placement and string length.

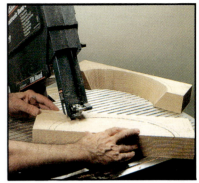

6 After sawing bowl blank along centerline, set band saw for 30° bevel and cut to the inside wall line on each blank half.

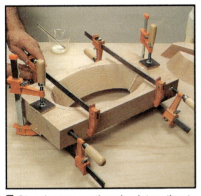

7 Glue the two sections back together to form a single block. Headless nails in waste area serve to keep the pieces aligned.

8 After smoothing inside walls and gluing bottom to bowl blank, saw to bowl outside line with band saw set at 30°.

9 Begin finishing outside with belt sander and move to orbital sander with 180- and 220-grit paper for final smoothing.

Stacked-Ring Bowl

Removing stock isn't the only way to shape a bowl. You can just as easily build the bowl by gluing pieces together. One advantage here is that the depth of the finished bowl isn't limited by the stock thickness.

The stacked-ring bowl shown measures about 4½ in. high and 11 in. diameter. It's made by gluing together rings cut from a 1×12 mahogany board and a ⅛-in. piece of poplar plywood.

Begin by cutting both the board and plywood to 11½ in. sq. and gluing the plywood to a board face. When the rings are stacked, the plywood edge will appear as a light, contrasting ring. Next, set the band saw to 30° and saw an 11-in.-dia. circle that will be the outer edge of the topmost ring. To cut this angle accurately (and the ones that follow), use a circle jig (Fig. 10). You can also lay out the circles with a compass and cut them freehand.

10 Circle jig guides 30° cut when making ⁷⁄₁₆-in.-wide rings. Circles also can be drawn with compass and cut freehand.

11 Glue together entry cuts on each ring before assembling rings. Small spring clamps apply pressure until glue sets.

12 Apply glue to all mating surfaces and allow to become tacky before assembling. Then, use weights for pressure.

13 Level the inside and outside of bowl walls with rasp or flexible drive tool. Bottom is installed after smoothing.

14 For final sanding, use a large diameter drum sander. Glue bottom in place, complete sanding and finish.

Saw the board into a series of four rings, each 7/16 in. thick. The rings are made by entering and exiting the circular cut at the same place on the board. Position the entry cuts so they are parallel to the grain and alternate them from one side to the other on adjacent rings. The solid disc that remains is used for the bowl bottom.

Glue shut the entry cuts (Fig. 11). When the glue has dried, apply glue to the adjoining ring faces, stack the assembly, and apply pressure with weights (Fig. 12).

Don't glue the bottom disc in place yet to facilitate smoothing the inside walls of the bowl.

You can level the stepped interior wall with a flexible shaft tool and a cone-shaped, structured-carbide bit. You also could use a sanding drum, half-round rasp or Surform tool (Figs. 13 and 14). Then, hand sand the inside wall smooth. After gluing the bottom disc in place, level and smooth the outer wall in the same way.

15 Use a compass to lay out the series of circles. Bore a 3/16-in.-dia. entry hole on each ring for the scroll saw blade.

Telescoping-Ring Bowl

Another novel way to obtain a 3-dimensional bowl from a flat board is to cut the board in a series of rings that telescope apart. Once glued together, the assembly is then turned on the lathe.

16 Tilt saw table to about a 5° angle to cut beveled rings. Use larger angle to reduce telescoping if kerf is too wide.

17 Apply glue to contact areas of rings. Align and press each ring into the next and let the glue dry.

18 Mount work on lathe faceplate. Use sharp gouge to trim steps on bowl surface. Stop cutting when steps disappear.

The rings are cut on a scroll saw with the table set a few degrees off horizontal. Both the thickness of the saw kerf and the bevel angle determine the degree to which each ring telescopes beyond the next. If the kerf is large and the angle small, the rings will slide completely by each other. Ideally, the kerf size and the bevel angle should combine to allow each ring to overlap the next one half the stock thickness. You may have to cut a few test rings first.

To avoid splitting, ¾-in.-thick Baltic birch plywood was used for the bowl shown. This material has 13 uniform layers that provide an interesting striped effect in the finished bowl. You could substitute a quality veneer-core plywood. A 8-in.-sq. board will yield an 8-in.-dia., 2½-in.-high bowl.

Lay out the rings starting with an 8-in.-dia. circle (Fig. 15). Start with a ⁷⁄₁₆-in.-thick ring and increase each succeeding ring by ¹⁄₁₆ in. to achieve a slightly curved profile.

Bore a centered ³⁄₁₆-in.-dia. blade entry hole at each circle and stagger alternately from side to side. Cut the rings on the scroll saw (Fig. 16) and begin gluing with the bottom piece and smallest ring. Apply glue to the side walls and press the parts together (Fig. 17). Align the entry holes for proper orientation. After the glue has dried, rebore the entry holes to clean out excess glue, and glue short dowels in place to plug the holes.

To mount the assembly on the lathe, first turn a ¾-in. plywood disc on the lathe faceplate, and mark the center while on the lathe. Remove the disc from the faceplate and bore a small, perfectly straight hole in the center. Slip a nail through the hole so that the center of the disc can be aligned with the compass center point on the bowl bottom. Then, glue the disc to the bottom and remount the disc on the faceplate. Trim the bowl surface until the steps of each ring are eliminated (Fig. 18).

Laminated and Turned Bowl

This lathe-turned bowl owes its unique appearance to the laminated construction of the turning blank. It's made of sections that feature light, thin poplar ply-

19 Sandwich of contrasting poplar plywood and walnut is made in two stages. Holes for alignment nails go into waste area.

20 Miter laminated stock into eight equal segments. Number each piece in order so grain will be continuous in final assembly.

21 After carefully aligning parts, use band clamp to hold ring segments in place after glue is applied to mating surfaces.

22 Glue plywood discs to top of bowl and to mitered walnut bottom piece. Discs permit work to be secured to the lathe faceplate.

23 Mount bowl blank on lathe and use a skew chisel to shape rabbet on inside bottom edge of ring for bowl bottom.

24 Then, attach bottom piece to lathe faceplate and turn down diameter until the piece fits snugly in bowl rabbet.

25 After bottom has been glued in rabbet, use a parting tool to remove the plywood disc that's glued to the bowl top.

26 Shape the outside profile of the bowl while periodically checking the design. Stop when the contour and pattern look right.

27 Turn inside wall of bowl with bowl scraper or roundnose turning tool. Check wall thickness regularly with caliper.

wood sandwiched between dark, solid walnut. The laminated stock is then cut and assembled in a ring shape that becomes the blank for the bowl. When the blank is turned on the lathe, the contrasting plywood is revealed in a regular geometric pattern on the bowl surface. The possibilities of this technique are as varied as the ways you can glue different woods together. You'll notice that the surface pattern changes as you shape the bowl on the lathe.

The first step in creating the bowl shown is to glue up the laminated stock as shown in Fig. 19. The size of this laminated piece can vary according to the size bowl that you're producing. For the 3¾-in.-high, 8¼-in.-dia. bowl shown, it measured 1½×3¾×32 in. Begin by gluing a strip of poplar plywood between two different thicknesses of solid stock so that the plywood strip is off-center. Then, true the edges on a jointer and add a layer of light and dark wood to the top and bottom to create the H-shaped cross section shown. Finishing nails inserted into pilot holes help to keep the pieces aligned while gluing.

After the glue is dry, joint the edges straight and square. Set your table saw blade to a 22½° angle, and cut the eight mitered staves that make up the bowl circumference (Fig. 20). The 8¼-in.-dia. bowl shown requires about 3½-in.-long mitered sections. Be sure to cut the stock so the off-center plywood strip in each piece will be closer to the outside of the ring when assembled.

To maintain a continuous grain pattern around the bowl, number the pieces so that they'll be assembled in the original order. Check the pieces to make sure they fit correctly, apply glue and use a band clamp to hold the assembly together (Fig. 21). Make sure the pieces are aligned so the plywood lines on the finished bowl appear uniform and continuous.

The bowl bottom is made by first gluing together four mitered pieces of 13/16-in.-thick walnut to create a square slightly larger than the finished diameter of the bowl. Lay out an oversize circle and saw to the line with a band saw or sabre saw. Then, center and glue the walnut bottom piece to a ¾-in.-thick plywood disc for mounting on the lathe faceplate.

Next, turn a second plywood disc on the faceplate so the diameter equals the distance between the outside corners of the mitered bowl ring. Center and glue the plywood disc to the ring (Fig. 22). Mount the assembly on the faceplate and turn a 3/8-in.-deep rabbet on the inside edge that will accept the circular bottom piece (Fig. 23). Secure the bottom assembly to the faceplate and turn down the diameter of the bottom until it fits snugly in the rabbet (Fig. 24).

Glue the laminated ring to the base and use a parting tool to cut away the plywood disc on the bowl top (Fig. 25). Then, use a gouge, spear-point and skew chisel to shape the outside to the desired contour (Fig. 26). Finish shaping the inside with a spear-point and roundnose chisel while continually checking wall thickness with a caliper (Fig. 27). The bowl shown is finished with a wall thickness of about 5/16 to ½ in. Sand the bowl on the lathe, finishing with 220-grit paper. Separate the bowl from the plywood disc base by cutting in with the parting tool to within about 1½ in. of the center. Cut through the remaining stock with a handsaw and sand the base smooth.

Cedar-strip canoe

■ If you've always dreamed of building a boat, but were intimidated by the special skills required, then this updated version of a traditional guide canoe may be the key to turning your dreams into reality. It's not only fun to build, but its unique construction virtually guarantees that you'll have a useful, durable craft— whatever your skill level.

The hull is planked with cedar strips and then entirely sheathed in fiberglass. This method eliminates internal frames and the canvas outer covering of traditional canoes. It also makes the canoe easy to carry since it weighs just 44 pounds.

While boatbuilding is woodworking, there may be a few unfamiliar terms. The most important is the word *fair*. This describes a curve with no bumps or irregularities. Checking for a fair curve is done by bending a straight, uniform-grained wood strip called a *fairing batten*. The *sheer* is the curve that runs along the top edge of the hull from one end to the other. The other special terms are defined in the drawing (page 46).

Be sure to use fiberglass cloth and epoxy resin on the canoe—polyester cloth and resin are not recommended. Always follow manufacturer's instructions and proportions of resin to hardener. To glue together the stem components, Coldcure or G2 epoxy are both appropriate. Use acetone for epoxy resin cleanup.

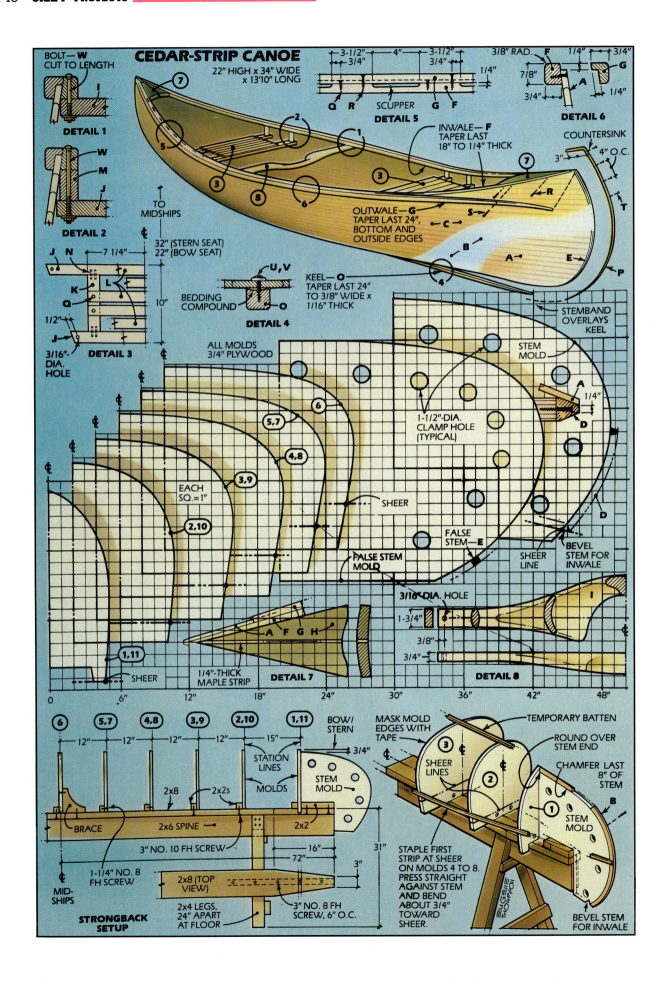

CEDAR-STRIP CANOE
22" HIGH x 34" WIDE
x 13'10" LONG

Cedar-Strip Canoe was written by Kim Aaboe. Photos by Thomas Klenck, Kim Aaboe and Pierre St. Jacques. Technical art by Eugene Thompson. Fiberglass cloth and epoxy available from Noah's, 2246 Lakeshore Blvd. W., Toronto, Canada M8V 1A5. Bronze carriage bolts available from Northwoods Canoe Shop, RFD 3, Box 118–2A, Dover-Foxcroft, ME 04426. Canoe strip flute (No. CS-AS) and cove (No. CS- BS) from Furnima Industrial Carbide, Inc., Beirnakie Rd., Barry's Bay, Ontario, Canada K0J 1B0.

MATERIALS LIST—CANOE

Key	No.	Size and description (use)
A		¼ x ¾" x 16' western red cedar (strip)—50 bd. ft. required
B*		5 yds. 38"-wide 6-oz. fiberglass cloth, 11 yds. 60"-wide 6-oz. fiberglass cloth
C*	1	6-liter kit 83-HA4 epoxy resin
D	2	¾ x ¾ x 42" ash (stem)
E	2	½ x ¾ x 42" ash (false stem)
F**	2	¾ x ⅞ x 165" ash (inwale)
G**	2	¾ x ⅞ x 165" ash (outwale)
H**	2	1½ x 4 x 13" walnut (deck half)
I**	1	2 x 6 x 34" ash (yoke)
J**	4	¾ x 1¼ x 30" ash (seat thwart)
K	4	¾ x 1¼ x 7½" (seat rail)
L	12	¼ x 1¼ x 14½" (seat slat)
M**	8	¾-in.-dia. x 3"-long dowel (spacer)
N	16	⅜-in.-dia. x 2"-long dowel
O	1	¾ x ¾ x 131" ash (keel)
P†	2	⅜"-wide x 48"-long brass stem band
Q	50	¾" No. 8 fh brass screw
R	50	1¼" No. 8 fh brass screw
S	10	2" No. 8 fh brass screw
T	25	¾" No. 4 fh brass screw
U	25	¾" No. 6 ovalhead brass screw
V	25	Finish washer for ovalhead screw
W†	10	³⁄₁₆-in.-dia. x 4" bronze carriage

Misc: Plastic resin glue, G2 or Coldcure epoxy*; microfibers*; acetone; glue syringes; Arrow Ceiltile staples; wood filler; sandpaper and discs; 5' 9" foam rollers; 4" autobody squeegee; disposable gloves; respirator with filters for organic vapors; marine bedding compound; spar varnish; ¼-in.-dia. canoe strip flute (No. CS-AS) and cove (No. CS-BS) available from Furnima Industrial Carbide, Inc., Beirnakie Rd., Barry's Bay, Ontario, Canada K0J 1B0
* Available from Noah's, 2246 Lakeshore Blvd. W., Toronto, Ontario, Canada M8V 1A5
** Cut to fit
† Available from Northwoods Canoe Shop, RFD 3, Box 118-2A, Dover-Foxcroft, ME 04426

Molds and Stems

Select straight, dry 2×6 and 2×8 stock for the strong-back spine and top. Plane the top edge of the spine perfectly flat. Cut both pieces to 12 ft. long and shape the ends of the top as shown in the drawing.

Secure the spine to the top with glue and screws. Screw the 2×4 legs to the spine and level the strong-back top along its length and across its width. Secure the legs to the floor.

Lay out a permanent centerline on the top surface by stretching a string from end to end. Then spray paint over the string so a line is left behind. Find the midpoint of this centerline and lay out the center mold position perpendicular to it. Then mark the remaining station lines.

Lay out the molds on ¾-in. plywood and mark the centerline and sheer position on each mold. Cut the molds on a band saw or sabre saw, and smooth the edges. Bore clamp access holes in the stem molds and screw 2×2 cleats to all molds as shown.

Clamp a mold to the strongback at station line. Note that all the cross-sectional molds are placed on the midships side of their station lines except the midships mold which is centered. Align the centerlines of the mold and strongback and check that the mold is square (Fig. 1).

Check the mold centerline for plumb (Fig. 2). Shim under the cleats, if necessary. Screw the molds in place from below (Fig. 3). At the midships mold, secure a right-angle brace so that the mold is plumb fore and aft. Plumb and secure the stem molds, and screw the first and last cross-sectional molds to them. Secure the remaining molds by tacking a thin strip along the mold tops (Fig. 4).

Check for fairness by laying a fairing batten across the molds to simulate the planking. If necessary, shift molds slightly forward or backward to smooth out a bump or hollow and shave down any high spots. Mask all mold edges with masking tape.

1 Clamp all molds square with center-line. Place every station mold except center mold on midships side of station line.

2 Use a level held against the mold centerline to check for plumb. Place shims underneath 2×2 cleat to adjust mold.

3 When each mold is plumb and square, screw to strongback from below. This allows hull to be removed later.

4 Tack a strip across all molds at the centerline. Adjust each mold for plumb with level. Then, check for fairness.

5 After steaming stem blanks, bend around mold. Clamp fits in holes and caul evens pressure on tight portion of curve.

6 When stems have cooled, replace clamps with screws. Brass screws do less damage to cutting tools if they're accidentally struck.

7 Use a fairing batten to determine stem bevel and check for mold alignment. Note rounding of stem end near first mold.

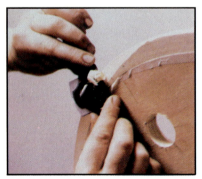

8 Bevel stem with spokeshave while continuing to check with fairing batten. Stop bevel about two-thirds of the way up.

Cut straight-grained ash stem planks to size. Then use a marking gauge to mark the centerline and two outside lines ¼ in. from the edges on one face of each stem, as shown on the drawing. Round one end of the opposite face as shown.

To bend the stems, first fill an electric kettle and allow the water to boil. Place a 4-ft. length of 4- or 5-in.-dia. duct over the spout. Place the stems in the duct, cover the top with a block of wood and let the stems steam for one hour.

Prepare a caul that matches the severest portion of the stem mold curve. When the stems are ready, pull one from the duct and clamp it to the stem mold near the first station mold. Carefully pull the stem around the mold, clamping as you go (Fig. 5).

After both stems have cooled overnight, install three 1½-in. No.6 brass screws in each stem and remove the clamps (Fig. 6). Bevel the stems about two-thirds of the way up to receiving the cedar strips, using a fairing batten as a guide (Figs. 7 and 8).

Planking

Rip ¾-in.-thick, 16-ft.-long cedar boards to ¼×¾-in. strips. The strips are routed with one concave and one convex edge so they will butt tightly around the hull. You can shape the edges with a ¼-in.-dia. canoe strip flute and bead cutters installed in a router and router table. Rout all the convex edges first. Then install the concave cutter and rout the opposite edges (Fig. 9).

Staple the first strip, concave side up, to molds No.4 through No.8 at the sheer marks using Arrow's Ceiltile staples (Fig. 10). Then, hold one free end against the stem mold without pushing it up or down. Shift the strip about ¾ in. toward the bow sheer mark, check that the curve is fair, staple in place and repeat at the other end. Apply Coldcure or G2 epoxy to the stems before stapling.

Apply a bead of plastic-resin glue to the first strip with a syringe (Fig. 11). Press the next strip in place and staple. Fasten three or four strips on one side, rough-cut the excess at the stems, and plank the other side. As you progress, double-check that the molds are fair and wipe off the excess glue. If a mold is low, don't staple to it. If it's high, shave it down. Use scrap strips to plank the bow sections toward the sheer (Fig. 12).

As you progress, finish shaping the stem bevel so the strips fit properly (Fig. 13). When you reach the point where the strips on one side will butt against those on the other, stop planking one side and continue the other side, letting the strips run across the centerline. Let the glue dry.

Snap a chalkline along the hull centerline (Fig. 14) and remove the waste with a handsaw. Then, plank in from the other side, mitering the ends to fit (Fig. 15). Don't staple the last three strips until the very last piece has been cut and fit. Then, spring them all into place and staple.

When the glue has dried, remove the stem screws and trim the strips flush with the stems. Steam bend each false stem around the false stem mold. After they've cooled, dry fit them to the stems with screws. Remove the stems and mix G2 or Coldcure epoxy adding microfibers to thicken the mixture to the consistency of heavy molasses. Apply the epoxy to the stems and use waxed screws to hold them until the epoxy has cured (Fig. 16). Remove the screws.

Use a can opener filed to a sharp point to remove all staples (Fig. 17). Fair the false stem to the hull with a spokeshave and lightly round the corners (Fig. 18). Plane the hull diagonally and then with the grain (Fig. 19). Fill all staple holes and gaps with wood filler, and orbital sand with 60- and 80-grit paper (Fig. 20). Finish by hand sanding with the grain. Cut the sheer slightly proud of the marks.

9 After ripping the ¼-in.-thick×¾-in.-wide strips, shape the ¼-in.-dia. convex and concave edges on a router table.

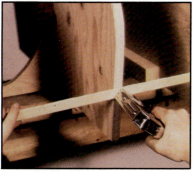

10 Staple the first strip to molds No.4 through No.8 at the sheer mark. Drop the strips about ¾ in. from straight at stems.

11 Apply glue to strip edge with syringe. Press next strip in place and staple. Alternate sides and epoxy strips at stems.

12 With the sides of the hull completed, move back to the bow areas and plank down to the sheer with short scrap strips.

13 As the planking nears the flat run of the stem, bevel the stem to accept the strips and align with first cross-sectional mold.

14 Complete one side of the hull, letting strips run over the centerline. Then, strike a chalkline along the center and cut to the line.

15 The remaining pieces are mitered at one end, pressed in place and marked for the miter at the other end. Cut and install.

16 After bending false outer stem on separate mold, secure with epoxy and screws. Remove screws after epoxy cures.

17 Use a can opener with the point sharpened to remove staples from hull. Fill staple holes and any gaps with wood filler.

18 After removing false stem screws, trim the stem flush with the planking. Taper stem to meet hull at hull bottom.

19 Smooth hull with a sharp hand plane. Work diagonally to remove ridges, dents and glue. Then plane with the grain.

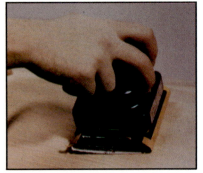

20 After planing, smooth the hull with an orbital sander. Follow by hand sanding with the grain until the hull is smooth.

Fiberglassing

Thoroughly clean the hull, lay 38-in.-wide fiberglass cloth over it and cut the cloth to a football shape that covers the bottom (Fig. 21). Smooth out the cloth by hand and then cut a 60-in.-wide piece about 2 ft. longer than the canoe. Lay this over the first piece and smooth out (Fig. 22). Cut the cloth at the sheer leaving a few inches overhang. Then, make a slit at each end to the point where the cloth leaves the hull (Fig. 23).

Before applying the epoxy resin, make sure that your workspace temperature can be kept at 70°F and you have appropriate respirators and gloves on hand for you and a helper. Mix the epoxy in 300-ml batches

as you need it. Follow manufacturer's instructions precisely.

Pour the first mixture in a tin pie plate and apply a small puddle to one side of the hull bottom at midships. Saturate the cloth by rolling with a foam roller (Fig. 24). Continue working down one side and toward the ends. At the ends, cut the cloth so it just overlaps the stem. Apply resin to the ends with a paintbrush cut short. Then, move to the other side.

After the entire hull is covered, wait a short time for the resin to begin curing (thickening). Then, starting where the resin was first applied, wipe the excess

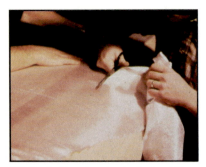

21 Begin fiberglassing by laying 38-in,-wide cloth over the hull. Cut to a football shape that matches the bottom.

22 Lay a 60-in-wide piece of cloth over the hull and cut it 1 ft. longer at each end. Smooth the cloth so it conforms to the hull.

23 Slit the cloth ends along the centerline to where the cloth meets the hull. Cut along the sides about 2 in. below the sheer.

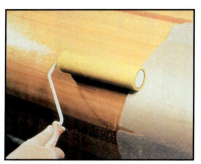

24 Mix 300-ml batches of epoxy resin at a time. Pour a small amount on the hull and work into the cloth with a foam roller.

25 After the hull is covered with epoxy, use a squeegee held at an angle to remove excess. Wipe waste into plastic container.

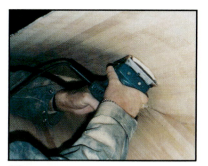

26 Inside of hull is smoothed by sanding. Start with disc sander and coarse paper. Finish with orbital sander and by hand.

away with a squeegee held at a slight angle (Fig. 25). Dispose of this resin. Squeegee out any small bubbles that appear.

When the resin has hardened, sand the hull lightly, cut the excess at the shear, wipe clean and coat the entire hull again. Repeat this until the weave of the cloth is completely filled.

When the last coat has cured, sand with 80-, 100- and 120-grit aluminum oxide paper. Then unscrew the molds, turn over the boat, and tap the molds free. Smooth the inside with a disc sander and 80-grit paper, moving the sander swiftly up and down the sides. Hand sand into the bows with a 40-grit sanding disc. Finish using an orbital sander with some foam between the paper and pad (Fig. 26).

Clean the hull, lay in fiberglass cloth and smooth it out. Let the excess overhang the sides. Apply only one coat of epoxy resin—the cloth texture will provide a nonskid surface inside the canoe. When the resin has cured, trim the sheer to a fair curve and apply epoxy resin to the edge.

Finishing

Make the outwales and inwales that comprise the gunwales from ¾-in.-thick ash ripped to ⅞ in. wide. If your stock isn't long enough to run the full length of the canoe, join two shorter pieces with a scarf joint and epoxy glue.

Check the gunwale bevel angle with a bevel gauge and staightedge laid across the midships section of the boat (Fig. 27). Then rip the outwales and inwales to the angle as shown.

Lay out the scuppers so they don't conflict with the seat and yoke bolts, and shape on the router table with a straight bit. To avoid tearout, move the stock into the bit at the right end of each scrupper, back the stock away and complete the cut from the other end against the bit rotation. Cut the inwales to fit and taper as shown. Clamp in place ¼ in. higher than the sheer and secure with brass screws.

Make the decks as shown in the drawing, fit them at each end and secure with screws. Use a table saw to cut the rabbets in the outwales. Then cut them to length and taper the ends. Clamp in place and secure with brass screws.

Cut the yoke on the band saw and use a gouge and disc sander to custom fit it to your shoulders. Apply varnish and install (Fig. 28). Construct the seats as shown in the drawing and fit them to the hull. Install the seats parallel to—and about 10 in. from—the hull bottom with dowel spacers as shown (Fig. 29).

Hollow the keel hull mating face by passing the stock at a 45° angle over a slightly protruding table saw blade with an auxiliary fence in place. Taper the keel and secure as shown. Then attach the stem bands. Wet sand the canoe with 180-grit paper and apply four coats of spar varnish that contains an ultraviolet screen.

27 Lay a straightedge across center of hull and use bevel gauge to determine gunwale bevel. Then bevel outwales and inwales.

28 Carved yoke makes canoe easy to carry on shoulders. Secure to inwale at midships with bronze bolts, washers and nuts.

29 Use ¾-in. dowels with holes bored through centers as spacers to align seats parallel to bottom. Secure with bolts.

Electric guitar

Electric Guitar was written by Thomas Klenck. Photos by Alex Layman and Thomas Klenck. Technical art by Eugene Thompson. Guitar hardware shown is available from WD Music Products, Inc., 261 Suburban Ave., Unit I, Deer Park, NY 11729 or from Woodworkers Dream, 510 Sycamore St., Nazareth, PA 18064. The small Blitz saw used to saw the fret kerfs on unit shown is available from Garrett Wade, 161 Avenue of the Americas, New York, NY 10013. Paint used on model shown is Martin-Senour Peanut Beige Spray Enamel No. 7872 and Gray Primer No. 7865.

■ There are few people today who haven't at one time or another played—or yearned to play—the electric guitar. The guitar shown here is based on the classic Fender Telecaster. A few changes have been made, however, such as adding two powerful double-coil pickups with independent volume and tone controls, a 3-way toggle switch for pickup selection, a tremolo bridge and custom pickguard.

Guitar hardware is available at most well-stocked music stores. If you choose components other than those specified, have them before you start construction so that any necessary design changes can be made.

Although the guitar is simple to construct, start with a full-size drawing from which you can transfer design details to your work. The neck requires special care to

1 After routing the channel for the truss rod in ¾-in.-thick maple, lay out neck outline and band saw to outside of line.

2 Use a sharp, finely set hand plane to joint and thickness fingerboard to ¼ in. Long bench hook holds work in place.

3 After installing truss rod in channel with epoxy, glue fingerboard to neck with carpenter's glue. Let glue dry overnight.

4 Shape head setback on band saw to bring head thickness to ½ in. Smooth sawn face with drum sander and by hand.

5 After laying out fret spacing, saw fret slots perpendicular to fingerboard centerline. Saw kerf must be .020 in. wide.

6 While hand planing the fingerboard camber, use a 7-in.-rad. template to gauge the arc. Then, sand the board smooth.

ensure that it's straight and that the frets are installed accurately.

Making the Neck

The guitar shown features a maple neck with a rosewood fingerboard. The neck is secured to the body with four screws and contains a box-type truss rod that can be used to straighten the neck, should it bend under the load exerted by the strings.

Select straight-grained maple for the neck, thick enough to be planed to a perfectly flat ¾-in.-thick board. After truing and thicknessing the neck stock, use a router with fence to cut the truss rod channel along the centerline. Check that the truss rod fits snugly and that the top of the rod is flush with the surface. Then, lay out the neck shape and band saw to the outside of the line (Fig. 1). Mark the nut position on the neck.

Plane the fingerboard stock flat and to a thickness of ¼ in. Keep the cutter sharp and finely set, and use a bench hook to hold the stock in place (Fig. 2). Scribe the centerline, edges, body end and nut position on the fingerboard. Cut off the excess at the nut end about 1 in. beyond the nut position and band saw to the outside of the remaining perimeter lines.

Apply slow-setting epoxy to the sides of the truss rod, set it in the channel and wipe away excess epoxy. Then, apply ordinary carpenter's glue to the neck

7 Install frets by first bending to tighter curve than board. Hammer ends in place and then tap from side to side to seat fret.

8 Use Surform tool to shape neck back near head and body joint. Finish between with spokeshave and sand smooth.

9 Carefully lay out spacing of holes for tuning machines and bore on drill press. Use backing board to eliminate tearout.

surface and clamp the fingerboard in place with the nut positions on the fingerboard and neck aligned (Fig. 3). Let the glue dry overnight.

Plane the neck sides to the scribed lines on the fingerboard. Smooth the edges around the head and lay out the line for cutting the head to a thickness of ½ in., as shown in the drawing on page 55. Band saw to the line using a block taped under the neck for support (Fig. 4). Use a drum sander to smooth the curve from the fingerboard to the head, and sand the head face. Trim the body end of the neck to length and round the corners to a ¼-in. radius. Check that the fingerboard is flat by laying it face down on a cast iron jointer or table saw top.

Use a vernier or dial caliper to lay out the fret spacing accurately. It's best to lay out the spacing between several frets, as shown in the fret detail. This reduces the chance of an accumulated error that can occur if each fret is spaced consecutively. Lightly scribe each fret location across the fingerboard centerline. The fret slots must be .020 in. wide. Some fine dovetail saws are appropriate, but be sure to check the kerf with a feeler gauge. A small Blitz saw will do the job.

Use the fret slot jig (right) to ensure that the slots will be perpendicular to the neck centerline. Line up the square with each fret location to guide the saw and cut the slots about ³⁄₃₂ in. deep (Fig. 5). If the saw binds, apply a little paraffin to the blade.

Plane the fingerboard top to a 7-in.-rad. camber. Use a template as a guide (Fig. 6) and periodically check that the board remains flat along its length. Sand with 120-grit paper and a long, straight sanding block.

Mark the pearl dot positions and use a drill press to bore holes just deep enough for the dots to protrude above the surface. Secure with fast-setting epoxy and sand flush, finishing with 220-grit paper.

Prepare to install the frets by ensuring that the fret slots are slightly deeper than the tang of the fret wire. It's a good idea to practice fretting on a small scrap block of maple. When you're confident, you can move onto the actual neck. Cut the first fret about ¼ in. longer than the slot. Use pliers to bend it to a tighter curve than the fingerboard camber. Place the ends over the slot and tap them gently but firmly into the slot. Then, seat the rest of the fret by gently tapping across the fret, working from side to side (Fig. 7). If the ends pop out, you're probably tapping the center too hard.

After the frets are installed, cut the ends flush and file to a 45° bevel. Shape the back of the neck by band sawing the taper that goes from 1 in. at the body joint to ¹³⁄₁₆ in. at the nut. Use files and Surform tools to shape the neck at each end (Fig. 8) and spokeshave the area between. Then finish by hand sanding the neck.

Saw the sides of the nut slot to the correct depth and add a saw kerf between them. Then, use a chisel to break away the waste, and clean out the slot with a file. Glue the nut blank in place with a dab of epoxy, file the ends flush and trim the height to the rough dimensions shown in the nut detail. Lay out the tuning

machine holes and bore them with a drill press (Fig. 9). Then, shape and install the truss rod cover block at the head.

MATERIALS LIST— ELECTRIC GUITAR		
Key	No.	Size and description (use)
A	1	1¾ x 13 x 16" basswood (body)
B	1	¾ x 4 x 25½" maple (neck)
C	1	¼ x 2⅛ x 19" rosewood (fingerboard No. 14FB18A)
D	1	⅜ x ⁷⁄₁₆ x ⅝" maple (access block)
E	1	tremolo assembly (No. STRB)
F	2	pickup (No. WPU 11 BL)
G	4	potentiometer (No. WD 500)
H	2	.022 uF capacitor (No. .022 CAP)
I	2	tone knob (No. KB 130 T)
J	2	volume knob (No. KB 130 V)
K	1	3-way toggle switch (No. WDE 7)
L	1	truss rod (No. 13BAR)
M	1	nut (No. BNF)
N	1	6-in-line tuning machines (No. SD 9105 MN)
O	1	9 x 15½" pickguard blank (No. GB-705)
P	17	pickguard screw (No. PGFC)
Q	2	strap button (No. EPB 2 C)
R	1	neck plate (No. NBS 3 C)
S	4	neck plate screw (No. FNC)
T	8	³⁄₁₆"-dia. pearl dot (No. 13DO8)
U	1	¼"jack (No. WDE 12)
V	1	jack plate (No. JCS 3 C)
W	1	60" fret wire (No. 13FWF020)
X	1	string retainer (No. RG 11 C)
Y	1	set strings
Z	1	tremolo cover plate (No. STB-3606)

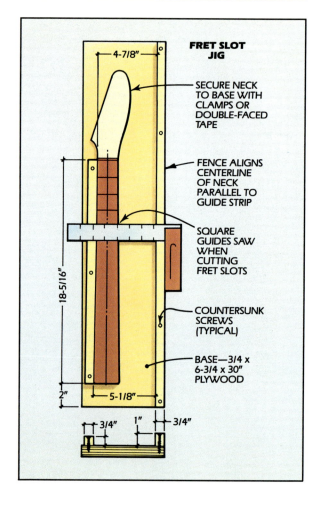

FRET SLOT JIG

4-7/8"

SECURE NECK TO BASE WITH CLAMPS OR DOUBLE-FACED TAPE

FENCE ALIGNS CENTERLINE OF NECK PARALLEL TO GUIDE STRIP

SQUARE GUIDES SAW WHEN CUTTING FRET SLOTS

18-5/16"

COUNTERSUNK SCREWS (TYPICAL)

BASE—3/4 x 6-3/4 x 30" PLYWOOD

2" 5-1/8"

3/4" 1" 3/4"

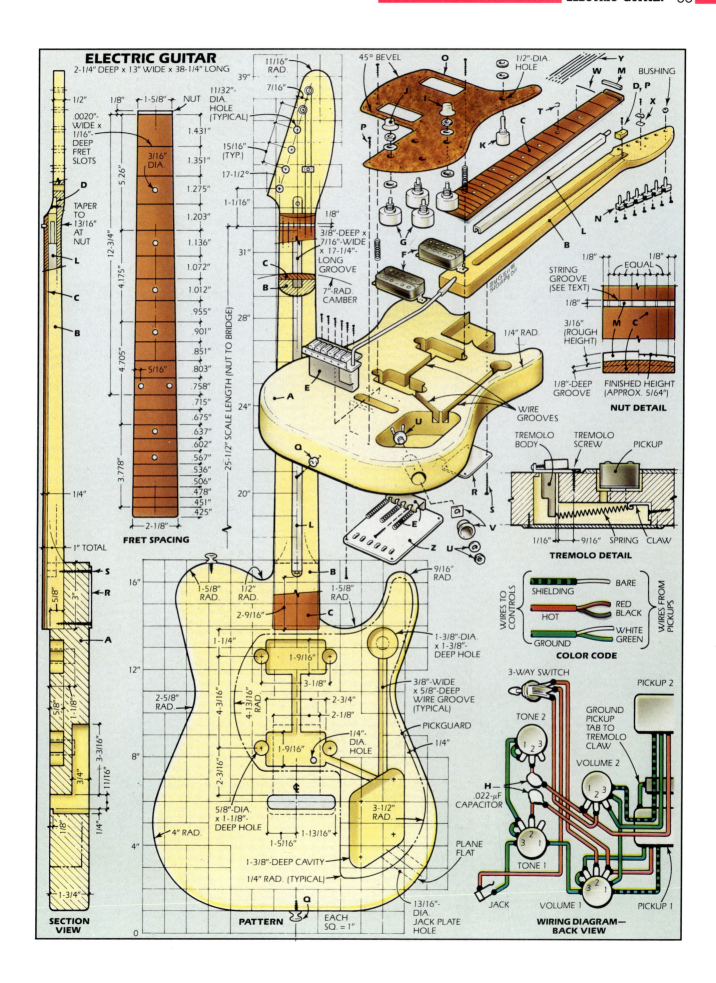

ELECTRIC GUITAR
2-1/4" DEEP x 13" WIDE x 38-1/4" LONG

FRET SPACING

NUT DETAIL

TREMOLO DETAIL

COLOR CODE

SECTION VIEW

PATTERN

EACH SQ. = 1"

WIRING DIAGRAM—BACK VIEW

10 After laying out body shape and centerlines on 1¾-in.-thick basswood, saw to the outside of the line on a band saw.

11 Plunge router with guide bushing follows plywood template for cutting all body cavities. Shown is the tremolo slot.

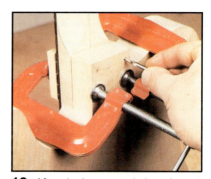

12 After boring screwholes through body, align and clamp neck in place and transfer pilot hole locations to neck.

Making The Body

Glue together 2-in.-thick basswood to create the 13×16-in. body blank, and then thickness to 1¾ in. Lay out the body shape and mark the centerlines on the front and back. Band saw to the outline and smooth with a drum sander and by hand sanding (Fig. 10).

The cavities for the pickups, controls, tremolo and neck joint are all made by using templates to guide a plunge router equipped with a guide bushing. To rout the neck cavity, use a ¼-in.-dia. straight bit and ½-in.-dia. guide bushing. Cut a template to the shape of the cavity, but ⅛ in. larger on each side to compensate for the bit offset from the guide bushing. Mark the centerline on the template so it can be aligned on the guitar. Make a trial neck joint in scrap stock to ensure that the template is correct.

Begin the pickup cavities by boring the ⅝-in.-dia. holes, as shown. Then, using the ¼-in. bit, ½-in. guide bushing and appropriate template, rout the cavities ⅝ in. deep. Follow by routing the control cavity, boring the hole for the 3-way switch, and routing the wire channels.

Lay out the tremolo slot and remove most of the waste with a drill press and ½-in. drill bit. Then, with a long ½-in.-dia. straight bit, ¾-in. guide bushing and appropriate template, rout the tremolo slot that extends through the body (Fig. 11). Next, use the same template, bit and bushing on the back of the body to rout the slot undercut shown on the tremolo installation detail. This time, however, set the template ¼ in. closer to the guitar bottom and stop the cut ⅛ in. from the front face, as shown. Complete the tremolo cavity by routing the recess in the guitar back that contains the tremolo springs and claw.

Use the neck plate (**R**) as a template for boring the screwholes through the body at the neck joint. Then, clamp the neck in place, check that it's aligned properly, and transfer the hole locations to the neck (Fig. 12).

Round the edges of the body with a ¼-in.-rad. rounding-over bit. Plane a slight flat at the jack hole location as shown and bore the jack hole to meet the control cavity. Then, bore the hole through the bridge pickup cavity for the ground-to-tremolo claw.

13 Use double-faced tape to attach pickguard template to pickguard blank. Then band saw blank roughly to shape.

14 Mount router in router table and use chamfering bit with pilot to bevel edges of pickguard. Work against bit rotation.

15 After cutting pickup holes, use drill press to bore control holes, pickup screwholes and pickguard mounting holes.

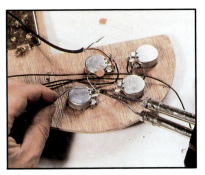

16 Install all of the electrical components in pickguard template and use a soldering gun or small iron to complete wiring.

17 Mount the completely wired assembly in the pickguard. Pickup screws and springs allow adjustment of pickup height.

Pickguard And Wiring

First, make an exact template of the pickguard from ¼-in. plywood and include all cutouts for pickups and controls. This template not only acts as a guide for shaping the pickguard, but serves as a temporary assembly board for the wiring.

Use double-faced tape to secure the template to the back of the pickguard blank (Fig. 13) and rough saw the shape on the band saw. Then, use a chamfering bit with ball-bearing pilot mounted in a router table to trim the pickguard edge (Fig. 14). Use a straight bit with pilot to cut the pickup holes after boring a starter hole with a drill bit. Bore the holes for the pickup mounting screws and controls, making sure to hold the pickguard firmly, as it tends to lift as the bit exits the material (Fig. 15). Countersink all pickguard mounting screwholes.

Place the controls and pickups in their positions on the pickguard template for wiring. Use ordinary 20-gauge hookup wire (from electronic supply stores) for connections. First, wire the hot leg of the jack to the center terminal of the 3-way switch. Be sure to use enough wire so the jack can be inserted in the jack hole during assembly. Connect the ground side of the jack to the bottom of the nearest pot (potentiometer).

Next, connect each side of the 3-way switch to the center tab of a volume pot. In this way, the hot side of the circuit can be routed to either or both volume controls through the 3-way switch.

Each double-coil pickup has four colored wires and a bare shield wire. Attaching the wires, as shown in the color-code detail, connects the two coils of each pickup in parallel for a bright sound. For a somewhat deeper sound with a slight increase in power, you can wire the coils of each pickup in series by connecting the white and red wires to each other and using the black and green for the hot and ground. The shield wire always goes to ground. Be aware that other pickups may have different color codings. Check manufacturer's instructions.

When soldering the pickup wires to the volume pots, also solder the capacitors that connect the volume pots with the tone pots (Fig. 16). Complete the wiring by connecting all grounds and soldering a grounding wire to the bridge pickup tab that will eventually be connected to the tremolo claw. Remove the wired components and install them on the pickguard (Fig. 17).

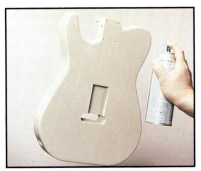

18 After priming guitar body, apply finish coats. Be sure to have adequate ventilation and observe all manufacturer's precautions.

19 Wet sand final finish with 400- and then 600-grit sandpaper to remove all imperfections. Then use polishing compound.

20 Install tremolo unit and wired pickguard assembly. Rotate controls clockwise and install knobs with No.10 facing up.

21 After fitting tuning machines, screw string retainer in place. This holds high strings down to bear tightly on nut.

22 Lay a large file along the fingerboard and move it carefully along the length to level all frets to same height.

Finishing

The guitar body shown was finished with an acrylic enamel paint and primer that's available in spray cans at auto parts stores. Be sure to follow all product warnings, provide adequate ventilation, and wear a respirator when using spray paints. If possible, do the job outside.

After sanding the body with 220-grit paper, apply 10 coats of primer. Allow to dry for one week, then sand with 400-grit wet/dry paper using water for lubrication and a piece of rigid foam as a sanding block.

Have three cans of the color coat on hand and apply light coats until the last can is empty (Fig. 18). After one week, wet sand with 400-grit paper until all surface imperfections have been eliminated (Fig. 19). Follow with 600-grit paper and then use auto body polishing compound, following the directions on the can.

Finish the neck by first masking the fingerboard and then applying about 10 coats of clear spray lacquer (available at hardware and paint stores). Then, join the neck to the body. Install the tremolo so the tremolo body is free to pivot on the mounting screws and doesn't touch the slot sides. Tighten the screws only until they contact the unit, and install the springs and claw.

Tap in place the jack plate and square washer. Install the jack and fit the pickguard to the body. Thread the grounding wire to the claw and secure it behind a claw screw. Turn each pot shaft clockwise all the way and press on the knobs with the No.10 facing up (Fig. 20). Install the tuning machines and string retainer as shown (Fig. 21).

Use a large file to dress the frets to the same height. Carefully move the file along the frets until a small flat spot appears at the top of each fret (Fig. 22). Then, mask the rosewood between the frets and use 400- and 600-grit paper to round and smooth the fret tops. Finish by applying a light coat of tung oil to the rosewood.

Guitar Setup

Lay out the string spacing at the nut, as shown in the nut detail (page 55). Use a triangular file to cut the string slots for the three lower, heavy strings, and the fretting saw for the remaining high-string slots. Cut the slots just deep enough to hold the strings in place. Then, install a set of strings and bring them roughly to pitch. Be sure to pass the two highest strings under the string retainer. Strings are generally classified by gauge and sets are often referred to by the diameter of the lightest string. The unit shown has extra-light gauge strings where the high string was .009 in. diameter.

Beginning with the lowest string, carefully deepen the nut string slot until the string just clears the first fret when it's pressed down at the second fret. The exact position is a matter of personal preference. If the slot is too deep, the open string will rattle on the first fret. If too shallow, the string will be difficult to fret.

Adjust the depth of all string slots and then trim the top of the nut to just below the top of the heavier strings. Make sure that the slots are angled back so the strings are clearly contacting at the foremost edge.

Next, check the fingerboard for straightness with the strings at full tension. A *very* slight forward bend is acceptable, since it provides room for the strings to vibrate. Check by holding down a string at the first and last fret while measuring the distance between the string and the 12th fret. There should be a gap of no more than 1/64 inch. If necessary, carefully tighten the truss rod to reduce the gap and straighten the neck. At the bridge, adjust each string saddle so that the strings are at a comfortable playing height and don't rattle.

The individual bridge saddles can also be moved forward or backward to adjust the intonation along the entire fingerboard. To adjust the intonation, first sound a harmonic tone at the 12th fret by gently touching the string over the 12th fret while plucking the string. Then, press down the string at the 12th fret and sound the string. If the fretted tone is higher than the harmonic tone, move the saddle backward. If it is lower, move the saddle forward.

Heirloom sled

■ A sled is a prized possession, especially one that's homemade. Long after we've outgrown it, we cherish the memory of receiving it while looking forward to the day when we can hand it down to another happy child. The sled shown is built from red oak, a wood noted for its strength and durability. Like any good sled, this one is sure to become an heirloom.

At 30 in. long, this petite coaster is designed as a child's first sled, one for sliding on gentle slopes. Its handle is securely anchored to the body for towing, and a railing helps keep the occupant safely aboard. Assembled with water-resistant glue and finished with exterior-grade polyurethane, it will take winter rigors in stride.

Heirloom Sled was written by Rosario Capotosto. Photos by J.R. Rost and Rosario Capotosto. Technical art by Eugene Thompson.

1 Tape a runner pattern to the stock. Mark the hole centers for the cutouts by poking an awl through the pattern.

2 Make straight cuts on runner with a table saw. Attach tape to the workpiece and saw table to mark the end of the cut.

3 Bore holes in the runners to start the cutouts. Saw between holes with a scroll or sabre saw to drop out the waste.

4 Using a router, cut the stopped dadoes in the runners that house the crossmembers. Guide cut with a scrap block.

Runners and Crossmembers

Begin by drawing the pattern of the runners onto thin cardboard. To do this, either buy 1-in. grid paper at an art supply store or simply draw a grid pattern on a piece of paper. Copy the shape of the runners, drawing freehand, on the pattern. Cut out the pattern and then trace it onto the runner stock. Be sure to tack or tape the pattern in place so it won't move. Poke an awl through the pattern, into the stock, to mark the center of the holes that are bored to form the cutouts in the runners (Fig. 1).

Make stopped cuts on a table saw to establish the straight portions of the upper edges of the runners (Fig. 2). To avoid cutting into the curved section of the runner, mark the table saw bed and the runner with a piece of tape, corresponding to where to stop the straight cut. Stick the tape on the table saw bed so its edge is even with where the tip of the blade's teeth meet the stock. This is important since this portion of the blade will be buried in the cut and will not be visible. Mark the runner with tape where the straight cut ends. When the two pieces of tape line up, stop the cut. Turn off the saw and wait for the blade to stop spinning, then pivot the runner off the saw blade.

The apparatus ahead of the saw blade (shown in Fig. 2) is a kerf splitter. It prevents the offcut side of the workpiece from flexing toward the saw blade and pinching it. This not only makes for easier cutting, but also reduces kickback.

Cut the curved ends of the runners with the band or scroll saw using a ¼-in.-wide blade.

Next, use the drill press with ⅜- and 1-in.-dia. bits to bore the holes for the curved runner cutouts. Draw connecting lines from hole to hole, then use a scroll saw or handheld sabre saw to drop out the waste (Fig. 3). Use a moderately coarse 10 tpi (teeth per inch) blade, which is ideal for straight-line cutting.

Mark the dadoes for the crossmembers in the side runners, including the dadoes for the heavy crossmember in the front. Use a router, with a straight mortising bit, to cut the stopped dadoes in the runners. Tack a straight board to the workpiece to guide the router for the side dadoes (Fig. 4). To guide the router for the wider front-end recesses, use a simple C-shaped guide cut from scrap plywood, 8 in wide by 10 in. long.

Regardless of the router bit diameter and the router's base diameter, the formula for determining the width of the guide's opening is as follows: Measure from the cutting edge of the bit to the outside of the base. Double this figure and add the desired width of the recess. Mark the width on a piece of plywood and cut it to shape. Be careful to cut the sides of the U-shaped opening smooth and parallel. Any irregularity in the cutout will be transferred to the router cut and will need to be straightened later.

Tack the guide to the workpiece, and align it with a spacing block (Fig. 5). The block's width is equal to the dimension from the cutting edge of the bit to the outside of the router's base. After routing, chisel the ends of the slots square.

Cut the crossmembers to size and dry fit them in place. Mark the projecting part of the front member prior to trimming it to fit the runner profile (Fig. 6). Hold the piece in a vise and shape it with a hand plane.

Simply attach a pair of small blocks to the top edge of the center and rear crossmember to provide a notch in which to seat the deck slats.

Use a 3/16-in.-rad. rounding-over bit in the router to ease all exposed corners (Fig. 7). Prevent tearout while routing over the notches for the front crossmember by inserting a pair of filler blocks in the notches. Make them so they fit snugly in the notches, then rout over them. Reposition the clamp as necessary to finish routing the runner edges.

Glue and clamp the two runners to the three crossmembers. Apply pressure with pipe or bar clamps, using clamping pads of scrap wood to distribute the pressure and to keep from marring the work. Note that the clamps are positioned in pairs, one below and one above the crossmember. This prevents uneven pressure on the joint, assuring that, when dry, it will be as strong as possible. Measure diagonally across the assembly for squareness (Fig. 8). Let glue set.

Rail and Deck

Resaw the 3/8-in.-thick deck slats from 3/4-in.-thick stock with a band saw or table saw (Fig. 9). Sand or plane out the saw marks. Cut the curved back rails to shape with a band saw or sabre saw and sand them smooth.

Bore the dowel holes in the side rails, clamp the rails on the runners and then bore the pilot holes (Fig. 10) for the screws that attach the rails to the runners.

Most dowels are less than their stated diameter, so the dowels may fit loosely in their holes. To prevent this, grind a 3/4-in.-wide spade bit to match the dowel diameter.

Cut the deck slats to size, then bore the countersunk holes for the oval-head screws that attach them. Countersink the holes slightly deeper for the two screws under the lower curved railing. When countersunk, oval screwheads project above their surroundings. The two screws would otherwise prevent the lower rail from being firmly seated on the deck slats.

Cut the dowels to size and dry fit the parts to check for fit (Fig. 11). Pin the rear posts where they project through the upper rails with a brass escutcheon pin. Bore pilot holes and drive the pins. Offset the pins so they won't meet. Attach the side rails and posts, then add the rear post and rail.

Hardware and Finish

The handle and bracket are made from 1/8-in.-thick ×3/4-in.-wide aluminum flat stock. To form the brackets, cut the stock to size, then bend each piece in a vise, applying pressure with a stout piece of wood.

The handle is formed with a simple jig consisting of two dowel posts and two backup blocks. Clamp an 11-in.-long piece of aluminum to the block and bend the legs of the bar around the posts (Fig. 12). Nail a

5 U-shaped plywood guides router to make the cutouts for the front crossmember. Chisel the ends of the cutout square.

6 Fit crossmembers to runners without glue. Mark the runner radius on the front crossmember and plane down to the line.

7 Ease corners with rounding-over bit. Place blocks in crossmember cutouts to prevent tearout as bit moves over edge.

8 Using water-resistant glue, clamp the crossmembers to the runners. Measure the diagonals to check for square.

9 Resaw the ⅜-in.-thick deck slats from ¾-in.-thick stock. Smooth away the saw marks by planing or sanding.

10 Bore post holes in lower rails, and clamp rails to runners. Bore pilot holes for screws that attach rails to runners.

11 First assemble rails and dowels without glue to test fit the parts. Rear and side dowels are pinned to top rail.

block centered on the jig, perpendicular to the backup block. Finish bending the handle using a parallel jaw clamp (Fig. 13).

On the sled shown, a coat of Krylon metal primer was applied and sprayed with two light coats of cherry red enamel to finish the handle and bracket. The wood portion of this sled received three coats of McCloskey's Gloss Polyurethane Exterior Varnish. Sand between coats with 220-grit sandpaper, wiping off the dust with a tack cloth before applying the next coat of exterior varnish.

12 Clamp aluminum flat stock to jig. Stock should be centered to produce a symmetrical handle, then bent to shape.

13 Nail block to jig and complete bend using parallel jaw clamp. Sand or file off sharp edges,prime and paint handle.

MATERIALS LIST—OAK SLED

Key	No.	Size and description (use)
A	2	¾ x 6 x 30″ oak (runner)
B	2	¾ x 2⅛ x 12″ oak (crossmember)
C	4	⅜ x ¾ x 1⅛″ oak (block)
D	1	$1^{1}/_{16}$ x 1¾ x 12″ oak (front crossmember)
E	2	⅜ x 2¼ x 27⅜″ oak (slat)
F	2	⅜ x 2¼ x 26⅞″ oak (slat)
G	1	¾ x 3½ x 10¾″ oak (lower rear rail)
H	1	¾ x 4 x 13¼″ oak (upper rear rail)
I	2	¾ x 1¼ x 19½″ oak (lower side rail)
J	2	¾ x 1¼ x 15″ oak (upper side rail)
K	1	¾ x 1 x 27″ oak (handle rod)
L	4	¾″-dia. x 6″ maple (post)
M	3	¾″-dia. x 6¾″ maple (post)
N	1	⅛ x ¾ x 11″ aluminum (handle)
O	2	⅛ x ¾ x 2½″ aluminum (bracket)

Misc.: 1, ¼-20 × 1½″ hexhead bolt and nut; 1, ¼-20 × 1¾″ hexhead bolt and nut; 2, ¼″ washers; 6, 1¼″ fh screws; 2, 1″ oval-head stainless-steel screws; 16, 1″ No. 8 oval-head stainless-steel screws; 4, ¾″ No. 15 escutcheon pins, from Garrett Wade, 161 Avenue of the Americas, New York, NY; Krylon metal primer, Krylon cherry red spray paint, McCloskey's Gloss Polyurethane Exterior Varnish.

OAK SLED

11-1/2" HIGH X 13-3/4" WIDE X 30" LONG

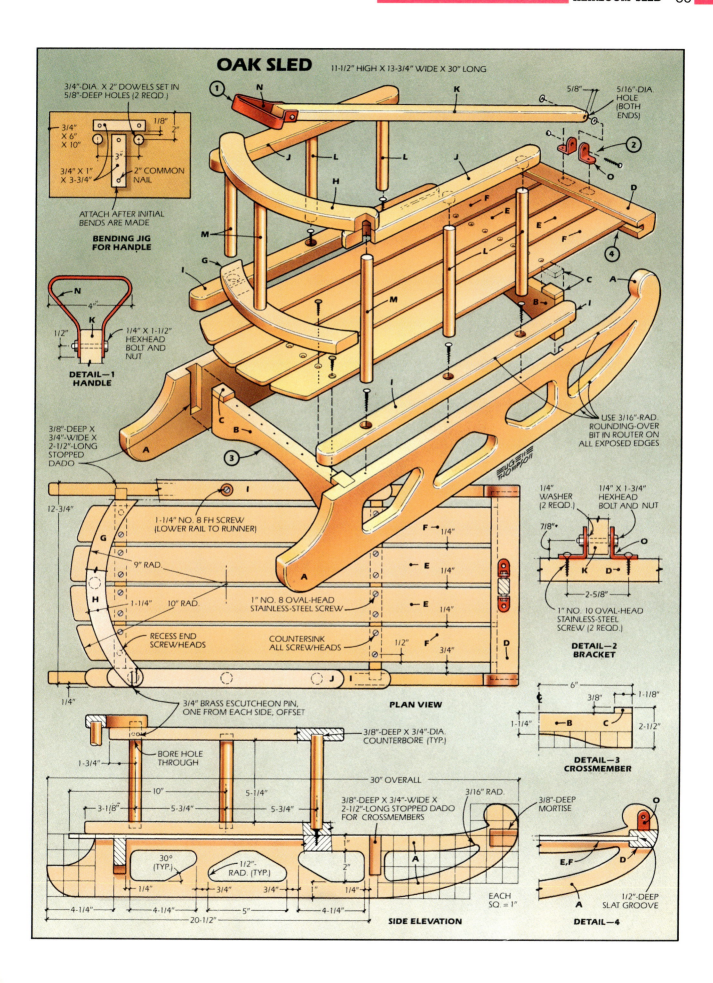

3/4"-DIA. X 2" DOWELS SET IN
5/8"-DEEP HOLES (2 REQD.)

3/4"
X 6"
X 10"

1/8"

2"

3"

3/4" X 1"
X 3-3/4"

2" COMMON
NAIL

ATTACH AFTER INITIAL
BENDS ARE MADE

**BENDING JIG
FOR HANDLE**

N

4"

K

1/2"

1/4" X 1-1/2"
HEXHEAD
BOLT AND
NUT

**DETAIL—1
HANDLE**

5/8"

5/16"-DIA.
HOLE
(BOTH
ENDS)

1/4" WASHER
(2 REQD.)

1/4" X 1-3/4"
HEXHEAD
BOLT AND NUT

7/8"

2-5/8"

1" NO. 10 OVAL-HEAD
STAINLESS-STEEL
SCREW (2 REQD.)

**DETAIL—2
BRACKET**

USE 3/16"-RAD.
ROUNDING-OVER
BIT IN ROUTER ON
ALL EXPOSED EDGES

3/8"-DEEP X
3/4"-WIDE X
2-1/2"-LONG
STOPPED
DADO

12-3/4"

1-1/4" NO. 8 FH SCREW
(LOWER RAIL TO RUNNER)

9" RAD.

10" RAD.

1-1/4"

RECESS END
SCREWHEADS

1" NO. 8 OVAL-HEAD
STAINLESS-STEEL SCREW

COUNTERSINK
ALL SCREWHEADS

1/4"

1/4"

1/4"

1/2"

3/4"

PLAN VIEW

1/4"

3/4" BRASS ESCUTCHEON PIN,
ONE FROM EACH SIDE, OFFSET

3/8"-DEEP X 3/4"-DIA.
COUNTERBORE (TYP.)

6"

3/8"

1-1/8"

1-1/4"

B

C

2-1/2"

**DETAIL—3
CROSSMEMBER**

1-3/4"

BORE HOLE
THROUGH

30" OVERALL

10"

5-1/4"

3-1/8"

5-3/4"

5-3/4"

3/8"-DEEP X 3/4"-WIDE X
2-1/2"-LONG STOPPED DADO
FOR CROSSMEMBERS

3/16" RAD.

3/8"-DEEP
MORTISE

O

30°
(TYP.)

1/2"-
RAD. (TYP.)

2"

1

E,F

D

1/4"

3/4"

3/4"

1"

1/4"

EACH
SQ. = 1"

1/2"-DEEP
SLAT GROOVE

A

4-1/4"

4-1/4"

5"

4-1/4"

20-1/2"

SIDE ELEVATION

DETAIL—4

Mahogany folding tables

■ Most households need extra table space when company comes. Typically, folding card or tray tables are pressed into service and are later put away in a closet. The folding tables shown here, however, are attractive enough to be stored out in the open. Considerably more elegant than a card table or sheetmetal tray tables, these are made from mahogany, although other hardwoods, such as cherry, walnut or oak will also look attractive.

Being able to store these tables in the open not only frees up closet space, but makes them more convenient. You'll never have to dig in a closet again to get at a folding table.

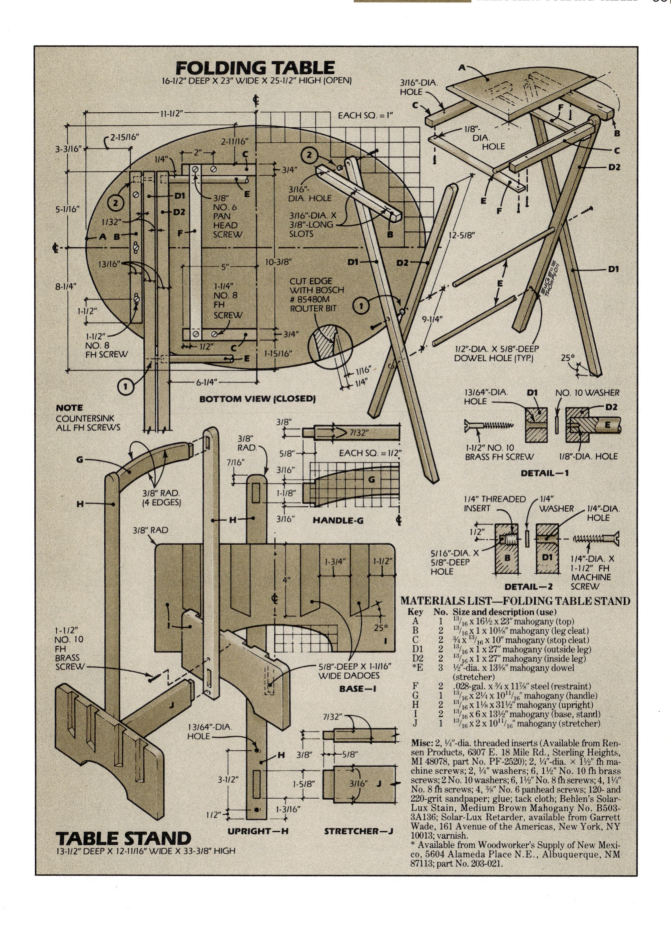

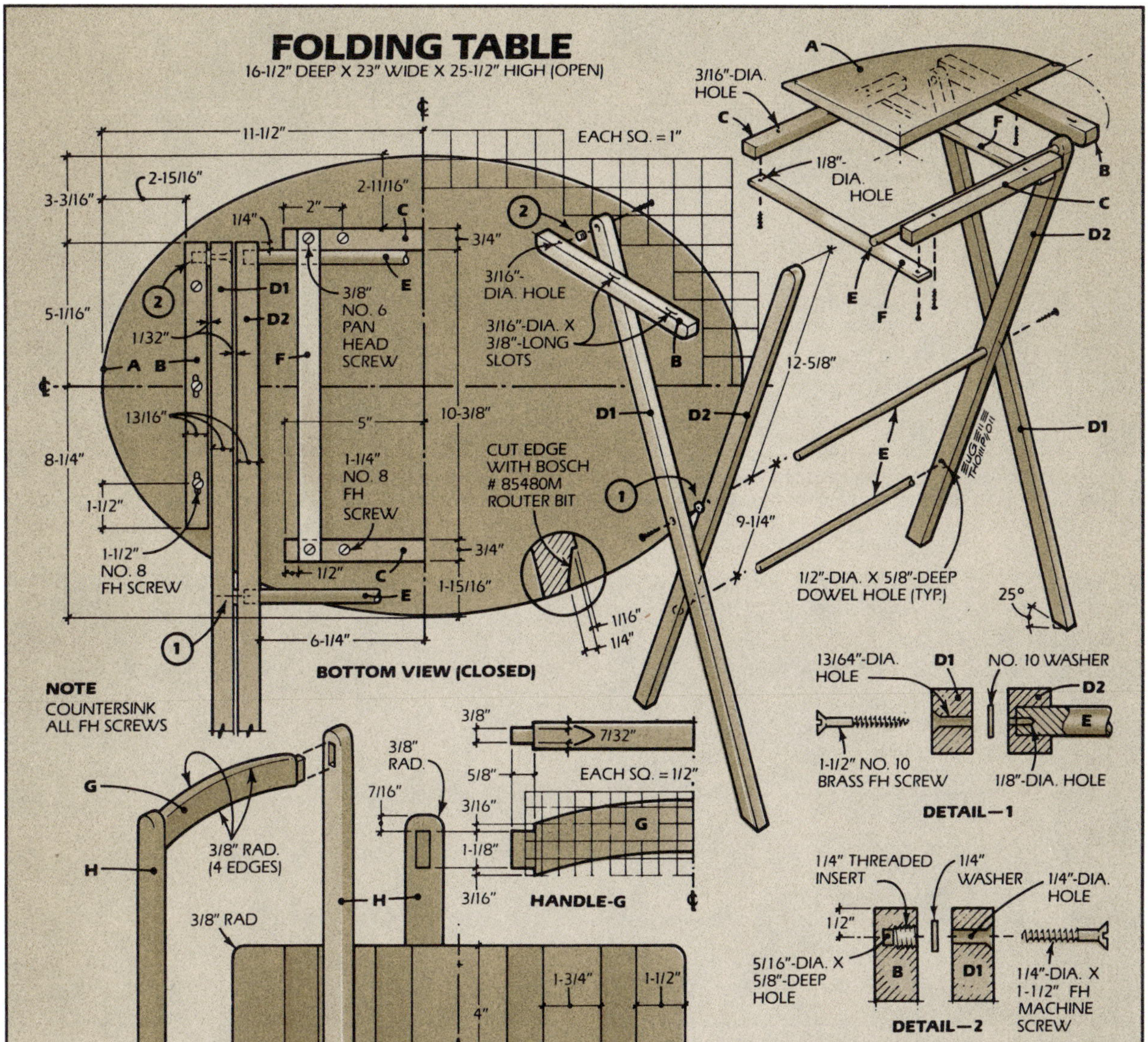
FOLDING TABLE
16-1/2" DEEP X 23" WIDE X 25-1/2" HIGH (OPEN)
EACH SQ. = 1"
11-1/2"
2-15/16"
3-3/16"
2-11/16"
2"
1/4"
3/4"
5-1/16"
1/32"
3/8" NO. 6 PAN HEAD SCREW
3/16"-DIA. HOLE
3/16"-DIA. X 3/8"-LONG SLOTS
13/16"
5"
10-3/8"
8-1/4"
1-1/4" NO. 8 FH SCREW
CUT EDGE WITH BOSCH # 85480M ROUTER BIT
1-1/2"
1-1/2" NO. 8 FH SCREW
1/2"
1-15/16"
1/16"
1/4"
6-1/4"
BOTTOM VIEW (CLOSED)
NOTE
COUNTERSINK ALL FH SCREWS
3/16"-DIA. HOLE
1/8"-DIA. HOLE
12-5/8"
9-1/4"
1/2"-DIA. X 5/8"-DEEP DOWEL HOLE (TYP.)
25°
13/64"-DIA. HOLE
NO. 10 WASHER
1-1/2" NO. 10 BRASS FH SCREW
1/8"-DIA. HOLE
DETAIL—1
1/4" THREADED INSERT
1/4" WASHER
1/4"-DIA. HOLE
5/16"-DIA. X 5/8"-DEEP HOLE
1/4"-DIA. X 1-1/2" FH MACHINE SCREW
DETAIL—2

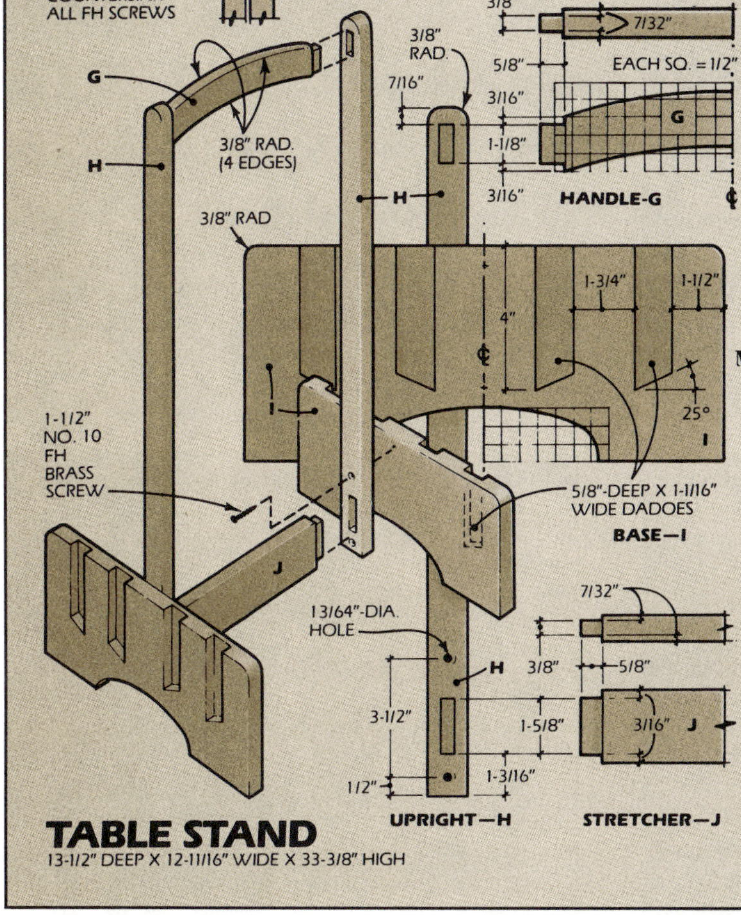
3/8"
7/32"
3/8" RAD.
5/8"
EACH SQ. = 1/2"
7/16"
3/16"
1-1/8"
HANDLE-G
3/8" RAD. (4 EDGES)
3/8" RAD
1-3/4"
1-1/2"
4"
25°
1-1/2" NO. 10 FH BRASS SCREW
5/8"-DEEP X 1-1/16" WIDE DADOES
BASE—I
13/64"-DIA. HOLE
3-1/2"
1-5/8"
1-3/16"
1/2"
UPRIGHT—H
STRETCHER—J
TABLE STAND
13-1/2" DEEP X 12-11/16" WIDE X 33-3/8" HIGH

MATERIALS LIST—FOLDING TABLE STAND

Key	No.	Size and description (use)
A	1	$^{13}/_{16}$ x 16½ x 23" mahogany (top)
B	2	$^{13}/_{16}$ x 1 x 10⅛" mahogany (leg cleat)
C	2	¾ x $^{13}/_{16}$ x 10" mahogany (stop cleat)
D1	2	$^{13}/_{16}$ x 1 x 27" mahogany (outside leg)
D2	2	$^{13}/_{16}$ x 1 x 27" mahogany (inside leg)
*E	3	½"-dia. x 13⅜" mahogany dowel (stretcher)
F	2	.028-gal. x ¾ x 11⅞" steel (restraint)
G	1	$^{13}/_{16}$ x 2¼ x $10^{11}/_{16}$" mahogany (handle)
H	2	$^{13}/_{16}$ x 1⅛ x 31½" mahogany (upright)
I	2	$^{13}/_{16}$ x 6 x 13½" mahogany (base, stand)
J	1	$^{13}/_{16}$ x 2 x $10^{11}/_{16}$" mahogany (stretcher)

Misc: 2, ¼"-dia. threaded inserts (Available from Rensen Products, 6307 E. 18 Mile Rd., Sterling Heights, MI 48078, part No. PF-2520); 2, ¼"-dia. × 1½" fh machine screws; 2, ¼" washers; 6, 1½" No. 10 fh brass screws; 2 No. 10 washers; 6, 1½" No. 8 fh screws; 4, 1¼" No. 8 fh screws; 4, ⅜" No. 6 panhead screws; 120- and 220-grit sandpaper; glue; tack cloth; Behlen's Solar-Lux Stain, Medium Brown Mahogany No. B503-3A136; Solar-Lux Retarder, available from Garrett Wade, 161 Avenue of the Americas, New York, NY 10013; varnish.

* Available from Woodworker's Supply of New Mexico, 5604 Alameda Place N.E., Albuquerque, NM 87113; part No. 203-021.

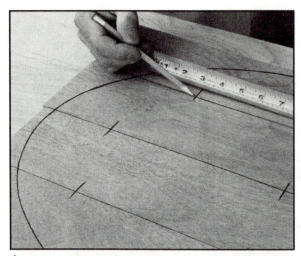

1 Lay out the joining plate positions on top. Keep the plates 3 in. back from top's edge and space them 6 to 8 in. on center.

2 Cut plate slots in boards. To ensure joiner and boards are on the same plane, the work surface should be free of debris.

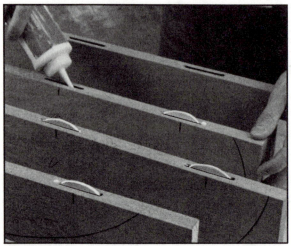

3 Apply glue sparingly to the plates and plate slots. Insert plates in slots and bring pieces together with hand pressure.

4 Bring the edge joints tight with bar or pipe clamps. Scrape off the excess glue after 20 to 30 minutes, before it hardens.

5 Tap the threaded inserts into 5/16-in.-dia. holes in top cleats. Inserts allow the folding leg assembly to screw to the top.

6 Bore pilot holes into the top. Elongated screwholes in cleats allow top to expand and contract without cracking.

The Top

Begin by making a template of the top from ¼-in.-thick plywood. Saw out the template, then smooth it to final shape by filing, sanding or using a block plane. Then, rip and crosscut four pieces of plywood, one for each top, measuring 4¼ in. wide by 24¹³⁄₁₆ in. long. Joint their edges to form a good glue joint.

Lay out the pieces for each top and trace the oval shape from the template on them. You can use joining plates (also called *biscuits*) to align the pieces during glueup, but dowels serve just as well. Lay out the location of the plates, keeping them at least 3 in. from the top's edge (Fig. 1) and about 6 to 8 in. on center. Cut the slots with a plate joiner, making sure than joiner and workpiece are held firmly to the bench (Fig. 2). The bench should be free of debris to ensure the joiner and workpiece are on the same plane.

Apply glue to the edges of each piece, to the plates and the plate slots (Fig. 3). Pull the pieces together with pipe clamps (Fig. 4), and scrape off glue squeeze out after 20 to 30 minutes, while it's firm but still soft enough to remove easily.

When the glue is dry, smooth the surface with a cabinet scraper. Retrace the top outline on the blank and cut out the top with a band saw or jigsaw. Cut on the waste side of the guideline and remove saw marks and refine the outline with a sharp block plane. Sand the edges smooth using 120- and 220-grit sandpaper.

You can cut the top's decorative edge with a Bosch panel raising router bit and an edge guide in your router. Clamp the top so half its edge overhangs the bench. Cut the molding on half the top, then clamp as before and finish routing the edge. Be sure the bit is razor sharp and advance the router slowly to avoid tearout.

Rip and crosscut the legs and cleats. Plane or sand away any saw marks, then cut the radiused ends on them and rasp each piece to shape. Sand them smooth with 120- then 220-grit sandpaper.

The two cleats which run crossgrain under the top are attached with three screws each. One screw fits in a round hole, while the other two fit into elongated holes to allow for expansion and contraction of the top with changes in humidity. Without the slotted holes, the cleats would restrict the top's movement and it would split in time.

Form the elongated holes by boring two holes side by side and chisel out the waste. Then counterbore each hole for the screwhead. Bore a ⁵⁄₁₆-in.-dia. hole in the side of each cleat as shown and tap in a ¼-in. threaded insert (Fig. 5).

Place a top upside down on the bench, bore the pilot holes (Fig. 6) and attach the cleats.

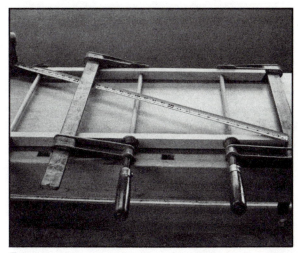

7 Glue and clamp together legs and dowels. Measure diagonals to ensure leg assembly is square, and let glue dry.

8 Use spring or C-clamps to hold the outside legs to the leg assembly. Bore the pilot holes for the screw at the pivot point.

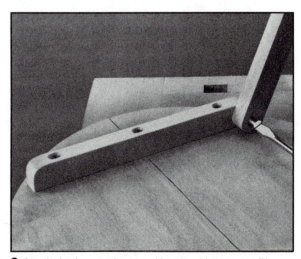

9 Attach the legs to the top with a machine screw. Place a washer between the leg and the cleat to reduce the friction.

10 Lay out dadoes and curved cutout on stand base. Make curved cut with a jigsaw. Remove saw marks with rasp, then sand.

11 Clamp base pieces to bench and run router against a fence clamped to base. Finish dadoes by chiseling them square.

12 Rip a 6-in.-wide×10¹¹/₁₆-in.-long piece and cut the tenons on both ends. From this, rip the stretcher and handle.

13 Cut out curved handle on band saw or with jigsaw. Smooth away saw marks with rasp or spokeshave, then finish sand.

14 With a ³/₈-in.-dia. bit in the drill press, bore overlapping holes to remove waste from the mortises in the stand uprights.

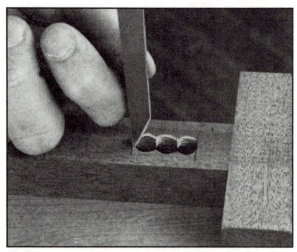

15 Use a sharp chisel to square the mortise ends and smooth its walls. Test fit mortise-and-tenon joints for a snug fit.

Leg Assembly

The inside pairs of legs are joined together with ½-in.-dia. mahogany dowels. To seat the dowels, bore ½-in.-dia. holes, ⅝ in. deep in each leg at the locations in the plan. Crosscut the dowels to length, and sand them with 120- and 220-grit sandpaper.

Cut a 25° angle at each leg bottom, arranging the legs in pairs so the angles match properly.

Spread glue in the dowel holes and on the dowel ends, and join them to the inner legs. Pull the assembly tight with clamps, and cross measure the diagonals to check it for square (Fig. 7).

Clamp the outside legs to the inside legs (Fig. 8) and bore a ⅛-in.-dia. pilot hole into the inner leg. Attach the legs with a washer between them.

With the tabletop upside down, screw the leg assembly to the top, driving the machine screw into the cleat's threaded insert (Fig. 9). Separate the leg and cleat with a washer.

Bore and counterbore pilot holes in the cleats that run with the gain and attach them to the top. Cut strips of sheet steel to length using tin snips, debur them with a file and bore a ⅛-in.-dia. pilot hole in the end of each strip. Attach strips to the cleats.

Open and close each table to check for smooth action and sand parts to eliminate friction between them.

Folding Mahogany Tables was written by Neal Barrett. Photos by J.R. Rost and Neal Barrett. Technical art by Eugene Thompson. Stain used on the tables shown is Behlen Solar-Lux. This stain should be used with Solar-Lux Retarder to prevent lap marks caused by rapid drying.

Table Stand

Rip and crosscut the pieces for the stand base, and lay out the dadoes and curved bottom edge. Cut the curved bottom edge with a jigsaw and smooth the cut with a rasp (Fig. 10). Rout the dadoes in them using an edge guide and a ¾-in.-dia. straight bit (Fig. 11). Guide the cut with a straightedge clamped to the workpiece, and chisel the cut square.

Rip and crosscut a block 6 in. wide by 10¹¹⁄₁₆ in. long. From this, cut the handle and bottom stretcher. Use the dado blades in the table saw to cut the tenons on this (Fig. 12).

Rip the stretcher off the block, then cut out the handle (Fig. 13). Smooth saw marks off the handle, and cut the shoulders at the top and bottom edge of each tenon with a backsaw. Round the handle's edge with a ⅜-in.-rad. rounding-over bit in a router.

Rip and crosscut the uprights to size and cut their curved ends. Bore out the bulk of the stretcher mortises on a drill press. Chisel the mortise ends square and smooth their walls (Figs. 14 and 15). Bore and counterbore pilot holes in the uprights for attaching them to the base. Sand the base parts with 120- and 220-grit sandpaper and wipe with a tack cloth.

Glue and clamp together the uprights, stretcher and handle, and check for square. After the glue sets, screw the uprights to the base.

Finish the stand assembled, but do remove the leg assembly from the tops and separate the outer legs from the inner leg assembly. Finish sand the parts, wipe them with a tack cloth and apply stain. When the stain has dried, wipe each part with a tack cloth and finish it with a good quality varnish. Assemble the tables when finishing is complete.

Ebonized writing table

This writing table is constructed with two of the most elegant hardwoods available, cherry and mahogany. Both have been prized by generations of woodworkers for their beauty and dimensional stability. The top panel is mahogany plywood edge banded with solid mahogany strips that are mitered at their corners and secured to the panel with splines. Using plywood, as opposed to solid wood, makes the top relatively simple to make.

The base is ebonized cherry. An ebonized finish is one in which the wood is considerably darkened to look like ebony, while still allowing its grain and character to be evident. The top is stained with aniline dye to bring out the mahogany's warm red tones, and then given a traditional brushed varnish finish. This gives the top a satisfying sheen and adequate protection against the abrasion that results from books, picture frames and, of course, writing on a blotter or the surface itself.

The result of combining tones and textures achieves a quiet elegance that belies the table's simple, but sturdy construction.

Legs

For the table legs, use either 3-in.-thick cherry, or glue up thinner stock. If gluing up the legs, start with slightly oversized stock and cut the workpieces to dimension after the glue has set. Use a radial-arm saw or table saw to crosscut the leg blanks. Clamp a stop to

Ebonized Writing Table was written by Neal Barrett. Photos by Neal Barrett and J.R. Rost. Technical art by Eugene Thompson. Fasteners used in the table shown are Knape & Vogt KV 1547. The table was finished with Behlen's Solar Lux stains, Medium Brown Mahogany (No. B503–3A136), Retarder (No. B500–00A25), Jet Black (No. B503–1A46), Medium Brown Walnut (B503–3A136). The proportions are two parts Jet Black, four parts Medium Brown Walnut and two parts Medium Brown Mahogany.

the radial-arm saw fence, or on an extension to the miter gauge, to ensure the legs are crosscut to the same length.

Lay out the octagon shape of the legs on the top and bottom ends of each leg blank. Note that the legs begin to taper 4 in. down from the top and they measure 1 in. across at the bottom.

Mark a line around each leg about 4 in. down from the top to indicate the start of the taper (Fig. 1). Extend the octagon corner marks down the face of the legs. Then mark the position of the apron mortises on the leg faces. Next, clamp a fence on a drill press table to help position the work, and use a ½-in.-dia. drill bit to bore overlapping holes. Remove most of the waste from each mortise (Fig. 2). Then, use a sharp chisel and mallet to square the ends and smooth the walls of the mortise (Fig. 3).

Use a band saw or sabre saw to make the taper cuts (Fig. 4). Cut on the waste side of the line. Then clamp the leg to the workbench, and use a belt sander to

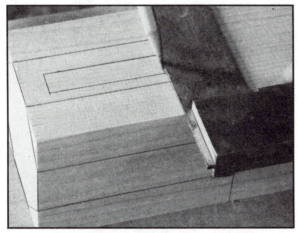

1 Draw line around leg to mark where it starts to taper, and extend taper lines down leg. Mark for apron mortises.

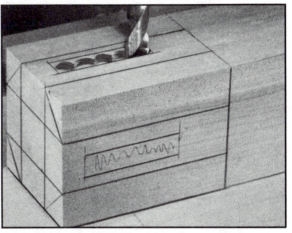

2 To clear mortises, butt leg against fence clamped to drill press table and bore overlapping holes with ½-in.-dia. bit.

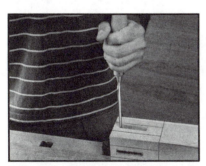

3 With leg secured between bench dogs, use a sharp chisel and mallet to square the ends and smooth walls of the mortise.

4 Cut the leg tapers on a band saw. Feed the leg smoothly into the blade, and cut just to the waste side of the taper line.

5 Use a belt sander to remove the saw marks and refine leg taper. Be sure that the workpiece is firmly held to the bench.

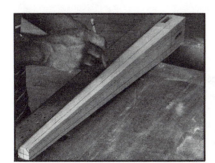

6 After the leg has been smoothed, connect the marks at the top of the leg to those on the bottom and draw the remaining facets.

7 Use a chamfer bit in a router to rough out remaining leg facets. Each chamfer should be about ⅜ in. wide.

8 Finish shaping the legs with a hand plane. Work in direction of grain. If used against grain, plane will tear out wood.

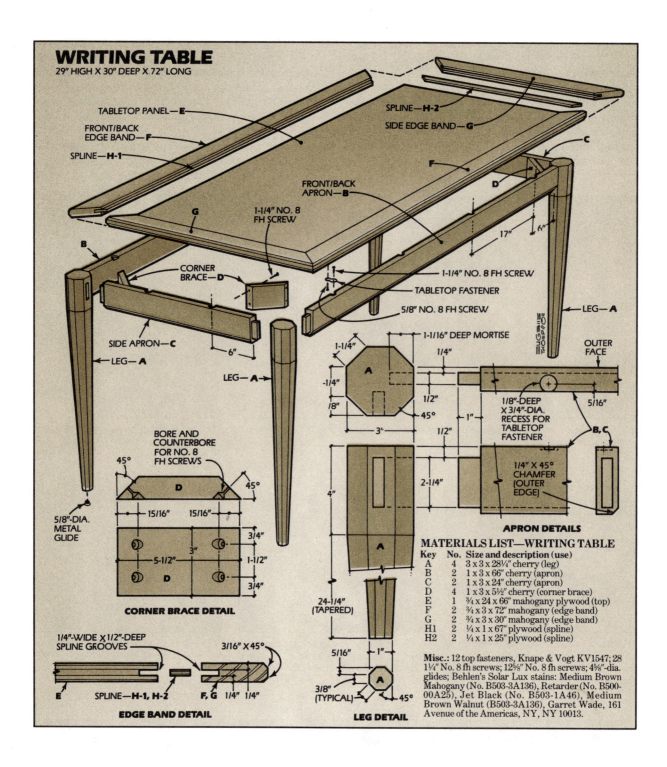

WRITING TABLE
29" HIGH X 30" DEEP X 72" LONG

TABLETOP PANEL—E

FRONT/BACK
EDGE BAND—F

SPLINE—H-1

SPLINE—H-2

SIDE EDGE BAND—G

FRONT/BACK
APRON—B

F

C

D

1-1/4" NO. 8
FH SCREW

G

17"   6"

B

CORNER
BRACE—D

1-1/4" NO. 8 FH SCREW

TABLETOP FASTENER

5/8" NO. 8 FH SCREW

LEG—A

SIDE APRON—C

LEG—A

LEG—A

1-1/4"

1-1/16" DEEP MORTISE

1/4"

A

OUTER
FACE

-1/4"

1/2"

1/8"

45°

3"   1/2"

1"

1/8"-DEEP
X 3/4"-DIA.
RECESS FOR
TABLETOP
FASTENER

5/16"

B, C

BORE AND
COUNTERBORE
FOR NO. 8
FH SCREWS

45°   45°

D

5/8"-DIA.
METAL
GLIDE

15/16"   15/16"

3/4"

5-1/2"   3"   1-1/2"

D   3/4"

CORNER BRACE DETAIL

2-1/4"

1/4" X 45°
CHAMFER
(OUTER
EDGE)

APRON DETAILS

4"

A

24-1/4"
(TAPERED)

A

MATERIALS LIST—WRITING TABLE

Key	No.	Size and description (use)
A	4	3 x 3 x 28¼" cherry (leg)
B	2	1 x 3 x 66" cherry (apron)
C	2	1 x 3 x 24" cherry (apron)
D	4	1 x 3 x 5½" cherry (corner brace)
E	1	¾ x 24 x 66" mahogany plywood (top)
F	2	¾ x 3 x 72" mahogany (edge band)
G	2	¾ x 3 x 30" mahogany (edge band)
H1	2	¼ x 1 x 67" plywood (spline)
H2	2	¼ x 1 x 25" plywood (spline)

1/4"-WIDE X 1/2"-DEEP
SPLINE GROOVES

3/16" X 45°

E   SPLINE—H-1, H-2   F, G 1/4" 1/4"

EDGE BAND DETAIL

5/16"   1"

3/8"
(TYPICAL)   45°

LEG DETAIL

Misc.: 12 top fasteners, Knape & Vogt KV1547; 28 1¼" No. 8 fh screws; 12⅝" No. 8 fh screws; 4⅝"-dia. glides; Behlen's Solar Lux stains: Medium Brown Mahogany (No. B503-3A136), Retarder (No. B500-00A25), Jet Black (No. B503-1A46), Medium Brown Walnut (B503-3A136), Garret Wade, 161 Avenue of the Americas, NY, NY 10013.

remove saw marks and bring the taper right to the line (Fig. 5).

Mark the taper for the remaining sides on the newly cut surface, and saw the next tapers. Again, smooth the tapers with the belt sander working down to the layout line.

Mark the lines for the remaining leg facets (Fig. 6). Rough out these facets with a ⅜-in. chamfer bit (Fig. 7). Clamp the leg to the workbench, and finish shaping the leg with a hand plane (Fig. 8).

Apron and Base Assembly

Rip and crosscut the 1-in.-thick stock for table aprons. Use a stopblock while crosscutting to ensure that the aprons are the same length.

Lay out the apron tenons. Using the dado blades in a table saw, make the cheek cut for the tenons (Fig. 9). You can leave the blade height in the same position to cut the shoulder at the apron's bottom edge (Fig. 10), but then raise the blade to cut the shoulder at the

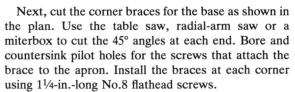

apron's top edge. Cut the tenons just a little large. Then hold the apron in a bench hook and, using a sharp chisel, pare away the ridges left by the dado blades.

Test fit each mortise and tenon joint. The joints should be snug, but should not require great force to bring them together. Finish shaping the aprons by using a chamfer bit in a router to cut the chamfer on the bottom edge of apron members.

Mark the locations of the tabletop fasteners along the apron's top edges, and use a ¾-in.-dia. multispur or Forstner bit in the drill press to cut each fastener's recess (Fig. 11). Clamp a fence to the drill press table to keep the apron aligned under the bit.

Begin the base assembly by joining two legs to each long apron. Apply glue to both mortise walls and the tenons, and use long bar clamps to bring the joints tight. To maintain equal spacing at the top and bottom of the leg, clamp a scrap board from the foot of one leg to the other (Fig. 12). Cross measure the diagonals to check for square, adjust the clamps if necessary, and let the assembly dry.

Complete the base assembly by joining the short aprons to each side (Fig. 13). Carry out this assembly on a flat surface to avoid imparting any twist to the base. Again, cross measure to check for squareness, adjust if necessary.

Next, cut the corner braces for the base as shown in the plan. Use the table saw, radial-arm saw or a miterbox to cut the 45° angles at each end. Bore and countersink pilot holes for the screws that attach the brace to the apron. Install the braces at each corner using 1¼-in.-long No.8 flathead screws.

Invert the base and install the ⅝-in.-dia. glides on each leg bottom.

Tabletop

Cut a piece of mahogany plywood to size for the tabletop. Although the unit shown here uses lumber-core plywood, other core types also work (veneer or flake core, and medium-density fiberboard, known as MDF). Use a table saw and crosscut jig, or a circular saw and a guide clamped to the panel (Fig. 14).

Rip ¾-in.-thick stock for the top edge banding. Use the miter gauge on the table saw to cut the 45° angles at their ends (Fig. 15). Next, use a slotting cutter and router to cut the spline grooves in the panel and edge bands (Fig. 16).

Cut the splines from ¼-in.-thick plywood or solid wood. Check that plywood fits snugly in the groove, because ¼-in.-thick plywood is often less than ¼ in. thick. If the spline is loose, it won't accurately align the panel and edge band.

9 Cut tenon cheeks on aprons using dado blades in table saw. Butt apron against fence, and use miter gauge to guide cut.

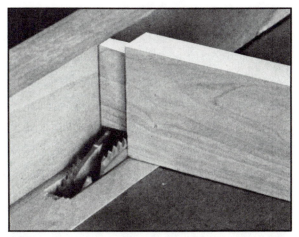

10 Tip the apron on its side to cut the bottom tenon shoulder. Lower the blade height to cut the top tenon shoulder.

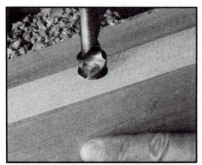

11 Butt apron to a fence clamped to the drill press table. Use multispur or Forstner bit to bore recess for top fasteners.

12 Glue and clamp a pair of legs with an apron. Clamp a temporary support at foot of the legs to maintain proper spacing.

13 Glue and clamp together subassemblies with short aprons. Cut corner braces to span long and short aprons.

Glue and clamp the end edge bands to the panel (Fig. 17). Spread glue on the panel and edge band and in the spline grooves. Clamp until the glue sets. Apply glue to the mitered surfaces, and apply the remaining two edge bands.

Use a chamfer bit in the router to cut the edge profile along the top and bottom edges of the tabletop.

Finishing

Sand the base and top with 120- and 220-grit sandpaper. Be careful throughout the sanding process not to sand through the panel's face veneer. Sand the underside of the tabletop first, to get the feel of sanding mahogany veneer, which is relatively soft and easily removed by sanding. Vacuum off the dust and wipe clean with a tack cloth before proceeding.

The top on the table shown was stained with an aniline dye. A retarder was added to prevent it from drying too rapidly and leaving lap marks. Let the stain dry 2 hours before applying the top coat. Use several heavy applications of aniline dye to ebonize the base (Fig. 18).

Mix the stains and apply the mixture with a cloth or a brush, add retarder to prevent leaving lap marks. Let the stain dry 1 hour, and apply a second coat. Let that coat dry, and apply a third coat, if you want the darkest color possible. When aniline stains dry, they appear considerably lighter than they will under the top coat. The color of the wet stain is closer to the finished color.

Next, brush on two coats of satin varnish to all parts, front and back. Let it dry overnight and sand between coats with 600-grit, wet-or-dry paper. As with all varnish finishes, you can apply more coats for greater protection and a deeper-looking finish. Because this is a satin varnish, however, adding more coats will not increase its glossiness. If you desire a high-gloss finish, then apply a gloss varnish. A high-gloss varnish requires more work to rub out dust specks and other imperfections, such as lap marks.

With a high-gloss finish, follow the finish manufacturer's directions, as explained on the can label. With the 2-coat finish, use a tack cloth to wipe up the varnish dust. Use 4/0 steel wool to remove dust marks from the second coat and apply a light coat of wax.

When the finish is dry, attach the tabletop fasteners to the aprons with 1½-in.-long No.8 flathead screws. Invert the tabletop on a padded surface, and invert the base over it. Check for uniform overhang on all sides. Then attach the top to the base using ⅝-in. No.8 flathead screws. When boring the top for these screws, use a stop collar on the bit to prevent you from boring through the top.

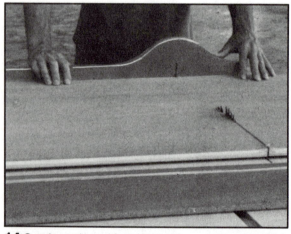

14 Cut plywood panel for tabletop. Here, a sliding table jig is used on a table saw, but a handheld circular saw works too.

15 Cut mitered edge band on table saw. The edge band is cut to length, and inside edge of the saw blade bisects corner.

16 Use slot cutter in a router to make a spline groove in panel and in edge band. Cut spline so it fits snugly in groove.

17 Clamp edge bands in place first. Prevent clamps from coming in contact with glue by supporting them on strips.

18 Apply the ebonizing stain with a rag, brush or by spray. Wear gloves and use organic filter cartridges in your respirator.

Oak writing desk

Oak Writing Desk was written by Neal Barrett. Photos by Neal Barrett and J.R. Rost. Technical art by Eugene Thompson. Hardware and finish used on the desk shown include 2 sets C2006 Accuride pencil drawer slides (18-in. slide length) order No. D7553, available from The Woodworkers' Store, 21801 Industrial Blvd., Rogers, MN 55374.

■ The design of this white oak writing desk is derived from the Mission furniture style that was popular in the early part of the 20th century. The slats lighten its appearance, so it can fit into any room without overpowering the decor. Two drawers keep paper handy.

Its construction is straightforward. The top panel is white oak plywood banded by four pieces of solid white oak. The base has four legs, three aprons and matching stretchers with decorative slats between. A tung-oil finish was used because it is tolerant of dust.

1 Glue up slightly oversize leg blanks. When the glue is dry, rip and crosscut the blanks to the finished dimension.

2 During crosscutting, butt legs against clamp or stopblock on miter gauge. This ensures the legs will be the same length.

3 Mark the mortise position on legs and remove waste by boring overlapping holes with ⅜-in.-dia. bit in drill press.

4 Hold leg securely to bench. Use a sharp chisel to square the ends of mortise and to finish smoothing the mortise walls.

Legs

Begin by gluing up stock for the leg blanks. Use two pieces of 6/4 stock for each leg (Fig. 1), or glue up the leg blanks from thinner material. The blanks should be slightly oversize. Clean off the glue squeeze-out while it's still rubbery, using an old chisel. Then, rip the blanks and plane off the saw marks. Crosscut the legs using a stopblock to ensure the legs are the same length (Fig. 2).

Lay out the apron mortises as shown in the drawing (page 80). Note that two legs have four mortises, while the other two have only two mortises each.

Use a ⅜-in.-dia. bit in a drill press to bore overlapping holes to remove waste from each mortise (Fig. 3). Clamp a fence to the drill press table and butt the workpiece up to it when boring the holes.

Finish the mortises by paring with a sharp chisel to square the ends of each mortise and smooth its sides (Fig. 4). The tenon should fit the mortise snugly, so be careful not to pare beyond the lines.

Aprons and Stretchers

Rip and crosscut the aprons and stretchers. Using dado blades in a table saw, make two passes to cut one cheek of each tenon. Clamp a stop to the table saw or use the rip fence as a stop to make the cuts (Fig. 5).

Leave the dado blades at this height and cut the ¼-in. shoulder on both aprons and stretcher. Then raise the blades to ½ in. high and cut the top shoulder (Fig. 6). Since the dado blades leave small ridges on the tenon, cut the tenons a little large and pare them to size with a chisel.

Test each mortise and tenon joint for proper fit. The tenons should be snug in the mortise, but should not require great force to bring tight. If the joint is too tight, pare the tenon. If too loose, glue some veneer to the tenon.

Use a router and slotting cutter with a 1⅜-in.-dia. bearing to cut the ¼×¼-in.-deep grooves in apron edges and stretchers (Fig. 7). Use a ¾-in.-dia. multispur or

5 Use dado blades in table saw, with stopblock or fence as guide, to cut the tenon cheeks on aprons and stretchers.

6 Cut the bottom apron shoulder with dado blades at ¼-in. height. Raise the blades to ½ in. high to cut the top shoulder.

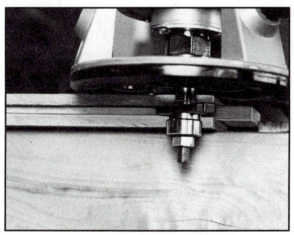

7 Use the slotting cutter in the router to cut the slat groove in apron and stretcher edges. Dado blades can also be used.

8 Use a ¾-in. multispur or Forstner bit in drill press to bore recess for tabletop fasteners in apron's top edge.

Forstner bit in the drill press to bore the recesses for tabletop fasteners on the apron's top edge (Fig. 8).

Slats and Base

Crosscut some 1¾-in.-thick stock to 15¼ in. long and rip that stock into strips to form slats (Fig. 9). Cut several extra slats as a hedge against defects in any of the pieces and to make the smaller filler blocks for between the slats. Finish plane the slats to ¼ in. thick.

Rip several ¼×¼-in. strips from the extra slats. Set up a stopblock on a table saw and crosscut the strips to ⅞ in long (Fig. 10). It's important that the strips be clear of the stopblock once they move into the blade. Otherwise, an offcut block could jam between the stopblock and the blade and shoot back at you.

To begin the base assembly, secure a side stretcher to the workbench with grooved edge facing up. Apply glue to the groove and place the first filler block at the

end of the groove (Fig. 11). Place the first slat next to the block and keep alternating block and slats until the groove is filled.

Apply glue to the apron groove and fit it over the slat ends (Fig. 12). Turn the assembly over and fill in between slats with filler blocks. Use pipe clamps to pull the assembly together. Compare opposite diagonal measurements to see if the assembly is square. Adjust the clamps if necessary to obtain square, then let the glue set up. Repeat this on the other side and the front.

Place a leg on the bench with the mortises facing up. Apply glue to the leg mortises and to the apron and stretcher tenons. Insert the tenons into the mortises, and use pipe clamps to pull the joints tight. Check the diagonals for square, and let the glue set (Fig. 13). Repeat the process to join the front assembly to the side legs. (Fig. 14).

9 Rip slats slightly oversized from 1¾-in.-thick stock. Then plane them to finished thickness to remove saw marks.

10 Rip ¼×¼-in. strips, then use the miter gauge with a stopblock on table to cut the filler blocks for between slats.

11 Apply glue to stretcher groove and position the filler blocks and slats. Slats and blocks should fit snugly in groove.

12 Next, apply glue to the groove in the apron and position over slat ends. Then, position filler blocks between slats.

13 Join the legs to apron-stretcher sub-assemblies with glue. Tap tenons into mortises, and clamp to bring the joints tight.

14 Use long pipe clamps to hold the front to side assemblies until glue sets. Pads under clamp heads prevent marring work.

Top

Using either a table saw or a circular saw and straight-edge, cut the plywood panel for the desk top. Rip ¾-in.-thick solid stock to width for the edge banding and carefully joint the edge that meets the panel. Butt the edge banding to the panel and mark the inside corners of the miters. Miter the edge banding on a table saw or miterbox (Fig. 15).

For this project, joining plates were used as a registration device between the plywood panel and the edge banding. These plates should be spaced 6 in. to 8 in. on center. If you don't own a plate joiner, a spline joint will work just as well.

Place the panel and edge band on a broad, flat surface. Clamp the edge banding to the panel and mark the plate locations on the panel and banding (Fig. 16). Hold the plate joiner and the workpiece firmly against the surface. Cut the plate housings in the panel and edge bands (Fig. 17).

Test fit the edge band to the panel (Fig. 18). Then, spread glue on the edge banding, the panel and the plate housings (slots). Clamp the end edge bands in place, and support the pipe clamps above the panel with thin wood strips (Fig. 19). After 15 to 20 minutes, remove the clamps and apply the remaining two edge bands, spreading adequate glue on the miters. Scrape off glue squeeze-out after 30 to 40 minutes.

Sand the base and top with 120- and 220-grit sandpaper. Attach the tabletop fasteners to the aprons using 1¼-in. No.8 flathead screws. Invert the top on a padded surface and place the base over it. Locate the base with 1½-in. overhang of top on all edges. Attach the top to the base with ⅝-in. No.8 flathead screws (Fig. 20).

Drawers and Finish

Make the drawer parts from ½-in.-thick birch plywood. Cut the dadoes and rabbets in the drawer sides and back using dado blades. Use a stop on the miter gauge to ensure uniform cuts. Cut the drawer bottom groove in the front and sides. Make a pair of plywood drawer bottoms. Sand the interior of drawer surfaces.

Assemble the drawer boxes with glue and brads. Slide in the bottoms and screw them to the drawer back with four ⅝-in. No.5 roundhead screws.

Rip, crosscut and sand the drawer faces. Clamp each face to the drawer box and attach it with two 1-in. No.8 roundhead screws (Fig. 21).

Attach the drawer slides to the drawers using the slotted holes (Fig. 22). Assemble the drawer slides, place the drawer upside down on the inverted desk top, and mark the position of the mounting tabs. Bore on the marks, and screw the slides to the desk with

15 Cut the edge band miters in the miterbox or table saw with miter gauge. Extreme accuracy is needed for tight joints.

16 Temporarily clamp edge band to the panel. Mark edge band and panel for joining plates centered every 6 to 8 inches.

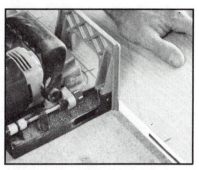

17 Position the plate joiner on a flat surface when cutting plate slots. Align mark on joiner with that on workpiece.

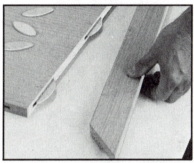

18 With panel and edge band on flat surface, dry fit pieces with joining plates before gluing and clamping them in place.

19 With top on sawhorses, use long pipe clamps to hold edge band to panel. Spread glue on joining plates and on edge band.

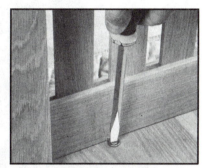

20 Screw tabletop fasteners to the apron edges, then invert base on top and attach, leaving 1½-in. overhang on all sides.

½-in. No.8 roundhead screws. Install the drawers (Fig. 23)

To complete the desk, apply three coats of transparent finish. Allow each coat to dry overnight, and sand lightly between coats with 220-grit sandpaper. Buff out the final coat with 4/0 steel wool.

21 Assemble the drawer box with glue and brads and attach the oak drawer face to it using a pair of 1-in. No.8 round-head screws.

22 Drive screws through slotted holes in the drawer slides. Install the remaining screws after slides are adjusted.

23 Position drawers over inverted desk top and mark position of mounting tabs. Attach drawers and adjust as necessary.

MISSION DESK

29" HIGH X 29-7/8" DEEP X 69-1/4" WIDE

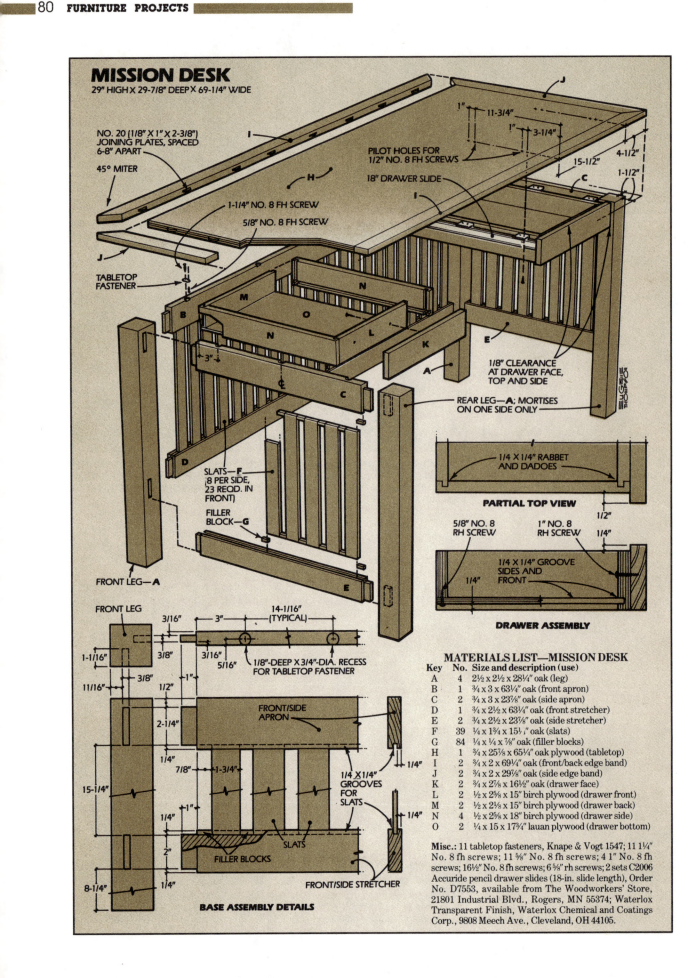

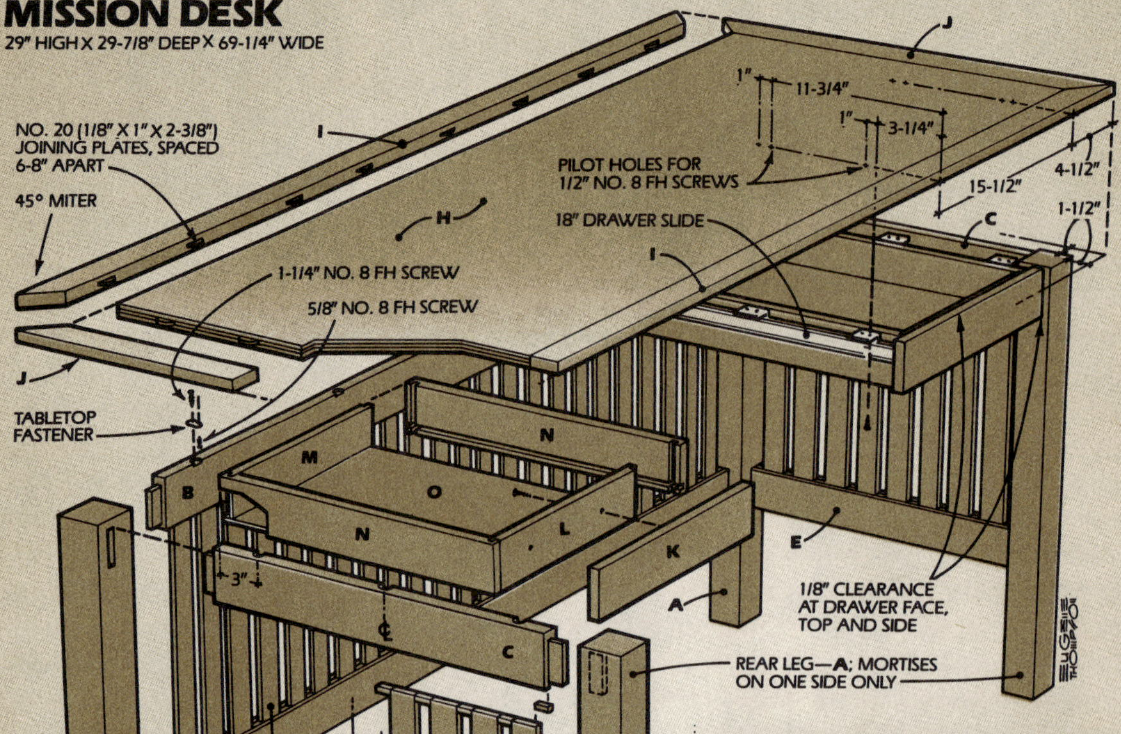
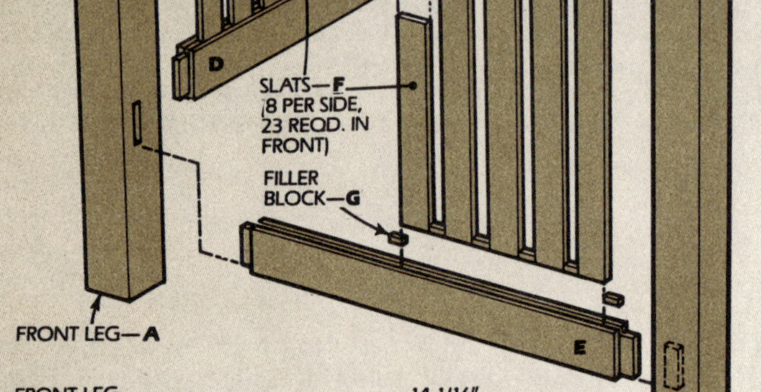
NO. 20 (1/8" X 1" X 2-3/8") JOINING PLATES, SPACED 6-8" APART
45° MITER
I
H
J
1"
11-3/4"
3-1/4"
PILOT HOLES FOR 1/2" NO. 8 FH SCREWS
4-1/2"
15-1/2"
1-1/2"
18" DRAWER SLIDE
C
1-1/4" NO. 8 FH SCREW
5/8" NO. 8 FH SCREW
TABLETOP FASTENER
B
M
N
O
L
K
3"
C
E
A
1/8" CLEARANCE AT DRAWER FACE, TOP AND SIDE
REAR LEG—A; MORTISES ON ONE SIDE ONLY
D
SLATS—F (8 PER SIDE, 23 REQD. IN FRONT)
FILLER BLOCK—G
FRONT LEG—A

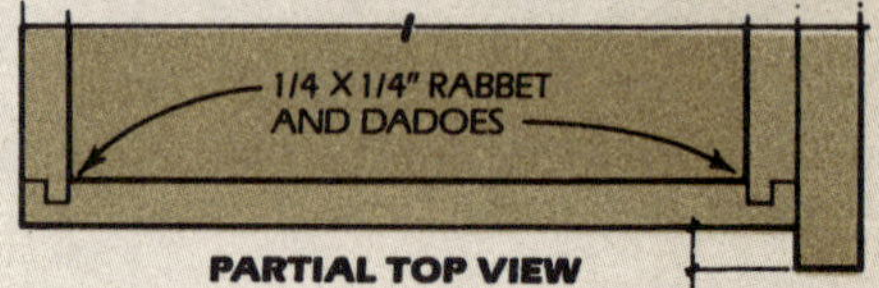
1/4 X 1/4" RABBET AND DADOES
1/2"

PARTIAL TOP VIEW

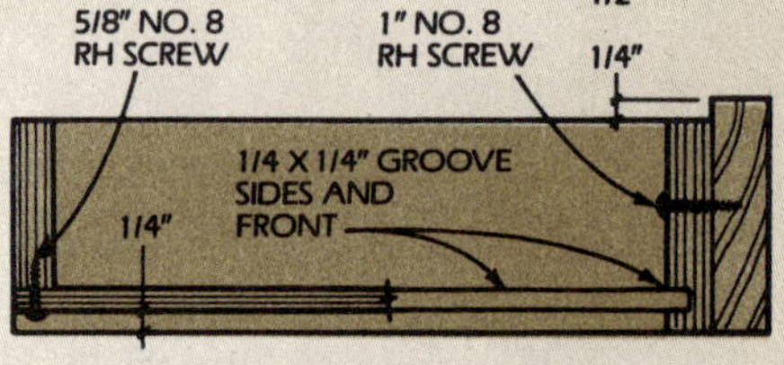
5/8" NO. 8 RH SCREW
1" NO. 8 RH SCREW
1/4"
1/4 X 1/4" GROOVE SIDES AND FRONT
1/4"

DRAWER ASSEMBLY

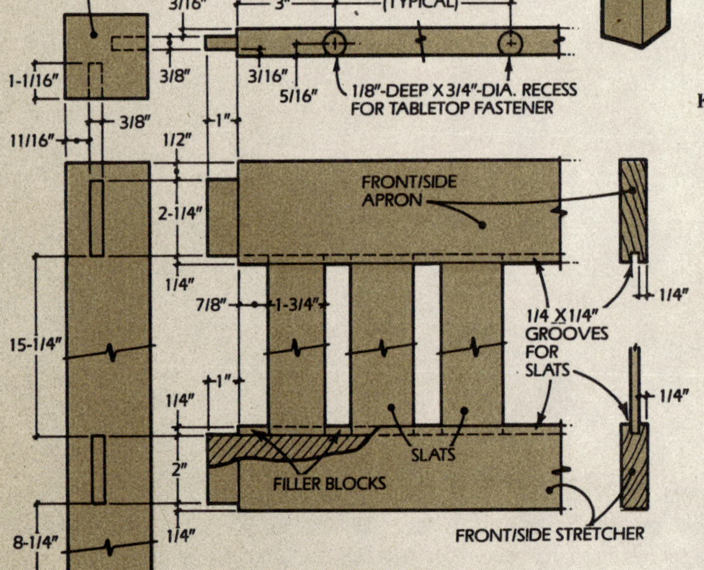
FRONT LEG
3/16"
3"
14-1/16" (TYPICAL)
1-1/16"
3/8"
3/16"
5/16"
1/8"-DEEP X 3/4"-DIA. RECESS FOR TABLETOP FASTENER
11/16"
3/8"
1"
1/2"
2-1/4"
FRONT/SIDE APRON
1/4"
7/8"
1-3/4"
1/4"
1/4 X 1/4" GROOVES FOR SLATS
15-1/4"
1"
1/4"
1/4"
2"
SLATS
FILLER BLOCKS
8-1/4"
1/4"
FRONT/SIDE STRETCHER

BASE ASSEMBLY DETAILS

MATERIALS LIST—MISSION DESK

Key	No.	Size and description (use)
A	4	2½ x 2½ x 28¼" oak (leg)
B	1	¾ x 3 x 63¼" oak (front apron)
C	2	¾ x 3 x 23⅞" oak (side apron)
D	1	¾ x 2½ x 63¼" oak (front stretcher)
E	2	¾ x 2½ x 23⅞" oak (side stretcher)
F	39	¼ x 1¾ x 15¼" oak (slats)
G	84	¼ x ¼ x ⅞" oak (filler blocks)
H	1	¾ x 25⅞ x 65¼" oak plywood (tabletop)
I	2	¾ x 2 x 69¼" oak (front/back edge band)
J	2	¾ x 2 x 29⅞" oak (side edge band)
K	2	¾ x 2⅞ x 16½" oak (drawer face)
L	2	½ x 2⅝ x 15" birch plywood (drawer front)
M	2	½ x 2⅛ x 15" birch plywood (drawer back)
N	4	½ x 2⅝ x 18" birch plywood (drawer side)
O	2	¼ x 15 x 17¾" lauan plywood (drawer bottom)

Misc.: 11 tabletop fasteners, Knape & Vogt 1547; 11 1¼" No. 8 fh screws; 11 ⅝" No. 8 fh screws; 4 1" No. 8 fh screws; 16½" No. 8 fh screws; 6 ⅝" rh screws; 2 sets C2006 Accuride pencil drawer slides (18-in. slide length), Order No. D7553, available from The Woodworkers' Store, 21801 Industrial Blvd., Rogers, MN 55374; Waterlox Transparent Finish, Waterlox Chemical and Coatings Corp., 9808 Meech Ave., Cleveland, OH 44105.

Painting walls and ceilings

■ Painting is the most popular do-it-yourself project for two very good reasons. Learning to paint is relatively easy, and your investment in paint equipment is minimal compared to the dramatic change created by a new coat of paint.

The secret to a professional-looking, long-lasting paint job is preparation. Unless your walls and ceilings are in unusually good condition, you will probably spend more time preparing to paint than actually painting.

Painting Equipment

Many time-saving painting devices are now on the market. Some are designed for professional use, but many can be used economically by the weekend painter. You'll find the best selection of paint equipment in a store that sells to painting contractors and consumers. A word of advice: Buy good quality equipment and paint.

Invest in a couple of canvas dropcloths. These are heavy enough to withstand rugged foot traffic and will protect your carpeting or hardwood floors. Paint splatters are absorbed in a canvas dropcloth, unlike plastic on which they dry then flake off in a snowlike flurry. An 8×10 ft. canvas is convenient to move around and costs about $30. Buy more than one dropcloth if you're painting a large area, such as the entire top floor of a house, at one time. It's inefficient and messy to constantly have to move one dropcloth as you paint.

Plastic dropcloths cost from $3 to $5. If there's a choice, go for the heaviest (highest mil number) plastic dropcloth. You can use these alone or under old sheets, blankets or draperies. Check to see that you do not have a slippery combination because some fabrics will slide on plastic.

Even though most of your painting will be done with a roller, you still need a brush to *cut in* or apply paint in the corners. A 2½-in.-wide brush is the best tool for cutting in. It carries enough paint for easy coverage but is lightweight and easy to handle. Nylon or polyester bristle brushes can be used with latex or oil (alkyd-based) paints. Bristle (also called China, hog or natural bristle) brushes are used with oil paints and go limp from the water in latex paints.

A 9-in.-wide paint roller is a good choice for the do-it-yourselfer. Buy a roller handle that accepts a screw-in extension pole. The roller handle's frame should be stiff enough to resist flexing. A cheap handle

will flex, leaving an uneven coat of paint, and the roller will keep running off the handle. A stiff frame handle lets you work the roller into corners.

Most good quality roller handles are sold without rollers (sometimes called covers or sleeves). Buy a roller labeled for walls and ceilings or one with a nap between ⅜ and ½ in. long. If you're painting a heavily textured surface, such as walls and ceiling that have received a stucco treatment, get a roller with a longer nap (more than ½ in. long).

The roller should fit snugly on the handle. The better quality rollers have a plastic core and will provide years of service if you clean them properly. You'll also find a cheaper line of disposable rollers with cardboard cores. Some are made of a spongelike material.

Purchase a sturdy metal roller pan. Inexpensive plastic pans are flimsy and flex when you pick them up, spilling the paint. A metal pan is sturdy and has legs or corner brackets so you can hook it over the top of a ladder.

If you're painting several rooms the same color, use a 5-gallon paint bucket with a lid and a roller screen that hangs in the bucket. You can buy a roller screen at paint stores that sell to professionals. The screen hooks over the bucket's edge and hangs in the container.

Fill the bucket with a couple gallons of paint, dip the roller into it, and work the roller up and down the screen to push out excess paint.

Painting Walls and Ceilings was written by Katie and Gene Hamilton. Illustrations by George Retseck.

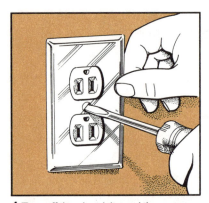

1 Turn off the electricity and then remove switch plates and outlet covers. Store them with their mounting screws in a plastic bag.

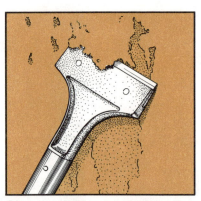

2 Scrape off loose paint, dirt, old wallpaper glue and high spots with a razor scraper. Change the scraper blades frequently.

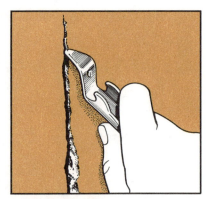

3 Widen small cracks in plaster walls into a wedge shape with a can opener. An old screwdriver blade also works well.

Screw an extension handle into the roller handle, and you can paint the walls and ceilings without using a step ladder. The extension handle also lets you spread paint on the roller without bending over. When it's time for a break, just drop the grate into the bucket, snap on the lid and wrap the roller in aluminum foil.

Estimating How Much Paint You Need

Figure 1 gallon of paint covers about 350 sq. ft., slightly less if the walls are unpainted drywall. To estimate the amount of paint you need, determine the paintable wall and ceiling area. Add the length of all the walls and multiply this by the ceiling height. From this total, subtract 20 sq. ft. for each door and 15 sq. ft. for each window. Divide this total by 350 to find out how many gallons of paint you need for the walls, Multiply the ceiling's length times its width to determine its area and divide it by 350 to arrive at the number of gallons required.

Wall and ceiling paint is sold in gallons and quarts, so round your paint estimate to the nearest quart. For example, if you need 1.33 gallons, purchase 1 gallon and 2 quarts. If you need more than 2 quarts, buy a gallon. You can use the extra paint for touching up later.

You will need two coats of paint to cover dark colors or if the walls are heavily patched. In this case, use a high-hiding (high solids content) primer which is less expensive for the first coat. Ask your paint store to tint the primer to bring it close to the final paint color.

Choosing Paint

Oil-based (alkyd) and water-based (latex) paints are the two major types of paint to use on walls and ceilings. Alkyd-based paints are durable and washable, but tools used to apply them must be cleaned with paint thinner.

Tools used to apply latex paints are cleaned with soap and water. Latex does not have the strong smell of alkyd-based paints—an important consideration if you're painting indoors in the winter and ventilation is less than ideal. Both alkyd and latex wall paint are available in a flat or semigloss finish.

Generally, flat latex paints are the best choice for the do-it-yourselfer to use on most walls and ceilings. Flat paint is easy on the eye since it reflects minimum light.

In heavy traffic areas, like the kitchen, bathroom, hallway or small child's bedroom, consider using a

4 Apply spackle into the crack with a putty knife. Press in spackle with blade at 30° angle. Scrape off excess with the blade at 45°.

5 Use drywall joint compound on small cracks and as a top coat for large cracks. It hardly shrinks and is easy to sand smooth.

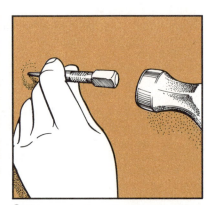

6 Drive protruding drywall nails with a nailset. Place a new nail above the popped nail, then fill the combined nail hole.

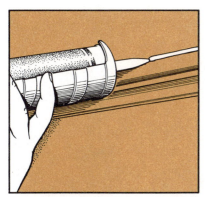

7 Fill gaps between walls or ceiling and moldings with inexpensive latex caulk. The caulk should be a thin, even bead.

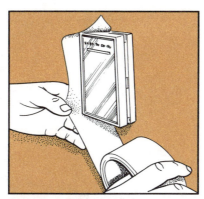

8 Mask off the thermostats, baseboard trim and wall fixtures to protect them from paint splatter thrown by the roller.

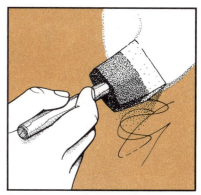

9 Stains bleed through latex paint, so hide them with a shellac-based primer. Apply the primer with a foam brush.

semigloss paint that can withstand several washings. Alkyd-based paint (flat or semigloss) is a good choice in the bathroom, especially if you like to take long, steamy showers, because it has good resistance to mildew. If mildew appears, it's easily removed with bleach and soapy water. The tough surface of alkyd semigloss finish withstands this kind of washing.

Quality paint gives better coverage and stands up better to washing than economy paints. Most good quality paints offer one-coat coverage under normal conditions and are actually easier to spread and level than inexpensive paints. The cost of even the most expensive paint is modest compared to the value of the labor involved in preparing and painting the walls and ceiling. Given the extra durability and better finish offered by quality paint, it makes sense to spend the extra $15 to $20 per room to buy it.

Getting Ready

Move as much furniture as you can into other rooms. What can't be easily moved, place in the center of the room at least 3 ft. from the walls. If it's a large room, stack furniture in two areas so there's ladder space in between.

Cover household furnishings and anything else left in the room with old bed sheets or plastic dropcloths taped closed. Completely cover wall-to-wall carpeting and hardwood floors with dropcloths and remove area rugs. Dropcloths should overlap each other by at least 1 ft., and they should reach well into corners and under radiators.

Paint sticks better to a clean surface, so thoroughly dust ceiling corners, baseboards and inside closets. Use a rag wrapped around a broom or vacuum's crevice tool and duster attachment to reach difficult areas.

Wash dirty walls and ceilings with a solution of trisodium phosphate mixed with water or Spic'n'Span to remove grease, grime and mildew. Use a strong household detergent if phosphate-based cleaners are not allowed in your area. Rinse the washed area with water and let it dry.

Remove electrical switch plates and outlet covers. Store the plates, covers and mounting screws in a plastic bag (Fig. 1).

Before painting, make repairs to the drywall and plaster surfaces so they are completely smooth and free of cracks and holes. Caulk the gaps between the walls or ceiling and the baseboards (Figs. 2 through 7).

Protect woodwork and thermostats from the fine splatter tossed by paint rollers by gently applying 1-in.-wide masking tape to them (Fig. 8). For maximum protection, use a flat knife to tuck masking tape into the corner where wall-to-wall carpeting meets the baseboard. The mastic used on masking tape will set if left in place too long, so remove all tape as soon as the paint has dried.

If it's feasible, remove hanging chandeliers and wall fixtures. Otherwise, wrap them in plastic bags and tape closed. Tape carefully, making sure that paintable surfaces are not covered by tape.

If there are any ink or marker pen stains, cover them with a stain killer, such as BIN, a widely available pigmented shellac (Fig. 9). To save cleanup time, line the paint pans with aluminum foil (Fig. 10). Dispose of or recycle the foil when you're done.

Paint Ceiling First

Paint the ceiling before you paint the walls. Since the paint roller cannot reach into the corners or paint right up to the woodwork, the first step is to cut in the ceiling (apply a 2-in.-wide band of paint around the ceiling) using a 2½-in.-wide brush. You may want to use an edge guard while cutting in the ceiling (Fig. 11). Wipe the guard frequently to avoid getting paint on the wall.

You don't have to complete the cutting in before you start rolling. One painter can cut in the ceiling while another rolls on the paint. Allow the cut-in person to get a head start, then begin rolling. Don't let the painter cutting in get more than 20 minutes ahead of the painter with the roller. Should the painted band dry, the paint applied by the roller acts as a second coat, and this 2-coat area becomes a lap mark.

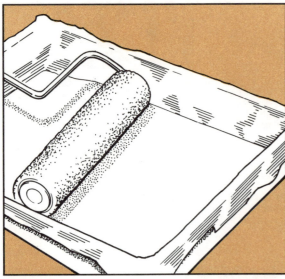

10 Save cleanup time by lining the paint pan with aluminum foil. At the end of the day, pour off excess paint, then dispose of foil.

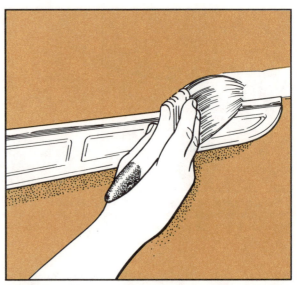

11 Hold an edge guard against the wall while you cut in the ceiling. Clean the guard occasionally by wiping it with a rag.

If you use the same color on the walls and ceiling, it's not as difficult to make accurate cutlines where the ceiling meets the wall.

Regardless of whether the walls and ceiling are the same color, paint the cut-in line as heavily as you can without dripping. Spread the paint evenly, but don't brush it too much. Use a damp rag to wipe off the walls.

To paint the rest of the ceiling, use a 4-ft.-long extension pole screwed into the roller handle. Start rolling at one end of the room and work the roller back and forth parallel to the longest wall (Fig. 12). Work your way across the ceiling in 3- or 4-ft.-sq. patches. When you reach the opposite wall, go back to the first wall. This technique lets you spread paint into new areas, but prevents lap marks.

Dip your roller in the paint, but don't submerge it, to avoid getting paint inside the roller (Fig. 13). This can cause runs and drips when the paint begins to leak out. Dip frequently and don't be stingy. If you try to spread the paint too far, you will not get even coverage. Similarly, don't roll paint too heavily. This can leave lap marks and runs.

When you are finished, move everything to the center of the room so you have free access to the walls.

Cut In and Paint the Walls

With the ceiling painted, start cutting in the corners of the room. Spread paint about 2 in. out from the

12 Use a 15-ft.-long extension handle when painting ceiling and walls. The extension screws into the roller handle.

13 To paint a large area, hang a roller screen in a 5-gallon paint pail filled with a couple of gallons of paint.

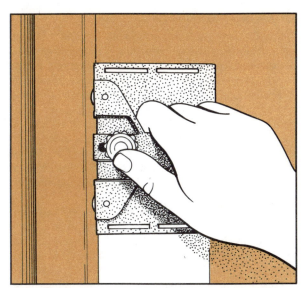

14 Cut in around door and window trim with a wheeled paint pad. If trim is wavy, however, pad leaves a wavy cutline.

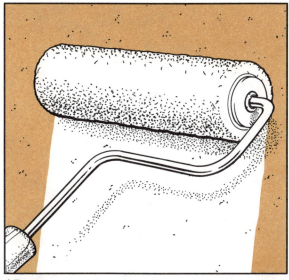

15 Use a roller with a nap length of more than ½ in. to paint rough surfaces like textured stucco walls or ceilings.

wall-ceiling corner. Outline one wall at a time, working along the ceiling and into the corners. Then, cut in around door and window trim and cabinets.

Instead of a brush, a paint pad with wheels on one edge can roll along the side of the trim to help make a clean cut (Fig. 14).

The roller person can use the extension handle when painting the upper half of the wall, then remove the handle and finish the wall. Overlap your strokes in the wall's center since this area takes the most abuse and it's the part most people look at.

With a little practice, you can use the pole to paint the entire wall. Roll the upper third of the wall and work the roller down. Step back a bit to roll the center, then move closer to paint the lower section. Roll out

small sections to avoid lap marks. Use a long nap roller for textured walls or ceilings (Fig. 15).

Finishing Up

Clean tools thoroughly when you're done. Before you wash the rollers, slice the paint out of them with a paint stirring stick (Fig. 16). Wash rollers and brushes in warm soapy water, then spin them dry with a brush/roller spinner (Fig. 17). Use paint thinner to clean brushes and rollers used with oil paint. Then wash them, spin them, and let them dry.

Store painting tools in the wrappers they came in. Store dropcloths in a dry area—someplace where mildew is not likely to form on them. Finally, keep a brush and some paint handy, even after you clean up, to touch up scuffs left by moving furniture.

16 To make cleanup easier, use a paint stirring stick to scrape the excess paint from the roller before you wash it.

17 Spin dry a roller after you wash it. Hold it in a bucket and pump paint spinner handle. Spinner also works on brushes.

Painting woodwork

■ Window sills, door trim, crown moldings and baseboard require a durable protective finish. A good, long-lasting paint job on woodwork and trim involves careful brush work that takes a little practice. It's worth the effort, though, to learn how to prepare and paint woodwork correctly because it really brightens a room. Done properly, a good paint job lasts for many years and withstands repeated cleanings.

In any painting project, first prepare the surface by cleaning and patching it, then paint it. If you're painting the walls and woodwork, begin by patching the walls and trim so all surfaces are smooth. Paint the trim first, then paint the walls. It's easier to wipe a little wall paint off woodwork than to get trim paint off a wall.

Wash the woodwork with a solution of water and Spic'n'Span or trisodium phosphate (TSP). If phosphate cleaners are banned in your area, use a good household cleaner. Rinse the woodwork and let it dry.

Choosing Paint

Latex or vinyl (water-based) paints are the predominant choice for the home painter and are best for walls. Latex semigloss and enamel (glossy), however, are not as abrasion resistant as oil-based paints (especially important on the window sash, handrails and sills) and can't be cleaned as often as oil-based paints. Latex trim paints dry quickly, and this makes it difficult to avoid lap marks—even for the most experienced painters. These paints dry to a softer and more flexible film than oil-based paints. Objects placed on latex paint can stick in place if left for a long time, even after the paint has dried.

On the plus side, latex paint is easy to clean up. Spills wipe up with water, and brushes can be quickly washed in the sink. Because it doesn't contain petroleum-distilled solvents, latex paint is less of a threat to the environment.

Oil-based paint provides a tough, durable finish that's ideal for woodwork. It dries slowly to a hard surface. This paint comes in four levels of gloss: flat, eggshell, semigloss and gloss. You clean up oil-based paint with paint thinner (also known as mineral spirits).

Estimating How Much Paint You'll Need

Most trim paints cover between 350 and 400 sq. ft. of surface per gallon. Painters allow about 8 sq. ft. of paintable area for each window and about 25 sq. ft. of area for each door. Extra paint is needed for the window's trim or casing and its jamb.

To determine the surface area of base and ceiling molding, estimate it at 6 in. wide (regardless of actual width) and multiply this by its length in inches. Divide this total by 144 to arrive at the square-foot surface area. The average room does not require much trim paint. A quart will usually do it. If you need 3 quarts, buy a gallon.

Paint Brushes, Buckets, Rollers and Trays

The material your brush is made from should be determined by your choice of paint. A brush with polyester or nylon bristles is suitable for latex of oil paint. If you're going to buy only one brush, make it polyester.

Brushes made from hog bristle (sometimes called China bristle) are best with oil paints and get limp when used with latex paint. Good quality bristle brushes are expensive. Don't buy inexpensive bristle brushes, though. They lose their bristles.

For a quick touchup, use a small inexpensive foam brush. Avoid the wide foam brushes because they tend to drip when loaded with paint.

Consider brush shape when you're buying your supplies. A sash brush with its bristles cut at an angle is designed for painting thin areas and getting into

Painting Woodwork was written by Gene and Katie Hamilton. Illustrations by George Retseck.

hard-to-reach corners. It's your best bet for cutting in (painting up to a line) and painting windows. A square cut brush is best for painting door panels or wide trim. Brushes with a long pencil-style handle give you a good grip and provide balance.

You should own at least three brushes: a 1-in. and 2½-in. sash brush and a 2½-in. straight brush. Buy the best brushes you can afford. Properly cared for, they will last indefinitely.

You can use a paint roller to work wide sections, such as flat doors. Use a roller with nap length recommended on the paint can.

Open paint cans by prying around the lid with a wide-tip screwdriver. Pour the paint into a paint pail or a clean paint can and stir it to make sure it's evenly mixed. You can pour some paint back into the paint can and work out of that or work out of the pail. If you use the can, don't fill it right back to the rim. It's a messy and inefficient way to work. Also, puncture the lid of the can in several places using a 4d finishing nail to help drain paint back into the can (Fig. 1).

Prepare the Woodwork

Paint sticks better to a dull surface. One way to remove its gloss is with a chemical solvent deglosser (Fig. 2). Rub on the deglosser with a clean rag. This is strong stuff, so allow plenty of ventilation.

You can also use 120-grit sandpaper with a sanding block or an electric palm sander to dull a surface or smooth out chipped areas. Feather rough areas smooth.

Remove several layers of deteriorating paint with heat guns or chemical strippers. Your paint store should have a variety of chemical strippers, among them low odor and water-soluble types. Stripping is a messy job, so protect the floor and surroundings by putting down a dropcloth. Wear old clothes and protective glasses.

Let the gun heat up and hold it about a foot from the paint. When the finish bubbles up, scrape it away using a paint scraper. Move the gun slowly forward, and you can keep the paint hot without burning it. Keep a fire

1 To allow paint to drain back into the can, punch a few holes in the lid groove with a 4d finishing nail. Keep groove clean.

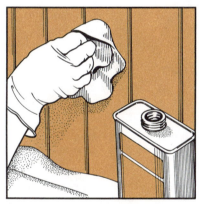
2 Degloss shiny surfaces with a chemical deglosser (paint adheres best to a dull surface). Solvent also degreases and cleans.

3 Fill any cracks or screwholes in the woodwork with spackling compound. Use wood filler for deep holes and cracks.

4 Wrap sandpaper around a sponge to sand curved areas like window or door trim. Sponge takes on molding profile.

5 Rub sealant on glass before painting. Afterward, scrape the window clean with a retractable razor scraper.

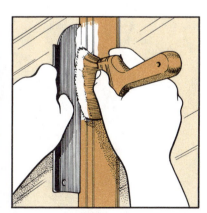
6 You can also keep glass free of paint with a trim guard. On bare wood windows let some paint seal against glass.

extinguisher handy when using a heat gun and don't set down the gun on a flammable surface.

Apply chemical strippers with an old paintbrush. When bubbles appear, use a scraper and steel wool to remove it. Clean off the residue on the scraper using the sides of a sturdy cardboard box. A second application is often required. Let the surface dry, then sand it lightly.

Fill Holes and Cracks

Most trim has some cracks and holes in it that should be filled with spackle or wood filler before applying paint. Spackle, premixed or two-part fillers are applied with a small putty knife (Fig. 3). Just overfill the hole or crack, smooth the filler and let it dry. Sand the filler flush and it's ready for paint (Fig. 4). You might have to use two coats on large repairs since some fillers shrink.

Window Painting—Protecting the Glass

When you're painting windows you can use masking tape or a wipe-on protective film that's dispensed much like a deodorant (Fig. 5). Another alternative is to skip this step and scrape off any paint from the glass with a razor. It's a case of spending your time masking or scraping, but if you paint carefully, you will spend less time scraping.

Apply the tape or film only after thoroughly dusting the corners of each window pane. The crevice tool of a vacuum works well for this.

If you paint the windows without tape or film, you can use a trim guard to protect the glass area. These come either as a small triangular-shaped piece of metal or a metal strip with a plastic handle. Hold the guard tightly against the muntins while you paint them (Fig. 6). After each use, wipe any paint off the backside of the guard.

7 Begin painting a window from the inside out. Paint the sides of the muntins, then paint the front surfaces.

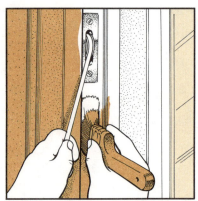

8 Paint the window jamb after the sashes. Pull the sash cords out of the way to avoid getting paint on them.

9 After the sash and jamb are painted, paint over the window trim. Begin next to the jamb, then do the outside edge.

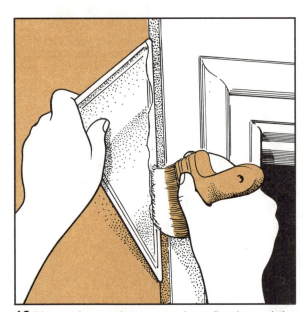

10 Use a trim guard to protect the walls when painting woodwork. Hold the guard tight in the corner between trim and wall.

11 Run razor scraper down the joint between the glass and frame, then scrape away the paint working toward the sash.

Hardware and What To Do About It

Should you remove hardware or should you paint over it? A purist will tell you to remove it before painting. Of course, that's the right answer. For practical purposes, it's not always the realistic one.

If a window lock is covered by several layers of paint but works properly, decide how much time you want to spend on the window. You will crack the existing paint if you remove the lock, and this also leaves a dent in the paint the shape of the lock. Unless you replace it with the same type, you will have to sand away the paint buildup in this area. If the hardware is not painted, it may be easier to remove it rather than paint around it.

Painting Windows

Paint windows from the inside out. Begin painting the thin vertical and horizontal dividers between the panes in double-hung windows (Fig. 7). The same holds for painting casement windows.

If your window has a removable window grille, take it out for a much easier job. Use a 1½-in.-wide sash brush, and don't drag your brush back across the edge because this will cause a run in the paint.

If you are painting a double-hung window and the upper sash is movable, reverse the position of the inner or lower sash and the outer or upper sash. Paint the lower half of the outer sash first, then paint the inside sash, but don't do the top edge where the lock is. Save that until last.

Return the sashes to their normal positions, but don't close the window completely. Then paint the top of the outer sash and the top edge of the inner sash.

Switch to a 2½-in.-wide brush and paint the window frame from the inside out moving the sash cord, if there is one, out of the way (Fig. 8). Next, paint the window casing (Figs. 9 and 10). Cut in a nice, clean line where the casing meets the wall. Then paint the sill and the apron, which is the trim beneath the sill. When the paint is dry, scrape it off the glass with a razor scraper (Fig. 11).

Of course, if the upper sash is painted shut, you can't move it, so paint the upper sash from the inside out. Then open the lower sash and paint it. Leave it open slightly so the paint will not get dirty at the bottom of the sash.

Painting a Panel Door

Like a window, paint a panel door from the inside out. Paint a small section at a time to avoid creating lap marks. A 2½-in.-wide brush should be used for this job.

Start with the decorative edge molding surrounding the door panel followed by the panel itself (Figs. 12 and 13). Then paint the stiles between the panels (Fig. 14). Next, paint the tip and bottom rails (Fig. 15) and work down the remaining stiles. Finish by painting the edges, cutting in cleanly around the hinges and avoiding drips (Fig. 16).

12 Start painting a paneled door by outlining the molding around each panel. Use a 2½-in.-wide square-tip brush.

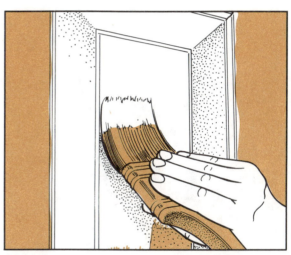

13 Next, work from top down and paint the panel's face. Work the paint into the outlined area to prevent lap marks.

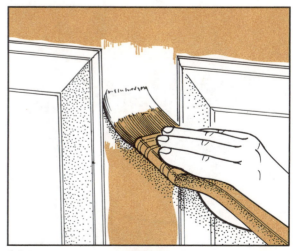

14 Paint the stiles between the panels. For a smooth finish, feather out the paint at the intersection of stiles and rails.

15 Paint the top and bottom rails and then the outside stiles. Paint the long surfaces with a continuous stroke.

16 Paint the door's side, top and bottom edges. Cut in cleanly around hinges, avoiding drips. Next, paint the door jamb.

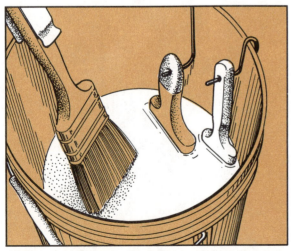

17 Suspend brushes in thinner at the end of the day. Keep the paint brushes off the bottom by using brush hooks or clips.

After the door is painted, do the door jamb. Start on the inside (door stop) and work out. Finish by making the cut along the outside edge and the wall.

When painting moldings, don't get too far ahead on one part of the molding. You don't want the paint to begin to dry or set up before you can finish. If you find your brush drags or sticks to an area where you have painted, don't try to smooth over it by brushing into the area. You'll just make it worse. In this case, let the lap mark dry, then sand it and repaint.

Painting Ceiling Molding and Baseboard Trim

To make a clean cut along a ceiling molding and the wall, hold your brush at an angle to the work surface and work away from the area you're painting. Don't set the ladder too close to the work. Move it often so you can easily reach the area you're painting. You can't paint a straight line if you have to stretch.

Cleanup

Latex paint is water soluble, so wash out the brush (or roller) under a steady flow of warm water until all the paint is removed. Then soak the brush in warm water and mild liquid soap. Towel-dry the brush and use a spinner to remove excess water. This device grips the paint brush and spins it as you pump the spinner's handle. Spin the brush holding it in a paint can or in a paint pail.

Oil paints require paint thinner for cleanup. Hang the brush in thinner using brush hooks or bent wire coat hangers. You can use handle clips for long-handled brushes (Fig. 17). Clean the brush completely at the end of the job.

Fill the container the brushes are hanging in about half full with mineral spirits. To store the brush for a couple of days, dip it in the spirits and work out most of the paint by spreading the bristles with your fingers. If you're concerned about getting the mineral spirits on your hands, wear a pair of rubber gloves. Use a brush comb to work out any stubborn paint deposits, especially those that accumulate near the ferrule (the metal band where the handle and the bristles meet). It's important to keep the tip of the bristles off the container bottom where pigment residue settles.

When you're ready to paint again, squeeze out the excess thinner from the brush. Then use a paint spinner to spin dry the brush.

Wrap a paint roller in plastic or aluminum foil overnight to keep it from hardening. You can clean or discard the roller at the end of the job. To clean it (or store it overnight), force out excess paint from its nap using a stirring stick. To clean it, pour some paint thinner in the pan and work the roller around in it. Force out the remaining residue, then wash the roller in soap and water. Blot it dry, then let it air dry.

After paint buckets and pans have been cleaned with thinner, wash them out with soap and warm water.

Exterior painting

■ Exterior painting has always been a chore that most people dread. The problem with it has very little to do with painting itself. The simple application of the paint is pretty easy. But the preparation is an entirely different matter. It takes time, energy and a willingness to work off ladders for long periods. It often involves pitched battles with wasps, bees and other annoying creatures. To make this necessary chore easier, the people at the Paint Quality Institute give this advice about the proper preparation techniques and the best kind of paint for the job at hand.

If your building is in bad shape, hand scraping would be a tremendous chore. Heat removal techniques may not be the answer because of the fire danger. You may want to go the power route. A power washer and a clever grinder designed specifically for removing paint can be used. To this add a simple palm sander and a portable drill outfitted with an assortment of abrasive wheels. Round out your tool selection with a couple of hand scrapers, wire brushes, sandpaper galore and an airless power painter for spraying the building once the surface is prepared. With these tools ready, the input of the Paint Quality Institute in mind, a generous supply of 100 percent acrylic primer and paint on hand and a can of insecticide spray within easy reach, you're ready for action.

The drawings here show the sequence that seems to work best. The house shown, however, had grooved

Exterior Painting was written by Steven Willson. Illustrations by George Retseck. The power washer shown is a John Deere model No. 117. The grinder is Porter-Cable's No. 303 with P-C's No. 5041 paint remover attachment. The airless paint system is Campbell Hausfield's Paint Pro AL 1200.

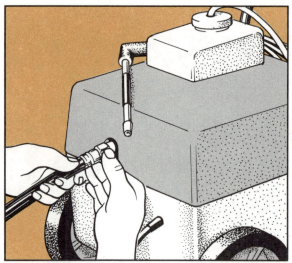

1 Electric power washer uses high-pressure stream of water to remove paint. Attach to water supply with garden hose.

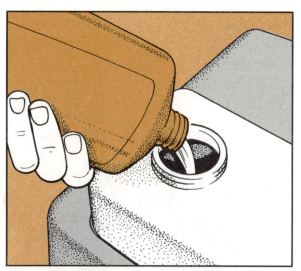

2 On washer with reservoir, pour cleaner into reservoir and set mixture control. Washer mixes cleaner with water stream.

3 Washer units require ground fault circuit interrupters. This model has TEST and RESET buttons built into electrical cord.

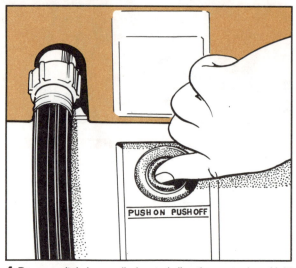

4 Power switch is usually located directly on washer. Hold spray wand in safe direction when power switch is turned on.

cedar shingles. If you have clapboard, board-and-batten or other types of smooth siding, your work should be easier and go faster. As always, there are no good substitutes for patience and hard work, but power equipment like the units featured here can make the job of exterior painting considerably more enjoyable.

Power Washer

It's always a good idea to wash the exterior of a building before painting to remove any residue that may have collected on the surface. Of course, you can do this by hand. But a power washer will not only clean the surface, it can also remove a great deal of loose paint in the process.

The sprayer shown is a John Deere model No. 117 power washer. The hookup is straightforward and the operation simple. You just attach a garden hose to one end of the unit, plug in the ground-fault-protected power cord and turn on the machine. It immediately starts pumping a stream of water that you direct with a handheld wand. Generally, power washers are rated by the pressure they deliver. The unit shown is listed at 750 psi, which seems to be the minimum pressure you'd want to handle any paint removal chores. Most experts suggest a washer in the 900- to 1200-psi range to remove paint. You may want less pressure on soft cedar shingles.

Though power washers are easily rented, if you'd like to have one for other chores around the house, a painting project can help you amortize the cost of buying one instead of renting. The unit shown worked very well and sells for about $450. Other types of washers, in different price ranges, are available from John Deere and a host of other manufacturers.

5 Beginning at top of building, wash all siding and trim with power washer. Keep wand moving to prevent surface damage.

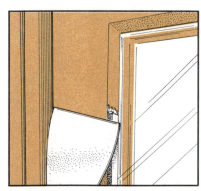

6 Once building is washed, make any necessary repairs, especially to windows. If old glazing putty is loose, remove it with knife.

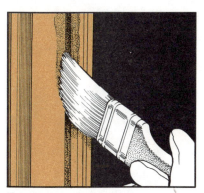

7 On broken windows, remove any glass fragments and old putty. Then coat sash—where glass will go—with mineral spirits.

8 Roll out thin rope of glazing putty, then press into sash. Mineral spirits keep wood moist so putty won't dry out too quickly.

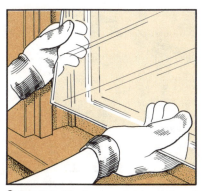

9 Carefully lift glass pane into sash and press into putty. Make sure putty seals the entire perimeter of back side of glass.

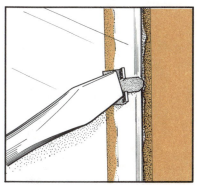

10 Install glazing points every 10 or 12 in. around perimeter of glass. To install this type of point, use flat blade screwdriver.

Grinder

Even though the power washer does remove the bulk of the loose paint, some blistered and cracked areas may remain—especially on flat surfaces that are not loose enough to scrape off. On these areas, a grinder with a paint remover attachment can be used. This attachment has a rubber-faced metal backer disc surrounded by a sturdy guard. The backer disc accepts flat aluminum abrasive discs that have carbide chips

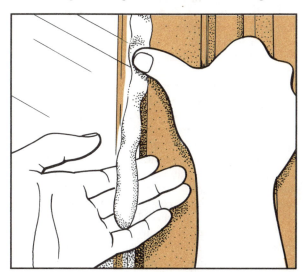

11 For outside perimeter of glass, roll out thicker rope and press into corner between sash and glass. Slightly overfill corner.

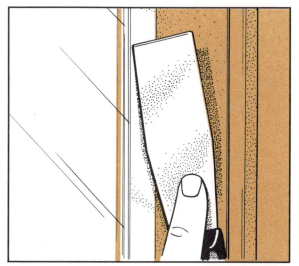

12 Smooth putty in place using stiff putty knife. Dip knife in mineral spirits before each stroke to get smoothest finish.

13 Once windows are repaired, return to siding and hand scrape any loose paint that was too stubborn for power washer.

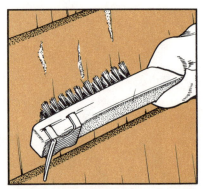

14 Once paint is scraped off, brush exposed areas with wire brush. Brushing loosens paint that scraper blade missed.

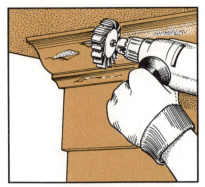

15 On curved surfaces, flat scraper blade doesn't work well. Drill-mounted abrasive flap sander works better.

16 On surfaces where lots of paint has been removed and exposed wood is rough, sand surface smooth with palm sander.

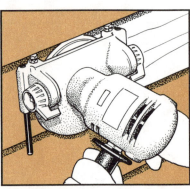

17 Grinder with paint removal attachment was designed primarily for clapboards but is great on flat surfaces, too.

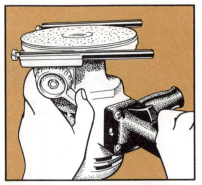

18 Grinder removes paint smoothly because one side of disc is higher. Side knobs raise and lower side support bars.

bonded to the surface. These discs come in coarse, medium and fine grits, and though they cost about $6 each, in the long run they are much cheaper to use than standard abrasive discs.

The guard features two adjustable support bars, one on each side of the disc. By setting one bar lower than the other, the leading edge of the disc rides above the paint, while the following edge grinds off the paint. The tool does take some getting used to. Once you master it, it will remove paint beautifully and leave a very smooth surface. The paint does tend to clog the abrasive, but by using two discs, you can put the clogged one in some paint remover while using the other. By the time the second is clogged, the first is ready to use.

This tool is designed primarily to remove paint from clapboards. As you'll see in Fig. 19, you can even remove the guard and use the tool freehand. With some practice and patience, you can control it easily. This allows you to work on flat but narrow surfaces where the guard would get in the way. The grinder with the paint removal attachment lists for about $340, but can usually be purchased for much less from mail-order tool discounters. If you do try out this tool, remember to wear eye protection, a dust mask and heavy gloves when grinding off paint.

Power Painter

The last piece of power equipment has nothing at all to do with the preparation. It is an airless spray system. Spraying, rather than brushing paint, makes the job go faster and requires practically no effort, though it does demand a couple of windless days.

An airless sprayer, as its name suggests, doesn't use compressed air to transport the paint. Instead, it simply forces the paint through a nozzle which atomizes it. Generally, airless sprayers come in two different configurations. The first is the one-piece version that has the power unit, paint reservoir and spray head all together. These painters tend to be heavy and somewhat difficult to maneuver. The second type is designed like the one shown here (Figs. 20-23). The spray head is separate from the power unit and paint reservoir—it's simply connected by a length of hose. In this design, the spray head is much lighter and more maneuverable, and the paint reservoir usually has a much larger capacity. The spray pattern is very controllable, and all coats should be relatively uniform.

One shortcoming with any spray painter is overspray falling on something you don't want painted such as your neighbor's house or car. For this reason, it's imperative to work on a calm day and make liberal use of dropcloths.

19 With practice and care, tool can be used without guard. This is especially helpful on large flat surfaces like door panels.

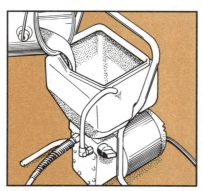

20 For big jobs, reservoir on power paint sprayer is more convenient. It holds more paint and reduces weight at spray head.

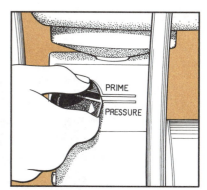

21 Painter must be primed before work begins. Once priming is complete, pressure is increased for spraying.

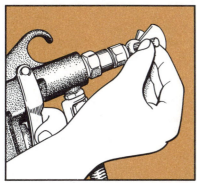

22 Turn adjusting screw on spray head to select spray pattern. For best results, spray pattern should be no more than 10 in.

23 Begin spraying building at top and moving across and down. Keep spray head perpendicular to surface at all times.

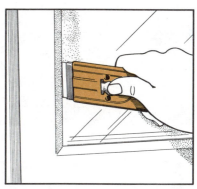

24 After primer is sprayed, scrape off any splatters from glass before they dry completely. If dry, they're harder to remove.

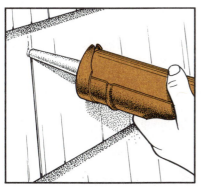

25 Fill cracks in siding, trim, doors and windows with caulk. For best results, apply after surface is primed but before painting.

26 Begin painting windows at sash. Be sure to cover new glazing putty completely, allowing paint just onto glass.

27 Once sash is painted, coat jamb and window trim. After all windows and trim are painted, spray rest of siding.

Like power washers, power painters are common rental items. You may, however, want to buy one if you have a large house to paint. The model shown here costs about $350 and it comes with a roller attachment for interior painting.

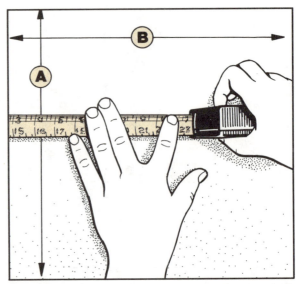

1 First, measure wall height, **A**. Now measure wall length, **B**. Multiply **A**×**B** and subtract door and window areas.

Hanging Wallpaper was written by Gene and Katie Hamilton with illustrations by George Retseck.

Hanging wallpaper

For your first wallpapering job, choose a paper that is easy to install, such as an inexpensive pretrimmed vinyl paper. Vinyl wallcoverings come paper-backed and fabric-backed and both go up nicely. These papers don't stretch out of shape, even if you reposition them several times on the wall. Fabric-backed papers are more expensive and well suited for bathrooms and kitchens where humidity can be a problem. Fabric-backed vinyls can be scrubbed and easily stripped off the walls later.

Look for a paper with a pattern repeat or drop of 10 in. or less. Pattern drop or repeat refers to a pattern's length (a repeat or drop of 10 in. is a pattern that repeats itself every 10 inches). The larger the drop, the more paper is wasted getting the pattern to align between pieces.

You'll find the pattern repeat on the back of each pattern in your wallpaper sample books and on the roll's wrapping. By choosing a pattern with a small repeat for your first project, you can avoid excessive waste.

Estimating Paper

First, look in the back of the wallpaper book for a notice that tells you the area of each roll. Most rolls of American wallpaper contain about 36 sq. ft. of material. Allowing for waste due to the pattern drop and trimming, the roll covers about 30 sq. ft. of wall. A roll of European (metric) wallpaper contains about 28 sq. ft. and covers about 23 sq. ft. of wall (these are based on wallpaper with a drop under 18 inches).

To calculate how much paper you need, first find the wall area. Add the length of each wall, and multiply this total by the ceiling height (Fig. 1). Multiply the height of each door and window by its width. Add the door and window areas and subtract this total from the wall area. This gives you the surface area to be papered. Add about 20 percent to the total papered area to allow for the few bad cuts you'll make (inevitable on your first job).

Divide this number by the area that your wallpaper roll covers, and that's the number of rolls you need.

Make sure the paper is from the same lot or batch. The batch number is stamped on each roll, and all the rolls should have the same number. If you run short and have to order extra paper later, you might get a roll from a different batch run. The color or repeat pattern might not match exactly, even if you order the same pattern from the same store.

Wall Preparation

Clean the walls thoroughly and repair holes, cracks or dents. Wash or paint the room's woodwork and trim. Unless the woodwork is natural or its paint is in good shape, it probably will look dingy next to the new paper. It's easier to paint it now than after the paper is in place.

Turn off the electricity to the room, and remove the light switch and outlet covers. You could hit an outlet or switch wire with your razor knife while trimming the paper and get a shock, so leave the power off while papering. Light the room with a lamp on an extension cord plugged into an outlet outside the room.

Next, size the walls. Sizing makes it easier to slide the paper around without tearing while you align the pattern. Because it seals the wall, sizing makes paper easier to remove later.

Premixed sizing is easier to use, but more expensive than the type you mix. Either is simple to apply. Use a paint roller and pan to spread the somewhat watery solution. When it's dry, the wall is ready for papering.

When hanging a wallpaper with a light-colored background on a dark wall, you may be able to see the wall where there's minute misalignment between seams. Prime dark walls with a coat of inexpensive white latex primer or use a combination primer and sizing.

Layout: Getting Started

Begin your paper layout by establishing vertical guidelines to help you position the paper. Even with guidelines, there's sure to be some misalignment between the first and last strip of paper you hang. To conceal this, lay out your job so you start and finish in an inconspicuous spot, such as over a door, a window or on the least conspicuous wall.

Hold up a roll of paper where you want to begin. Make a pencil mark equal to the paper's width minus ½ in. Use a carpenter's level or a chalkline to make a vertical plumb line through this mark (Fig. 2).

Align the edge of your first strip to be parallel and about ½ in. inside this layout line. This prevents the line from showing through the seam, but keeps the paper's edge close enough for accurate alignment.

Don't cut the first strip by measuring it. Take the roll over to the wall and unroll enough paper to reach from the floor to the ceiling. Hold the paper in place at the ceiling and move it up and down so you have a complete pattern at the top (if your paper's pattern requires alignment).

Make a light pencil mark on the paper at the ceiling. Remove the paper and place it on a flat surface. Trim the paper 2 in. above the mark you made at the ceiling,

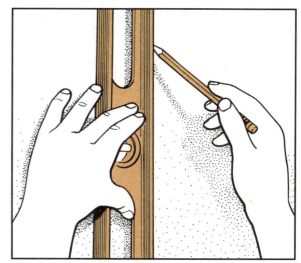

2 Use a level or chalkline to make a vertical layout line on the wall. Align the first strip of paper with this line.

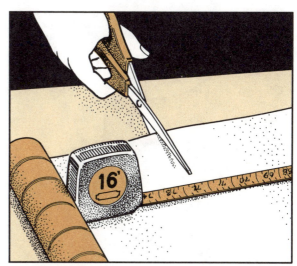

3 Unroll paper and measure the length of the strip allowing for pattern drop and trimming. Mark with a small scissor cut.

4 Fold the roll back on the paper you just measured. Crease the paper at the small cut and use it as a cutting guide.

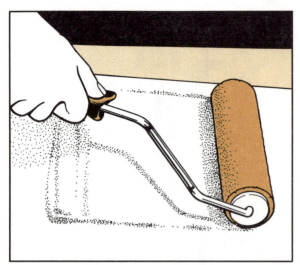

5 Apply wallpaper paste using a paint roller or a wallpaper brush. Spread paste evenly over paper's back and edges.

6 To prevent paste from getting all over when you handle the strips, fold the paper back over itself (pasted sides together).

7 Align first strip with vertical layout line. Smooth strip with wallpaper brush, working out from its center to the edges.

and mark the distance that the wall is high. Add 2 in. to this measurement for trim at the bottom. Make a small cut with a pair of scissors, fold across the paper at the cut, then use the fold as a guideline to cut the strip (Figs. 3 and 4). Test fit this strip.

To cut the second strip, unroll the paper and lay it next to the first strip. Move the paper up until the pattern matches (the wasted paper should always be located at the top of the roll). Cut the paper so it's 2 in. longer at the bottom, leaving some paper to trim at both the ceiling and baseboard. Avoid cutting a large batch of strips until you've tested a few pieces of paper to see how the pattern is lining up.

Hanging Paper

If you're using a prepasted wallcovering, use an inexpensive plastic container called a water box or trough. Fill this about half-full with warm water and place it on a plastic garbage bag covered by old towels to blot up spilled water. Let the strips of paper soak for the time specified by its manufacturer (usually less than a minute). Keep the paper rolled loosely from bottom to top and rotate it in the water.

Follow the manufacturer's advice for wallpaper that requires adhesive. A vinyl paste is usually a good choice because it resists mildew. If you have had a mildew problem in the room, buy a mildewcide additive and mix it in the paste.

Smooth the paste onto the paper's back with a paint roller or wallpaper brush (Fig. 5). Spread the paste evenly, including the edges. To keep the paste from getting over everything, fold the pasted side of the paper back on itself (Fig. 6). This also prevents the adhesive from drying out. Work ahead and paste up a couple of strips so one strip can soak while you work with the other.

Wait at least 5 minutes after brushing adhesive onto a strip of wallpaper for it to set, or *wet out* as it's called, before you hang it. Wallpaper expands when wet and contracts as it dries, so this wetting out lets it reach its maximum expansion and prevents bubbles from forming behind the paper once it's hung.

Have your ladder in place and your tools at hand before bringing the folded and pasted strip to your starting point. Unfold the top section and position the strip so it lines up with the plumb line. Don't forget that you allowed for an extra 2 in. at the top of the piece. Hold the top in place and unfold the pasted bottom section so it drops to the floor. Work your way down the strip checking alignment with the plumb line.

Press the strip firmly against the wall. Work out from the center of the strip using a brush or sponge to push air bubbles or wrinkles to the edges (Fig. 7). If you are very careful, you also can use a broad knife (a 6-in.-wide scraper, also called a flat knife) to do this (Fig. 8). Wipe off excess glue that oozes out of the edge of the strip. Hang the next strip and align the pattern by eye or with a level (Figs. 9 and 10). Use a seam roller to press the edge in place and again after each strip is hung to prevent the seams from opening.

Trim the paper at the top and bottom after you've hung several strips. This is best done using a broad knife and a razor knife. Press the knife into the corner where the wall meets the ceiling and draw the razor along it (Fig. 11). Move the knife over as the razor reaches its end, then repeat the cut. Trim the paper at the floor the same way.

You have to negotiate around doors, windows, cabinets and other projections. To get the paper to lie flat next to these protrusions, use a pair of small pointed scissors or a razor to make relief cuts.

A window frame is a good example. Carefully align the strip so it's plumb and its pattern matches the piece next to it. Smooth out the paper as much as possible. Make a 45° relief cut starting at the corner of the window trim, extending into the waste paper (Fig. 12). Then, finish smoothing the paper and work out remaining wrinkles and air bubbles. Trim the paper flush against the edge of the opening the same way you trimmed up against the ceiling (Fig. 13).

Hanging Corners

There's a great temptation to wrap a strip of wallcovering around an inside or outside corner, then continue by butting the next piece of paper to it. This often results in a sloppy looking job. Corners are seldom square, and wrapping the paper around the corner will cause the pattern to run out of plumb. For best results, use a lap joint or double cut the seams.

To make a lap joint in an inside corner, trim the last strip so it's up to the corner and overlaps the adjoining wall by a couple of inches (Fig. 14). Push the broad knife into the corner and cut off the paper that overlaps onto the adjoining wall (Fig. 15). This leaves about ¼ in., or less, paper overlapping.

Make a plumb line on the new wall to align the first adjoining strip. This first strip on the new wall should wrap around the corner and overlap an inch or so into the wall you just papered. Carefully match the patterns of the overlapping paper in the corner and check the new strip for plumb.

Trim the new strip flush in the corner. Use a light touch and a sharp blade in the razor knife to cut through the top strip only (Fig. 16). This overlaps about ¼ in. and covers any gap between the new strip and the wall.

Add more adhesive to the joint by peeling the strip you just trimmed back and applying the adhesive with an artist's brush. Then smooth out the joint and sponge away excess adhesive.

Wrap the paper around an outside corner and trim it back so ½ in. of paper rounds the corner (Fig. 17). Mark a plumb layout line on the unpapered adjacent wall. Align the first strip with the layout line and trim it flush with the corner.

The inside and outside corner joints described here overlap. Some heavy papers will show a lump at the joint and other vinyl papers do not stick well to one another. In these cases, and anywhere you want a joint that butts perfectly, you can use the double-cut method.

8 If you work carefully, you can smooth paper with a broad knife. Pull knife gently across paper to avoid tearing it.

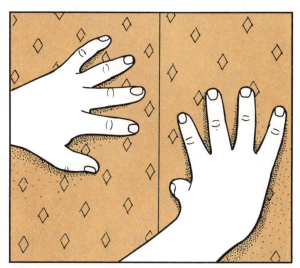

9 Slide next piece of paper into position while adhesive is still moist. Smooth paper after pattern is aligned.

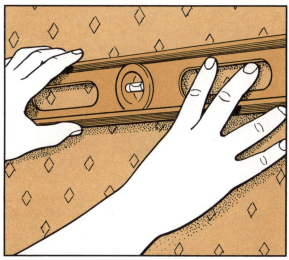

10 When working with small patterns, check alignment between strips using a level. This assures pattern stays even.

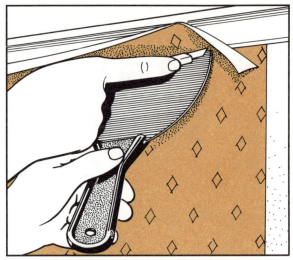

11 Push broad knife into corner at ceiling (or molding). Run razor knife along broad knife to cleanly sever scrap.

Overlap the strips where you want the joint, then cut through both strips with a sharp razor guided by your broad knife. The trimmed piece will fall away from the top strip, but you have to peel back the top strip to remove the trimmed piece from under it (Figs. 18 and 19). Smooth the top strip back in place.

While the paste is still soft, sponge away excess paste from the wallpaper's face and woodwork. Go back several times with a clean sponge to be sure you get it all.

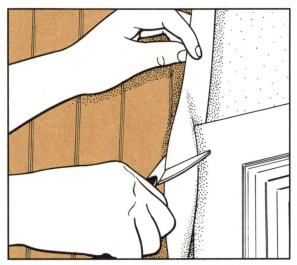

12 Make diagonal relief cut from corner of window or door trim to paper's edge. This lets you work around projection.

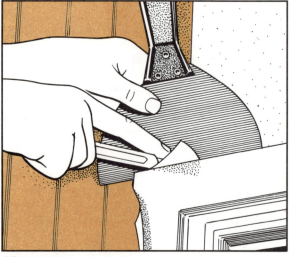

13 Guide cut around window and door trim using broad knife. Trim away scrap before hanging next strip of paper.

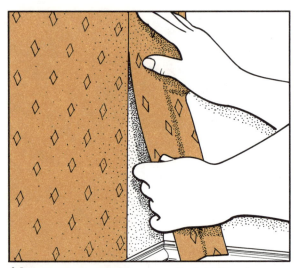

14 Hang strip on an inside corner with about 2 in. of scrap on adjacent wall. Smooth paper toward corner and to seam.

15 Trim paper flush working with broad knife and razor. This leaves a small bit of paper overlapping in the corner.

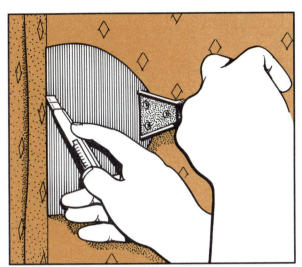

16 Start next paper strip with an overlap. Match the pattern and plumb the strip. Cut through top strip to remove overlap.

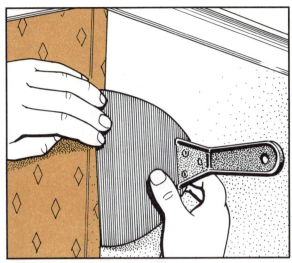

17 Overlap around outside corner should be under 1 in. Next strip should cover overlap. Then, trim strip flush to corner.

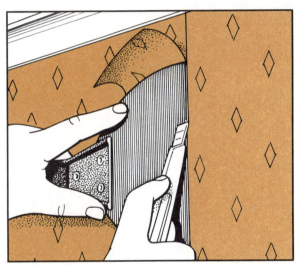

18 To make a double-cut joint, align the pattern with the strips overlapping. Press hard enough to cut both strips.

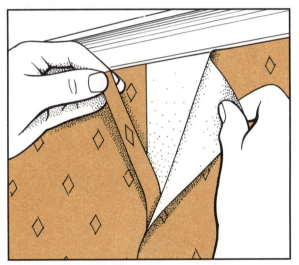

19 The overlap falls away, but you must peel back the top strip and remove the cut off section. Then, roll the joint tight.

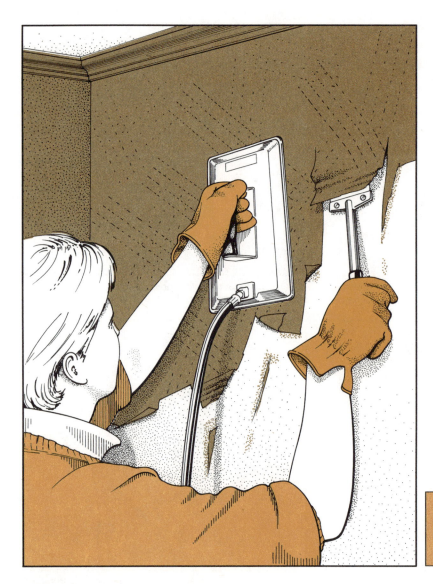

Removing Wallpaper was written by Gene and Katie Hamilton. Illustrations by George Retseck. A good tool for perforating painted wallpaper is the Paper Tiger by Zinsser (William Zinsser, 39 Belmont Dr., Somerset, NJ 08875, Dept. PM).

Removing wallpaper

■ Removing wallpaper is a messy job. Finding someone to do it is almost more difficult than doing it yourself. Professional paperhangers often don't want to do it and when they do, they charge you a premium rate.

Fortunately, this job is more messy than it is difficult. It's a good example of the kind of grunt work homeowners can do themselves. The job requires little skill and few tools, just scraping and patience. With the advent of improved wallpaper removing tools, teamed with time-proven methods, the job is easier than ever.

Different Papers, Different Problems

Some wallcoverings are more difficult to strip than others. The easiest papers to remove are the *strippable* wallpapers. They can be removed without tearing and without being loosened by water or steam.

Slightly more difficult to remove are old, untreated and uncoated wallpapers. They simply need to be wetted and scraped loose.

The most difficult to remove are the papers with vinyl coatings (washable wallpapers) or those with laminated surfaces of woven fabric or foils. Wallpaper that's been painted falls in this category. These papers are difficult to strip because water doesn't penetrate their surface as readily as with uncoated paper.

Stripping on Drywall or Plaster

Painted plaster is the easiest surface from which to strip wallpaper. Unpainted drywall is the most difficult.

Before you start, check to see what type of wall you have. Your stripping method depends on the type of paper and what's beneath it.

Most newer houses have drywall, and most houses over 50 years old, have plastered interiors. Plaster is rock-hard and smooth. Drywall is softer than plaster and easily punctured. Its paper facing has a slight *tooth* that becomes more apparent after you've gained some experience distinguishing drywall from plaster.

You might see rows of small bumps or dents where wall compound covers the nails hold drywall to the framing. Another telltale sign of drywall is a long, but shallow lump where the compound covers the tape that hides the seam between sheets. But be careful here, because the tape may conceal a crack in a plastered surface, not a drywall seam.

If after looking for these signs you still can't tell which wall material you have, look at the material you find behind the faceplate for a light switch or outlet (you have to remove these faceplates to strip the wallpaper anyway).

Drywall is thin and a uniform thickness, usually ½ or ⅝ in., and is attached directly to the studs. Plaster varies in thickness and is applied over wood, gypsum or metal lath that's attached to the studs. The electrical box will fit through a hole cut into the drywall. Since plaster is applied to a wall and not installed as a sheet, you'll find it has been troweled right up to the box.

It's important to check what wall material you're working on in the part of the house you'll be stripping. In an older house, the wall material may vary. If you're stripping wallpaper from a relatively recent addition to an older house, chances are the addition has drywall, while the rest of the house has plaster. Also, the plaster may have been removed in rooms that have been extensively remodeled.

Paint seals plaster and drywall, and makes removing wallpaper easier. Removing wallpaper from unpainted or unsized (*sizing* is a solution applied before papering that further seals the wall surface) drywall is hard, because the glue used to attach the paper penetrates the drywall's face and forms a strong bond. You have to use water to soften the glue that holds the wallpaper, but this also softens the drywall paper facing. Be careful not to tear the paper face of the drywall as you remove the wallcovering.

Preparing the Area

First, prepare the room. Remove phones, pictures, lightweight furnishings, and move the heavier furniture and area rugs to the center of the room (Fig. 1). Cover remaining objects and the floor with dropcloths. Although old bed sheets will do in a pinch, wet globs of wallpaper can soak right through them and damage the floor or furnishing beneath. Water-resistant plastic or canvas dropcloths are better and prove to be a good investment for future projects. Plastic sheeting and combination paper/plastic dropcloths are another alternative. Although somewhat slippery to work on, these coverings can be disposed of after the project. Next, turn off the electricity and then remove any remaining faceplates.

To stop soggy wallpaper from hitting the floor, tape the dropcloth to the baseboard with masking tape at least 1½ in., wide (Fig. 2). Tape the dropcloth's edge to the baseboard and unfold it into the room.

Stripping Without Steam

Old-fashioned wallpaper comes off the wall easily if you get enough moisture behind it. It's held up with wheat paste adhesive, a substance easily softened by water. These porous papers absorb water, hastening the decomposition of the paste.

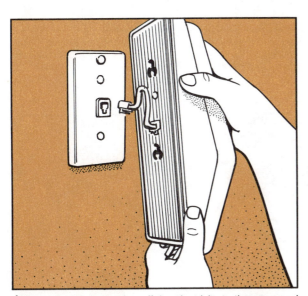

1 Begin the job by turning off the electricity to the room and removing the telephone, and faceplates for outlets and switches.

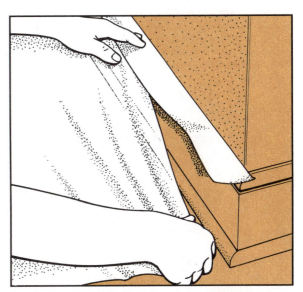

2 Tape the dropcloth to the baseboard molding and unfold it into the room. Use masking tape at least 1½ in. wide.

Stripping the paper is even easier if you mix some wallpaper remover in the water. The remover, sold at paint and hardware stores, has wetting agents that penetrate the paper and soften the paste. Some strippers also have enzymes that attack the wheat paste and dissolve it. Mix the remover in a pail or directly in a garden sprayer (Fig. 3). The sprayer should be clean and free of pesticide residue. Start applying the remover at the wall's top and work down. Work on 6-ft.-wide areas, soaking the area with the solution (Fig. 4).

Another effective way of applying the remover is with a sponge mop or paint roller (Fig. 5). A hand sprayer is effective for spraying hard-to-reach areas (Fig. 6), such as the thin strip of wallpaper between a window casing and a kitchen cabinet.

The paper will darken as it absorbs water. Apply only as much solution as the paper can absorb. Excess solution just runs down the wall and onto the floor. Let the solution soak in, then resoak it.

Let the solution do the work. You'll have to rewet the paper several times during a ½-hour period. A lot of water is needed to saturate it and soften the glue. Prepare another section while the first is soaking.

Test that the wall is ready to strip. If you can easily run a scraper from the baseboard molding to the ceiling, the wall is ready (Fig. 7). Let the paper fall on the dropcloth. For plaster walls, use a broadknife scraper or wallpaper razor scraper. On drywall, use a putty knife with a dull edge to avoid gouging its paper face.

Preparing for Steam Stripping

Vinyl, foil-faced and other moisture-resistant wallpapers are designed to be cleaned. The challenge, then, is to get moisture behind their water-resistant face to soften the glue. Wallpaper remover is not as effective on coated papers as on uncoated. The solution is to steam the paper loose, then scrape it off the wall.

You have to prepare these papers before steaming them. The easiest way to get steam or water behind a coated wallcovering is to score the surface to allow moisture to penetrate. There is a tool on the market for this job. It has small wheels with sharp spurs on them that make holes in the wallcovering (Fig. 8). Its cutting depth is adjustable so, with care, you can use it on drywall.

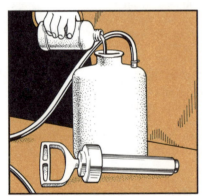

3 Use a garden sprayer to soak uncoated wallpaper. Fill sprayer with a solution of wallpaper remover and warm water.

4 Spray remover from the top of the wall down. Soak the paper during a 15- to 20-minute period, then soak a second area.

5 A floor mop can spread wallpaper remover. Soak the paper, but avoid letting the solution run onto the floor.

6 Apply the remover with a hand sprayer on hard-to-reach areas, such as a strip of paper between a cabinet and window trim.

7 The soaked paper should strip off the wall easily. If it doesn't, resoak. Use a wide, dull scraper to remove large pieces.

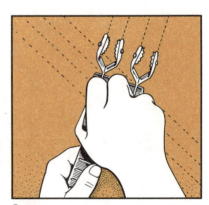

8 Perforate painted or waterproof wallpaper to prepare for steaming. Holes let the steam penetrate the paper.

Painted wallpaper may be difficult to score. With several coats of paint, it can take an almost canvaslike quality. Begin at the top of the wall, concentrating on an area that you can comfortably reach, and work down. Score the paper thoroughly, crisscrossing the surface. Time and effort invested at this stage results in a cleaner strip because the steam better penetrates the paper. If the paper is old and there are several painted layers, most of the layers can be scraped off with a razor scraper. This is harder work than steaming off the individual layers, but it's much faster than trying to steam down through the individual layers.

Steam Stripping

For about $20 a day, you can rent a wallpaper steamer. This tool has a small electric boiler tank that holds about 1.5 gallons of water. It plugs into a standard 15-amp household outlet, but draws a lot of current, so use a heavy-duty extension cord rated to carry that amperage. The boiler connects to a perforated steam plate with a hose. When the tool starts producing steam, press its plate against the wall to loosen the paper.

First, snap the cleaner's hose onto the tank and to the steam plate while the parts are cool and easy to handle (Fig. 9). Remove the heavy steel stopper covering the tank's fill hole and insert a funnel. These tanks are hard to fill without a funnel because the fill hole isn't very large. Fill the tank with tap water (don't use wallpaper remover). Let the steamer heat up for about 10 minutes. Fill the tank again when it's half empty, so you won't have a long wait for the water to boil.

Wear heavy work gloves, old clothing and especially an old pair of shoes or work boots. Stepping around all day in piles of soggy wallpaper will quickly ruin a pair of sneakers. Most importantly, avoid touching the hot hose or steam plate. You can't turn off the steam without shutting down the boiler, so rest the steam plate on a heavy towel when you change areas or want to take a break.

Hold the steam plate at the top of a wall and follow a wallpaper seam (Fig. 10). When the seam is loose, work onto the perforated area. Gently pull a corner of paper toward you when it starts to come loose. Move the steamer ahead as you pull the paper off the wall. If the paper does not readily come off, steam the area

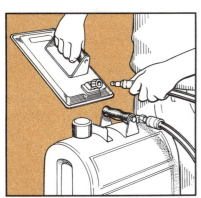
9 Plug steamer's hose into the tank and into the steam plate before letting it heat up. Parts are too hot to do this afterward.

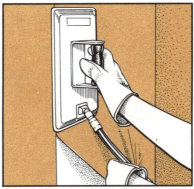
10 Start steaming the wallpaper along a seam. Hold the steam plate on the wall for 10 to 20 seconds or until the glue softens.

11 Hold the steam plate over perforated areas. Use a razor scraper or flat knife to scrape softened paper off the wall.

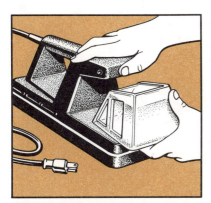
12 You may consider buying Black & Decker's Steamworks instead of renting. Tool combines water tank and steam plate.

13 Let Steamworks heat up, and use it as you would a rented steamer. Tool weighs about the same as steam plate and hose.

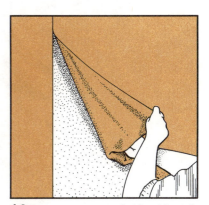
14 Pry up one corner of strippable wallpaper using a putty knife or scraper. Slowly peel the paper off the wall.

more thoroughly. Allow the steam to penetrate. If you rush the process, you'll have to scrape off a lot of small pieces.

Even when you are patient, however, wallcovering may separate from its backing. Give the remaining paper a second shot of steam, and pull or scrape it off.

The procedure is the same for painted wallpaper (Fig. 11). Work a small area to allow the steam longer to penetrate. If you uncover another wallpaper layer, attack it as you did the previous one.

If, as you progress, the steamer seems to be working less efficiently than it should, check that the tank isn't low on water or that the steam plate hasn't been clogged with bits of paper. Lightly scrape off any paper stuck to the steam plate using a broadknife.

If you are removing the paper from several rooms, or you need the steamer for a couple of days, consider buying Black & Decker's Steamworks (Fig. 12). They are available at about $50 at hardware stores and home centers.

It's used the same as a rented steamer, but it can be less cumbersome, even though it weighs about the same. Plug it into a 3-prong outlet or extension cord, fill its tank with water, and a minute later, it's ready to use. Its steam plate area is smaller than a rented unit, but there's no hot hose to worry about (Fig. 13).

Removing Wallpaper from a Ceiling

This is the worst wallpaper stripping job, because of the additional challenge of working overhead. Set up a pair of stepladders, spanned by a short section of scaffold or painter's adjustable plank (either may be available at your rental center). Working on the planking or scaffolding will save you countless trips up and down a ladder.

Observe several precautions when stripping the ceiling. First, wear goggles to keep pieces of wet paper, condensing steam or drops of wallpaper remover out of your eyes. Also, watch your step—it's easy to step off your scaffold when looking overhead. Keep the scaffolding clear of slippery bits of paper and work with it aligned in the direction you are stripping. You can insert a pole into the scoring tool so you can score the paper from floor level or the scaffold.

Strippable Wallcoverings

Strippable wallpapers simply peel off the wall when gently pulled from a corner (Fig. 14). At a seam, lift the corner of the paper with a putty knife or scraper and pull toward you. Carefully remove the adhesive left on the wall with a fresh blade in a razor scraper. Since the paste is dry and hard, most of the heavy residue can be scraped off. Then wash the walls with warm water and detergent.

Cleanup

Once the paper is off the walls, most of your work is done. After each wall is stripped, and still moist, wash off remaining paste and paper bits. Use a large sponge soaked in a warm solution of TSP (trisodium phosphate) and water (Fig. 15). If phosphate-based detergents are banned in your area, use a powerful household cleaner, like Spic'n'Span, instead.

Remove the masking tape and dropcloth from the baseboard. Pick up the four corners of the dropcloth to keep the water from running out (Fig. 16). If the dropcloth is disposable, simply tie or tape the cloth around the debris left as if it were a giant garbage bag and throw it in the trash.

15 Wash glue residue and bits of paper off the wall using a solution of TSP and warm water, or use a household detergent.

16 To complete the job, fold up debris in disposable dropcloth and throw it out. Let the walls dry before painting them.

Repairing damaged finishes

■ Ordinary use, abuse and the ravages of time can damage a furniture finish, but fortunately most of this damage is easily repaired. All that's required is some time and a minimum of materials and expense. In most cases, it's better to preserve and repair a finish than it is to replace it (strip it off and refinish the piece). It's amazing what a difference a thorough cleaning and repair job can make. Also, repairing instead of replacing a damaged finish preserves the character of a piece of furniture.

Most of the tools and materials to make these repairs are available at your local paint store or home center.

Identify Finish

The first step is to identify the finish used on the furniture being repaired. Ideally, you'll overcoat the repaired area with the same finish. Shellac, lacquer and varnish are common finishes. To identify them, apply a solvent to an inconspicuous area on your piece of furniture (Fig. 1).

Repairing Damaged Finishes was written by Rosario Capotosto. Illustrations by George Retseck. Materials not at your local hardware or paint store may be available from Constantine's, 2050 Eastchester Rd., Bronx, NY 10461; Garrett Wade, 161 Avenue of the Americas, New York, NY 10013; The Woodworkers' Store, 21801 Industrial Blvd., Rogers, MN 55374.

Start by applying denatured alcohol. Alcohol will readily dissolve shellac, and it will slowly soften lacquer. Lacquer thinner will readily dissolve lacquer and will soften shellac. The thinner will cause varnish to start to swell, crinkle and lift.

Cleaning, Minor Repair

Next, clean the surface using a soft cloth dampened with mineral spirits (also known as paint thinner) or commercial furniture cleaner. This removes built-up dirt and wax and gives you a clearer idea of what the finish actually looks like. After cleaning, you may discover the damage is really just a light scuff. If so, you may be able to hide the scuff by applying paste wax or polish.

You can also hide a minor scratch by rubbing over it with a furniture-wax pencil or by applying some liquid touchup solution (Figs. 2 and 3). Both are available in a variety of wood colors. Touchup solution stains and overcoats in one step.

Crazing or Alligatoring

Crazing and alligatoring describe a pattern of fine, irregular cracks in the finish usually caused by excessive heat or long exposure to sunlight.

Alligatored shellac or lacquer usually responds nicely to amalgamation (applying a solvent to partially dissolve the finish). Stroke on the appropriate solvent with a fine artist's brush until the finish softens and fills the cracks (Fig. 4). Let the finish harden overnight, then buff over the repair with some paste wax. Amalgamation doesn't work on varnish, however. The condition can be lessened slightly by varnishing over the affected area.

Gouges

Fill a gouge with wood filler, either premixed or a powder which is mixed with water. Most are buff-colored, while others are wood-toned. Colored compounds rarely match the wood so you need to stain them.

1 First identify the finish on furniture being repaired. Test it with solvent.

2 Hide minor scratches by rubbing over them with a furniture touchup pencil.

3 Stain and overcoat small blemishes in one step with a touchup solution.

4 Apply solvent to an alligatored finish. Softened finish flows into the cracks.

5 Firmly pack wood filler into gouges using a putty knife. Strike off excess.

6 Once filler is dry and sanded level, apply wood stain with a cotton swab.

First, scrape away loose finish around the gouge. Next, press the compound firmly into the gouge with a putty knife (Fig. 5). Shave off the excess, then sand the filler flush with a sanding block and 320- or 400-grit sandpaper.

Stain the patch with a cotton swab, and draw grain lines on the patch with a felt-tip pen when the stain is dry (Figs. 6 and 7). Marking pens are sold in a variety of colors at art supply stores. Seal the stained patch with a coat of dilute shellac (refer to the thinning instructions on the can), then apply the same finish on the patch as was used on the rest of the piece. Blend in the patch by rubbing it with 4/0 steel wool dampened with mineral spirits.

If you don't know what the original finish is, use padding lacquer, available from most mail-order woodworking supply houses. This lacquer is compatible with any finish.

Wrap a soft lint-free cloth into a tight pad over a ball of cotton. Moisten the pad in the padding lacquer and tap this on your palm to disperse the lacquer throughout the pad.

Stroke the pad briskly in a pendulum motion (Fig. 8). If you stop on the patch, the cloth will stick to the fast-drying lacquer. Build up the lacquer in several coats until the patch is level with its surroundings. For a satin sheen, rub the spot lightly with 4/0 steel wool.

Shellac Sticks

Fill small gouges and holes with melted shellac. Special burn-in shellac sticks, in a variety of colors, are sold through woodworking supply houses. You'll need a burn-in knife (or substitute a grapefruit knife), an alcohol lamp, a shellac stick of appropriate color, 400-grit waterproof abrasive paper, a felt block and leveling solvent (usually alcohol). These materials are also available through woodworking supply houses. This technique is somewhat difficult so you should practice before you try a real repair.

Heat the tip of the knife over an alcohol lamp (Fig. 9). Hold the hot knife over the gouge, and press the stick against the blade until the shellac melts into the gouge (Fig. 10). Reheat the blade, wipe it clean with fine steel wool, and spread the shellac level (Fig. 11).

7 Draw grain on patch with a fine-tip pen. Soften sharp lines with a cotton swab.

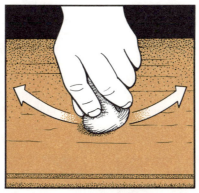

8 Apply padding lacquer in quick, pendulum-like strokes without stopping.

9 Heat burn-in knife or grapefruit knife over a soot-free alcohol lamp.

10 Press burn-in knife on shellac stick and let shellac melt into damaged area.

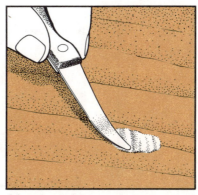

11 Reheat knife, wipe it clean with 4/0 steel wool and smooth the shellac patch.

12 Gently rub on toothpaste to remove white ring from shellacked surface.

13 Apply a thin coat of paste wax over area polished with toothpaste, then buff.

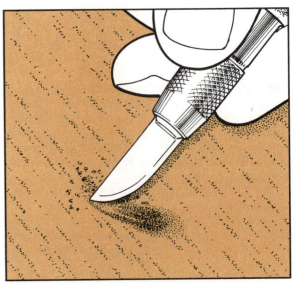

14 Use a curved razor knife to scrape away material charred by a cigarette.

Avoid touching the surrounding finish. If some melted shellac does get on the surrounding surface let it get firm, but not hard, then gently scrape it off. Remove any residue with a piece of cloth moistened with alcohol.

Moisten the felt block with leveling solvent and rub it briskly over the hardened shellac. Dry sand the area with 400-grit paper, and use a felt-tip marker to draw grain lines. Seal the patch with shellac and apply finish.

White Spots

To remove the white spots or rings on a shellacked surface left from a wet glass, simply rub a little toothpaste over the spot with the tip of your finger (Fig. 12). If this doesn't remove the stain, rub the surface with a soft cloth lightly moistened with denatured alcohol or lacquer thinner, depending on the finish. Apply paste wax and buff (Fig. 13). The white spot or ring should disappear.

Burns

A cigarette burn—or any other deep localized burn—is repaired by patching with wood filler. Scrape away charred wood using a razor knife with a curved blade (Fig. 14). Clean the depression with a cloth dampened with paint thinner, then pack it with a filler that's colored to match the wood, or stain the filler to match. When the patch is dry, sand it smooth and level to the surrounding surface (Fig. 15). Use a felt marker to draw grain lines, seal the spot and apply the top finish.

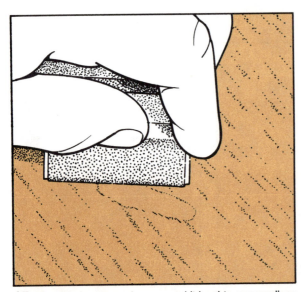

15 After filling a scraped area, sand it level to surroundings with fine sandpaper.

16 Slit the center of veneer blister with a razor knife. Make the slit along the grain.

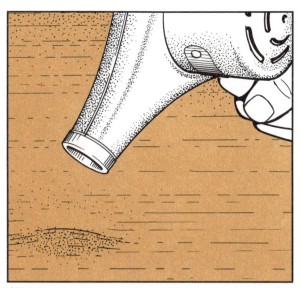

17 Soften the glue under the veneer blister by blowing on it with a hair dryer.

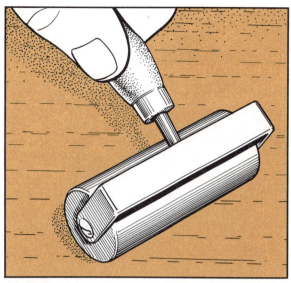

18 Press veneer down with roller and leave a weight on it until glue sets.

Blistered or Peeled Veneer

A veneer blister may be flattened by heating it and pressing it down. The finish on and around the blister may have been damaged as the blister formed. Gently scrape off any flaking or cracked finish before repairing.

Cut into the center of the blister, along the grain, with a razor knife to let the air escape (Fig. 16). Heat the blister with a hair dryer to soften the adhesive (Fig. 17). Then roll the blister flat with a veneer roller (Fig. 18), weight it down, or clamp a small block of wood over it.

A blister that formed at the edge of a surface is easily repaired. Gently slide a little glue under the peeled section and clamp a block over it.

On large veneer blisters, make an X-shaped slit to permit access for cementing. Regardless of whether the veneer was originally applied with glue or contact cement, use contact cement to make the repair.

Gently bend back each flap of the X, and apply cement to the veneer and the substrate with a small brush (Fig. 19). Allow the cement to air dry, then press the veneer back in place. Apply pressure with a roller or by placing a wood block on the repair and tapping it with a hammer.

Veneer Patch

Seriously damaged veneer can be repaired with a patch of closely matched veneer. Start by using a knife and straightedge to make a diamond-shaped cut around the damage (Fig. 20). Use a sharp chisel and a

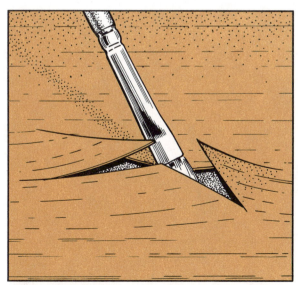

19 Make X-shaped slit on a large blister. Peel back the flaps and brush on cement.

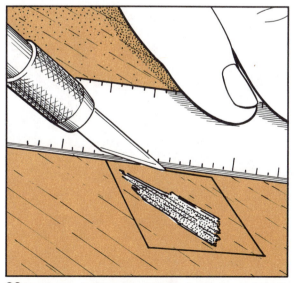

20 Use a razor knife and straightedge to cut diamond shape around damage.

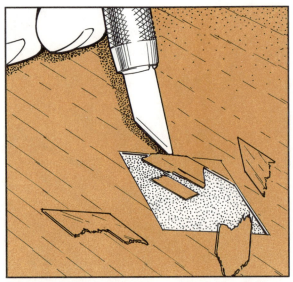

21 Pry up the damaged veneer from inside diamond cutout using razor knife.

22 Lay tracing paper over cutout and rub over paper with a pencil.

knife to remove the veneer inside the cutlines, and scrape the recess clean (Fig. 21). If the substrate is gouged, fill it with compound and sand it level.

Hold a sheet of tracing paper over the recess and rub over the recess with a pencil to obtain a pattern (Fig. 22). Select a piece of veneer to match the original and attach the pattern with rubber cement.

Cut out the patch (Fig. 23). Peel off the paper and test fit the patch. Pare the patch to fit and apply contact cement to the veneer and the substrate.

Insert the patch in the recess when the cement has set. Apply pressure by rolling or tapping, then sand the patch level to the surrounding veneer (Fig. 24). Stain the patch, then apply several coats of finish.

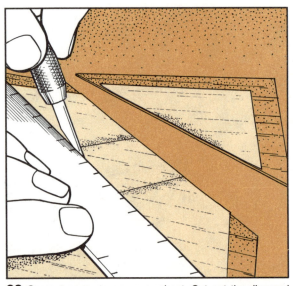

23 Cement paper to a veneer sheet. Cut out the diamond tracing with razor knife.

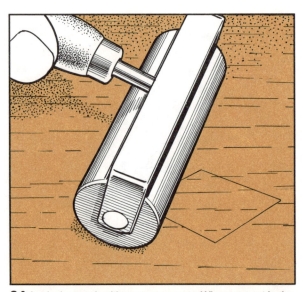

24 Apply the patch with contact cement. When cement is dry, roll over the patch.

Furniture stripping begins with these basic ingredients: rubber gloves, goggles, dust mask, bristle brush, putty knife, paint remover and, of course, a piece of furniture.

Furniture refinishing

■ Half the fun in finding a great piece of country furniture is anticipating how fantastic it will look after it's been stripped and refinished. Nothing is quite so satisfying as being able to do the entire job yourself. The finishing products available today not only make the job fast and easy, but offer endless possibilities for achieving the exact look that you're after.

The country cabinet shown had a dark paint finish. The goal was to remove the paint and refinish the piece in a way that combined the warm, well-used appearance of Early American country furniture with the look of a natural-wood finish.

Text and photographs for *Furniture Refinishing* by Frank Canovatchel. For more information on the chemical stripper, stains and tung oil used for the project shown, contact ZAR, United Gilsonite Laboratories, Box 70, Scranton, PA 18501.

1 Apply stripper with brush in single strokes—avoid brushing back and forth. Work on horizontal surfaces if possible.

2 After about 15 minutes, scrape off old finish with wide-blade putty knife. If paint remains, repeat the stripping process.

3 Use 2-part bleach, available at paint stores, to remove stains and discolorations apparent after stripping.

Before starting any finishing job, make sure you have the right protective equipment on hand, such as rubber gloves, goggles and a respirator.

Step 1—Stripping

The first step in a typical refinishing job is to remove the old finish with a chemical stripper. Be sure to read the label on the can to determine whether the stripper requires a neutralizing agent, such as water or mineral spirits. To speed up the stripping process, use paint remover that doesn't require a neutralizing agent.

Before you apply the stripper, carefully examine the workpiece. If carpentry repairs are necessary, it's often best to do these after the old finish has been removed. Small repairs, such as renailing loose trim, can be done before you start stripping.

Remove all hardware, such as hinges and latches, and set these aside with the original screws. If possible, plan to reuse the original hardware to maintain the character of the piece. If the components are heavily caked with paint, soak them overnight in paint remover. After the hardware has been thoroughly cleaned, lightly oil any components that have moving parts. It was decided not to strip the interior of the cabinet shown because the small compartments made it difficult work. If you're refinishing a similar piece, and you wish to remove the paint on the inside, first check to see if the shelves can be taken out to make the job easier.

Apply the paint and varnish remover with single strokes going in one direction—don't brush the liquid back and forth (Fig. 1). Try to adjust the workpiece so that you're always applying the stripper to a horizontal plane. In this way, the chemical will stay put and soften the finish quicker.

After about 15 minutes, scrape away the old finish with a wide putty knife. Scrape with the grain. If the finish is particularly heavy, you may have to repeat the process (Fig. 2).

4 After the bleached wood is dry, finish sand with 120-grit paper. Since bleach is in wood, be sure to wear respirator.

5 If the interior is difficult to strip, you can paint this unit after wiping the surfaces with a turpentine-dampened rag.

6 After applying thinned pine stain to color wood, white stain is applied and then wiped off to give whitewashed look.

7 When the stain has dried for 24 hours, apply the tung- oil finish with a rag. Apply a second coat after buffing with steel wool.

8 Additional surface protection and luster is achieved with a thin coat of paste wax. Apply with a rag or extra-fine steel wool pad.

9 After the wax has dried for a few minutes, buff the entire surface with a soft, clean lint-free cloth to produce a satin luster.

Step 2—Coloring the Wood

If areas of the wood appear stained or discolored after the finish has been completely removed, apply a commercial 2-part bleach that's available in paint stores (Fig. 3). Follow the directions on the label carefully.

After bleaching, and when the wood is completely dry, smooth the surface with 80- then 120-grit sandpaper (Fig. 4). If you use an orbital sander, follow by hand sanding with the grain. Be sure to wear a respirator for this job. Brush or vacuum away all dust and wipe the wood with a tack cloth.

After thoroughly sanding the outside, clean the inside with a turpentine-dampened rag in preparation for painting. Then, apply two coats of an oil-based paint to all interior surfaces and to the back of the door (Fig. 5).

Colonial Pine stain was used to color the wood on the outside of the cabinet shown. This is a pigmented oil stain that must be stirred to keep the pigment in suspension and ensure uniform color. Apply the stain with a rag or bristle brush. Let the stain stand for about 10 minutes and then wipe away with a lint-free cloth. The longer the stain is left to stand, the darker the color. A second coat can also be added to darken the color.

To get the popular whitewashed country look, thin the stain slightly with turpentine to impart a lighter, warmer tone to the wood. Then apply a tinted-white stain without thinning and let it remain on the wood for about 20 minutes. After the excess is wiped away, some of the white remains in the crevices and corners of the piece (Fig. 6).

Step 3—Final Finish

There's no faster or easier way to a successful natural-wood finish than with tung oil. Tung oil stands up well to daily use and resists moisture and most stains. It dries to a traditional, hand-rubbed finish with little effort.

Apply the tung oil by pouring a liberal amount on a lint-free rag and then rubbing it into the surface (Fig. 7). Let the finish dry for at least 12 hours. For extra protection, add one or two additional coats, buffing between each coat with 4/0 steel wool. For the final touch, apply a coat of paste wax with a rag or extra-fine steel wool pad. Then buff with a clean fiber bristle brush and follow with a soft, lint-free rag (Figs. 8 and 9).

Compost bin

■ Backyard composting facilities are often unsightly arrangements best relegated to a hidden area of your yard. But not so with the version that's shown here. It is attractive enough to be prominently located anywhere on your property. It's dimensioned to process about 2/3 cubic yards of organic material in each bin, yielding an ample supply of compost for the average garden on a continuing schedule.

Materials

The bin is built of redwood—the ideal lumber because of its pleasing appearance and remarkable resistance to decay and insect infestation, particularly termites. Not all redwood will serve the purpose, however. Only the reddish-brown heartwood from the tree's core contains the substances that render it decay resistant. The creamy-colored sapwood that makes up the outer layer of the tree is not insect and decay resistant.

Therefore, try and get Construction Heart grade redwood. If this is unavailable or too expensive, the next best grade is Merchantable Heart grade. Both these grades are suitable for soil-contact applications. The former has knots of varying sizes and minor imperfections. The latter has larger knots, some splits and some manufacturing flaws. Also, request either grade as surfaced, not unsurfaced (rough sawn).

The bin features removable front slats for easy access to the compartments, which are lined on the sides, back and bottom with wire mesh (also known as hardware cloth). This keeps out animals while allowing air to circulate and water to drain. The mesh floor prevents ground-burrowing pests from getting in, but allows beneficial earthworms to migrate up into the pile. The plastic Filon panel lid is extremely durable, keeps the compost from getting soaked when it rains and tends to let through some solar energy—especially in cooler months—to keep the piles warm.

Compost Bin was written by Rosario Capotosto. *Using the 3-Bin Composter* written by Kathleen Bond Borie. Photos by Rosario Capotosto. Technical art by Eugene Thompson. Lumber by California Redwood Association, 405 Enfrente Dr., Suite 200, Navato, CA 94949. Fiberglass Filon panels shown are Cool Rib panels in Cool White from BP Chemicals, Commercial Composites, Filon Products 12333 Van Ness Ave., Hawthorne, CA 92050. Compost bin design by Kathleen Bond Borie.

Frame Construction

The construction is relatively simple and can be accomplished with a circular saw, an electric drill and several hand tools.

Begin by cutting the 2×4s to length for each frame. The top of the frame is pitched down 2 in. across the bin's width. To achieve this pitch, crosscut the tops of the front and rear frame members at a 3° bevel. Use a crosscutting guide to ensure accurate, smooth cuts (Fig. 1).

Assemble the end and divider frames using two 16d common galvanized nails at each joint (Fig. 2). Label each frame and position them bottom side up as they will be when assembled. Place the 2×6 base members on top of the frames using a scrap block to position

them with a ¾-in. overhang at the ends, front and back (Fig. 3).

Hold the frame and base pieces in position with a clamp at each point where the frame and base pieces overlap. Bore the ½-in.-dia. holes for the carriage bolts as indicated in the drawing (Fig. 4). Temporarily insert the bolts, then rip and crosscut the bottom mesh nailers to size and attach them to the bottom frame members with 6d galvanized common nails (Fig. 5).

Attach Wire Mesh

Remove the frames from the base pieces to permit the nailing and stapling operations that follow. Start by

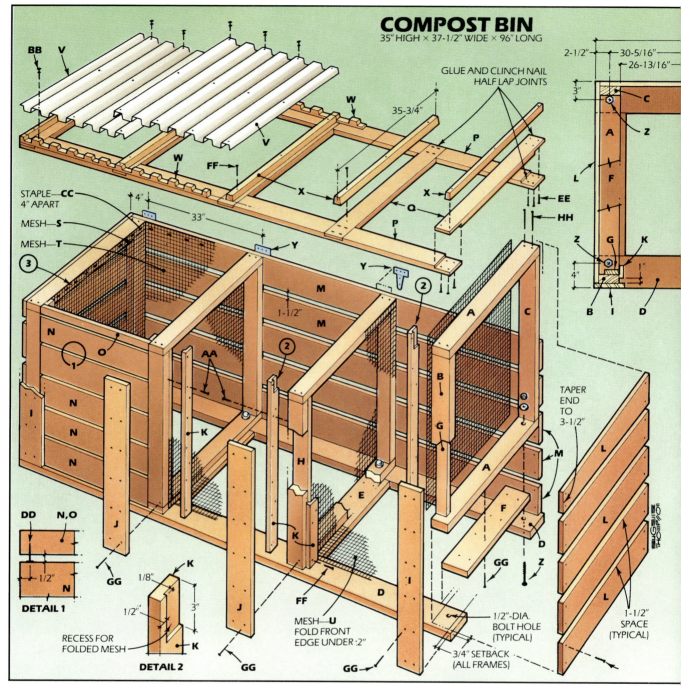

COMPOST BIN
35" HIGH × 37-1/2" WIDE × 96" LONG

GLUE AND CLINCH NAIL
HALF LAP JOINTS

BB
V
35-3/4"
W
W
FF
X
Q
P
X
P
EE
HH

2-1/2"   30-5/16"
26-13/16"
3"
C
A   Z
L
F
Z
G   K
1"
B   I   D
4"

STAPLE—CC
4" APART
33"
4"
MESH—S
MESH—T
3
Y
Y
2
M
M
1-1/2"
N
O
AA
2
A
C
1
B
G
TAPER
END
TO
3-1/2"
N
K
A
I
N
M
N
H
F
E
D
J
K
GG
Z

DD   N,O
1/2"
N
DETAIL 1

K
1/8"
1/2"   3"
K
RECESS FOR
FOLDED MESH
DETAIL 2

J
GG
GG
FF
MESH—U
FOLD FRONT
EDGE UNDER 2"
GG
1/2"-DIA.
BOLT HOLE
(TYPICAL)
3/4" SETBACK
(ALL FRAMES)

L
L
L
L
1-1/2"
SPACE
(TYPICAL)

1 For neat crosscuts, make a T-guide from scrap wood. Run saw's shoe against guide for straight and bevel cuts.

2 Each frame section is made up of four pieces nailed together and marked with chalk to indicate placement.

3 With frame inverted, position the base-boards using a scrap block at edge of frame to gauge ¾-in. overhang.

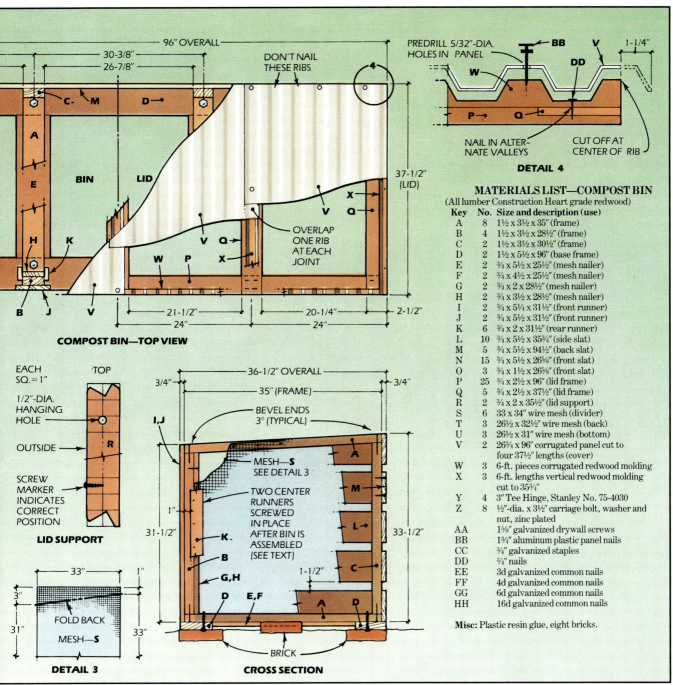

DETAIL 4

MATERIALS LIST—COMPOST BIN

(All lumber Construction Heart grade redwood)

Key	No.	Size and description (use)
A	8	1½ x 3½ x 35" (frame)
B	4	1½ x 3½ x 28½" (frame)
C	2	1½ x 3½ x 30½" (frame)
D	2	1½ x 5½ x 96" (base frame)
E	2	¾ x 5½ x 25½" (mesh nailer)
F	2	¾ x 4½ x 25½" (mesh nailer)
G	2	¾ x 2 x 28½" (mesh nailer)
H	2	¾ x 3½ x 28½" (mesh nailer)
I	2	¾ x 5¼ x 31½" (front runner)
J	2	¾ x 5½ x 31½" (front runner)
K	6	¾ x 2 x 31½" (rear runner)
L	10	¾ x 5½ x 35¾" (side slat)
M	5	¾ x 5½ x 94½" (back slat)
N	15	¾ x 5½ x 26⅝" (front slat)
O	3	¾ x 1½ x 26⅝" (front slat)
P	25	¾ x 2½ x 96" (lid frame)
Q	5	¾ x 2½ x 37½" (lid frame)
R	2	¾ x 2 x 35½" (lid support)
S	6	33 x 34" wire mesh (divider)
T	3	26½ x 32½" wire mesh (back)
U	3	26½ x 31" wire mesh (bottom)
V	2	26¾ x 96" corrugated panel cut to four 37½" lengths (cover)
W	3	6-ft. pieces corrugated redwood molding
X	3	6-ft. lengths vertical redwood molding cut to 35¾"
Y	4	3" Tee Hinge, Stanley No. 75-4030
Z	8	½"-dia. x 3½" carriage bolt, washer and nut, zinc plated
AA		1⅝" galvanized drywall screws
BB		1¾" aluminum plastic panel nails
CC		¾" galvanized staples
DD		¾" nails
EE		3d galvanized common nails
FF		4d galvanized common nails
GG		6d galvanized common nails
HH		16d galvanized common nails

Misc: Plastic resin glue, eight bricks.

4 Clamp the baseboards to the frames and bore the holes for the carriage bolts that attach the baseboards.

5 With the frame inverted, attach the mesh nailers to the bottom of each frame using 6d galvanized common nails.

6 Remove baseboards from the frame and attach the front mesh nailers to each frame. Again, use galvanized nails.

7 Position mesh over frames with overhang at the front. Clamp a board over the mesh and fold it with a block.

8 Place mesh on a flat surface and hammer over the fold. It's faster to tap on the block than hammer the mesh itself.

9 Nail front and rear runners to frame. The rear runner is notched to accommodate the mesh's fold at the corner.

10 Bolt end frames to baseboards after mesh is installed. On end frames, bolts are positioned to clear nailers.

11 Don't nail mesh at the bottom of the two center frames so you have access to nut. Tighten the nut until bolt digs in.

12 Complete the structural assembly before attaching the side and back slats and the rest of the wire mesh.

fastening the nailer strip to the back of each 2×4 front vertical member (Fig. 6).

Next, cut six pieces of wire mesh 33 in. long from a 36-in.-wide roll. Lay the mesh across each frame, clamp a strip of wood across it and fold over the mesh so it conforms to the slope of the frame. Use a block of wood to distribute the pressure evenly across the mesh (Fig. 7). Finish folding over the edge by placing the mesh on a flat surface and working over the fold with a block of wood and a hammer (Fig. 8). This produces a neat exposed edge, free of sharp points that could easily injure even the most careful user.

Use ¾-in. galvanized staples (also called poultry net nails) to attach the mesh, spacing them 4 in. apart. Attach the mesh to both sides of the dividers. Leave about 1 ft. unstapled at the bottom on one side of each divider frame so later you can tighten the nut on each bolt that fastens the base pieces to the frames.

Rip and crosscut the rear and front runners to size. Chisel a slight recess at the top of the rear runners to allow them to fit tightly against the frame where the mesh is doubled over. Nail the rear runners on the end frames and on one side of each divider frame, where the mesh has been fully attached (Fig. 9). Attach the remaining two rear runners with drywall screws after the divider frames have been bolted to the baseboards.

End Frames

Bolt the end frames to the baseboards (Fig. 10). Prop up the unattached mesh while you tighten the bolts that attach the divider frames to the baseboards (Fig. 11). Tighten the nut so the square section of the carriage bolt bites firmly into the baseboards. After the frames are bolted in place, fold down the mesh on the remaining two divider frames and screw down the last two rear runners. This completes the bin assembly (Fig. 12).

Use the same galvanized drywall screws to attach the side and rear slats. Screws are used instead of nails because the free-standing frames tend to bounce if nailed. Use a pair of 1½-in.-wide blocks to gauge the spacing between the side and back slats as you screw them in place (Fig. 13).

Attach the back mesh pieces after the rear slats are attached. The bottom mesh pieces go on last. Crosscut the drop-in front slats to size. The drop-in slats are separated by nails that are driven partially into the edge of each slat. Leave ½ in. of each nail exposed to provide the needed ventilation gap. To drive these nails to a uniform height, butt a piece of ½-in.-thick hardwood against the nail after it has been started. Drive the nail until the head touches the guide block.

13 Screw slats to end frames. For correct spacing, support each slat while fastening with 1½-in.-wide blocks.

14 Use a T-guide to make the repeated kerf cuts in the lid frame. Kerfs should be no more than ¼ in. apart.

15 Clean out between the kerfs with a sharp chisel. The overlap's depth equals half the stock's thickness.

The Lid

Assemble the lid frame with half lap joints. Mark the width of each frame member on the ends of the pieces where appropriate. Set the saw blade to cut a ⅜-in.-deep kerf (half the thickness of the stock) and, running the saw against a T-guide, cut a series of kerfs no more than ¼ in. apart. Chisel out the waste (Figs. 14 and 15). Cut two or more frame pieces at a time during this operation. The combined width makes a more stable base for the saw, as opposed to cutting one piece at a time.

The five crossmembers are attached to the two lengthwise members with plastic resin glue and clinched nails (Fig. 16).

The lid is surfaced with four pieces of fiberglass-reinforced plastic Filon panel cut from two 8-ft.-long panels. These panels are sold at lumberyards and home centers. The panels are attached to matching corrugated redwood molding that is sold with the panels.

Lid Assembly

Support the panels while cutting them by resting them atop the corrugated redwood molding (Fig. 17). Cut two panels at one time. Mark the appropriate length on one panel and fasten a piece of tape across its width. Mark the cutting line on the center of the tape and clamp a fence across the panel to run the saw against. Make the cut with a fine-toothed plywood or crosscut blade. To fit the four panels across the 8-ft. length of the lid with a 1-rib overlap, trim off 1¼ in. from the first and last rib using tin snips.

Nail the corrugated molding strips to the front and rear of the frame after cutting off the starting end to conform to the trimmed panel. Nail Filon vertical molding strips centered on the crossframe pieces (Figs. 18 and 19).

Use aluminum nails with neoprene washers to attach the Filon panels to the moldings (Fig. 20). Bore the nail holes in the panels and the molding with a ⁵⁄₃₂-in. bit. Nail the panels as shown in the drawing and when this is completed, attach the lid to the bin with four hinges.

Level the bin across eight bricks, one under each carriage bolt location. Slightly recess the bricks into the soil and check with a long board and level to obtain a true plane.

To prevent the weight of the compost from depressing the bottom mesh and loosening it, position a brick under the center of each bin. Of course, you can substitute any large flat stones for the bricks. Just be sure the whole unit is relatively level so the bin's lid will be able to work properly.

Complete the bin by nailing down the back and bottom mesh. The front edge of the bottom mesh is folded like the sides (Fig. 21).

USING THE 3-BIN COMPOSTER

Imagine loading up your bagged leaves, grass clippings and piles of brush from your yard, heading to your landfill and being turned away at the gate by a large sign saying: "Yard wastes are now banned from this landfill." This scenario is happening all across the country. At last count, nearly 20 states have passed or are considering legislation banning yard wastes from landfills because there simply isn't enough room for it anymore. When you consider that food and yard wastes account for about a quarter of our nation's garbage, it's not surprising that states and municipalities are setting up programs that encourage one alternative to landfilling it all—composting.

Composting is not only one solution to solid waste woes, it also is the least expensive and best way to improve the poor excuse for soil that surrounds your house. Compost can loosen clay soil and improve the water-holding capacity of sandy soil. It can supply your plants with nutrients, neutralize soil toxins and metals, and act as a pH buffer so your plants are less dependent on a specific soil pH. No need to buy peat moss and topsoil. Compost does the job of both.

You can build an outdoor compost pile by simply layering organic materials on the ground. If left alone, in a year or more you'll have compost. Or you can get the compost in a matter of weeks with this 3-bin composter. This method requires more of your time and energy than the laissez-faire approach. But you'll

16 Glue together the frame members with water-resistant plastic resin glue. Then, clinch nail the pieces together.

17 Support the panels on corrugated molding. Mark a cutline with tape and run the saw's shoe against a fence.

18 Nail the corrugated redwood molding through alternate valleys. Molding is sold with the corrugated panels.

be aptly rewarded with a continuous supply of compost to enrich your soil.

Materials

Collect a variety of organic materials. Leaves, grass clippings, tree and brush prunings, sod, seaweed, garden plants pulled up at season's end, manure, hay, straw, black-and-white newspaper (shredded, minus the colored advertising supplements) and even your kitchen scraps (minus meat, bones and fat) will turn into rich compost. The smaller the pieces of materials, the faster the microorganisms can break them down. So chop up those baseball-bat-sized zucchini from your garden, and rent or borrow a chipper/shredder to cut up any big branches. Avoid all colored paper and all glossy paper because some inks contain heavy metals. Pet litter and sewage should be avoided because they contain toxins that a backyard pile cannot eliminate.

When deciding what to add to your pile, consider the needs of bacteria—the organisms that are doing most of the work of decomposition. They digest organic materials and release bound-up nutrients. To do this efficiently, they need a certain ratio of carbon to nitrogen in the pile. Although impossible to measure exactly, the ratio that works best in the compost pile is approximately 30 parts carbon to one part nitrogen. Sawdust, leaves and other dry, tough, fibrous materials are high in carbon. Manures, grass clippings and green plant vegetation are nigh in nitrogen. Think of carbon as the food and nitrogen as the digestive enzymes. Add roughly 30 times as much carbon as nitrogen.

Mix your materials on the ground and add them to the first bin. If you cannot mix them first, alternate layers of carbon and nitrogen materials. Your pile will soon tell you if the carbon/nitrogen ratio is out of kilter. If there's too much nitrogen, you'll notice the unpleasant odor of ammonia gas emanating from the pile as the excess nitrogen is released. To remedy this, you can add more well-chopped carbon materials and mix them into the pile. If you have the opposite problem of too much carbon, decomposition slows down. In this case, try mixing in a nitrogen source such as fresh grass clipping, fresh manure or blood meal. If you can't mix the materials easily, make holes in the pile and pour in the nitrogen materials.

Activators

You may want to add an activator to make sure your pile has the necessary microorganisms. Finished compost, soil and manure are excellent activators. You can also use commercially available activators which contain dormant bacteria and fungi. These activators come in powdered form and a little bit will activate a large amount of compost. They can be sprinkled on top of each layer of materials you add to your pile. Many garden centers carry activators or you can order directly from the manufacturer.

Moisture

Microorganisms need adequate moisture to decompose organic matter. Try to keep the materials in your pile as moist as a well-wrung sponge. As you build your pile, sprinkle water on top of each layer, but take care not to saturate. Then reach into your pile occasionally and squeeze a handful of materials. If they are too wet, turn the pile to help it dry out. If you need to add more water, insert your garden hose or watering can into the middle of the pile in a few places.

Oxygen

To stimulate the most efficient bacteria, keep your pile well aerated. The aerobic or oxygen-loving bacteria are 90 percent more efficient at breaking down organic matter than the anaerobic bacteria that take over in a pile devoid of oxygen. Furthermore anaerobes produce substances that smell like ammonia and rotten eggs.

You can encourage airflow through the bottom of the pile by using bulky materials such as corn stalks for the bottom layer. Commercially available aerating tools cost about $15 from garden centers. These work best if the materials in your pile are well chopped. Large, fibrous materials are difficult to lift with the tools.

Turning

When you turn a pile, you're taking advantage of the intensified microbial activity in the middle of the pile. Once the microorganisms have broken down the materials in the center, their activity slows and the pile begins to cool down. Turning the materials from the edges of the pile into the center provides additional food for the microorganisms, and as their activity increases, so does the temperature. Turning can help raise the temperature high enough to kill weed seeds and disease organisms (about 150°F). If you want to keep your pile at maximum heating capacity, it's worth investing in a compost thermometer, which is basically a round thermometer face with a long metal probe that reaches into the compost pile. Turn your pile whenever your thermometer tells you the temperature in the center of the pile has dropped below 100°F. When turning no longer raises the temperature, your pile is probably well decomposed and ready to use. Keep in mind that turning is only beneficial up to a point. Turning too frequently can cause a disruption in the process that outweighs any benefit. In a fast-cooking pile, every three days is often enough. In a slower pile, every three weeks may be sufficient. Also remember that you can make compost year-round in moderate climates. But in colder regions, you and the microorganisms can take the winter off.

19 Vertical redwood molding is installed on the frame so it aligns precisely with ridges on corrugated molding.

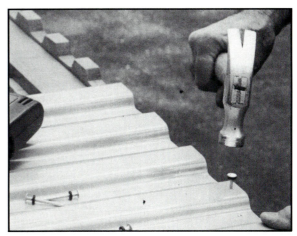

20 Bore clearance holes in panel ridges and molding. Attach panels with aluminum nails that have rubber washers.

21 Situate the bin on level ground and place a brick at the center of each bin to support mesh. Nail the bottom mesh.

The original front porch, with tapered and chamfered columns, rich molding details and stately proportions forms the inspiration for this reproduction back porch project.

The site before construction shows an extension on the right that abuts a bland expanse of wall. Proportions of the new porch are determined by existing roof, door and windows.

Traditional porch

■ If you're interested in adding a porch to your home, you may be disappointed to find out that there's no one design to meet every situation. Each porch, down to the last detail, must be appropriate to the house that it graces. The process of developing your own porch design, or duplicating an original porch, is the same no matter what style your home.

The porch shown completes the back facade of a 100-year-old country home. It fits neatly in the corner created by the main structure and a kitchen extension. The basic look and molding details are taken directly from the original front porch of the home. The proportions, however, were altered to suit the new location.

The porch features a typical sloped, tongue-and-groove floor; box-type posts complete with distinctive, yet easy-to-make, molding details; a hip roof; beaded tongue-and-groove ceiling; and traditional rails, balusters and newel posts. While modern materials and lumber were used, construction is entirely in keeping with the spirit of the original front porch. Where heavy 4-in.-thick beams support and tie together the original model, the new porch is constructed from up-to-date equivalents with 2×8s, construction adhesive and nails. The old classically turned balusters were easily replicated with today's pressure-treated variety.

Before you begin your porch, plan the details such as moldings, post design, proportions, roof slope and rail design to suit your house. Then, have your design and framing details approved by your local building inspector, if required.

Traditional Porch was written by Thomas Klenck. Photos by Stan Silver and Thomas Klenck. Technical art, Eugene Thompson.

The reproduction moldings captures the shape and depth of originals, but are made from profiles made with router.

Rails are made from ordinary lumber shaped to the original design. Balusters are standard pressure-treated type.

Box-type step construction matches original front porch, as does turned lower newel posts and square upper posts.

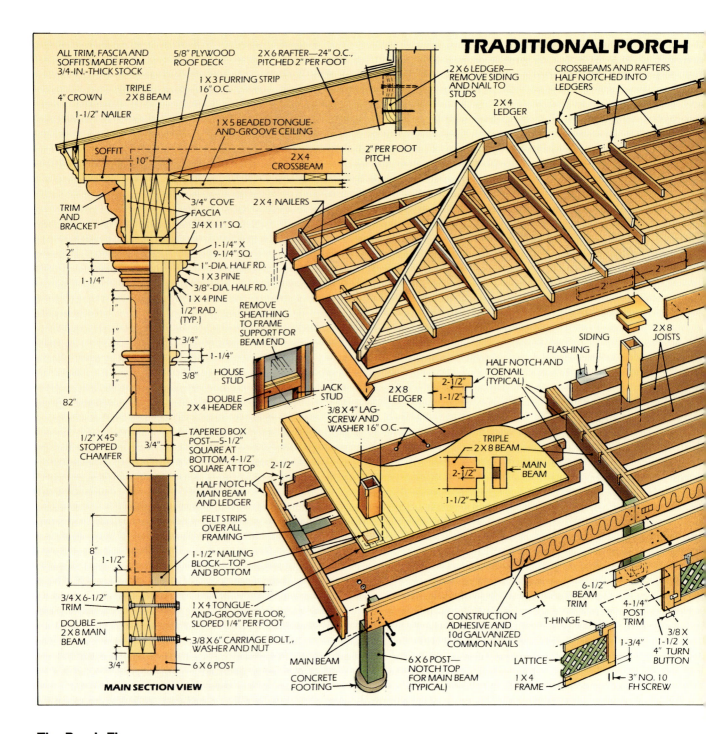

TRADITIONAL PORCH

ALL TRIM, FASCIA AND SOFFITS MADE FROM 3/4-IN.-THICK STOCK

5/8" PLYWOOD ROOF DECK

2 X 6 RAFTER—24" O.C., PITCHED 2" PER FOOT

2 X 6 LEDGER—REMOVE SIDING AND NAIL TO STUDS

CROSSBEAMS AND RAFTERS HALF NOTCHED INTO LEDGERS

4" CROWN

TRIPLE 2 X 8 BEAM

1 X 3 FURRING STRIP 16" O.C.

2 X 4 LEDGER

1-1/2" NAILER

1 X 5 BEADED TONGUE-AND-GROOVE CEILING

SOFFIT

10"

2 X 4 CROSSBEAM

2" PER FOOT PITCH

TRIM AND BRACKET

3/4" COVE

FASCIA 3/4 X 11" SQ.

2 X 4 NAILERS

2"

1-1/4" X 9-1/4" SQ.

1"-DIA. HALF RD.

1 X 3 PINE

3/8"-DIA. HALF RD.

1 X 4 PINE

1-1/4"

1/2" RAD. (TYP.)

REMOVE SHEATHING TO FRAME SUPPORT FOR BEAM END

2 X 8 JOISTS

SIDING

FLASHING

1"

3/4"

HALF NOTCH AND TOENAIL (TYPICAL)

2-1/2"

1-1/2"

1"

3/8"

HOUSE STUD

82"

DOUBLE 2 X 4 HEADER

JACK STUD

2 X 8 LEDGER

3/8 X 4" LAG-SCREW AND WASHER 16" O.C.

TRIPLE 2 X 8 BEAM

2-1/2"

MAIN BEAM

1-1/2"

1/2" X 45° STOPPED CHAMFER

3/4"

TAPERED BOX POST—5-1/2" SQUARE AT BOTTOM, 4-1/2" SQUARE AT TOP

2-1/2"

HALF NOTCH MAIN BEAM AND LEDGER

FELT STRIPS OVER ALL FRAMING

8"

1-1/2"

1-1/2" NAILING BLOCK—TOP AND BOTTOM

1 X 4 TONGUE-AND-GROOVE FLOOR, SLOPED 1/4" PER FOOT

6-1/2" BEAM TRIM

4-1/4" POST TRIM

3/4 X 6-1/2" TRIM

3/8"

T-HINGE

1-3/4"

3/8 X 1-1/2 X 4" TURN BUTTON

DOUBLE 2 X 8 MAIN BEAM

3/8 X 6" CARRIAGE BOLT, WASHER AND NUT

CONSTRUCTION ADHESIVE AND 10d GALVANIZED COMMON NAILS

LATTICE

3/4"

6 X 6 POST

MAIN BEAM

CONCRETE FOOTING

6 X 6 POST—NOTCH TOP FOR MAIN BEAM (TYPICAL)

1 X 4 FRAME

3" NO. 10 FH SCREW

MAIN SECTION VIEW

The Porch Floor

Although the original front porch was supported on posts that simply rested on flagstones, you might want to consider poured concrete footings set below the frost line. Begin by laying out the positions of the posts and the main front beam with stakes and string. Make sure that the post positions are evenly spaced and run parallel to the house. Then, dig holes for the footings. For concrete forms, use 10-in.-dia. cardboard construction tubes cut to protrude a few inches above the grade. Plumb the tubes, backfill and pour the concrete (Fig. 1). Because the job is small, you can use bags of premixed concrete, prepared by hand or with a power mixer.

Strike a chalkline along the wall at the finished height of the floor, plus ½ inch. Double-check the dimensions between the footing centers, and mark the corresponding post and crossbeam positions on the wall. You can use a circular saw to cut the clapboard siding along the chalkline (Fig. 2). After prying off the siding, slide aluminum flashing up under the siding to protect the sill and ledger from moisture. Fold up the flashing using a ¾-in.-thick board—held under the edge of the siding—as a spacer (Fig. 3). The framing

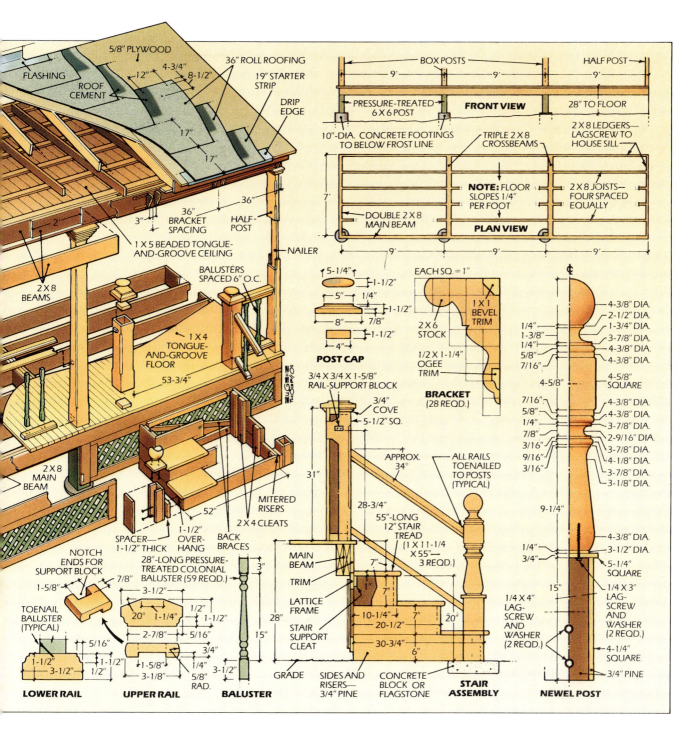

goes under the flashing and the flooring fits over it. If one end of your porch abuts a house wall, lay out the sloped floor line, remove the siding and install flashing in preparation for an end ledger.

Unless your porch is short, you'll need to make up the ledger from several lengths of stock. Plan the joints to fall between crossbeam positions. Mark the crossbeam notches on the ledger stock and cut the notches with a sabre saw (Fig. 4). Then, tack-nail the ledgers in place, check that they're level and secure to the house sill with ⅜×4-in. lagscrews and washers (Fig. 5). Install the end ledger at the correct slope.

Cut the 6×6 post stock oversize in length, and cut a crossbeam for each post. Clamp or tack-nail each beam to its post, and use a line level to check that the beams are at the right height and slope. Then, mark the post notch lines under the beam edges (Fig. 6), and cut the notches. Cut the inside main beam 2×8s to length so their ends join on the post centerlines. Use a drill and sabre saw to cut the crossbeam mortises as shown, and test fit the inner main beam, single crossbeams and posts (Fig. 7).

Cut the outer main beam pieces so the joints are centered between the posts. Then, assemble the dou-

1 Use 10-in.-dia. cardboard concrete forms to pour footings below frost line. Premixed bags of concrete can be mixed by hand.

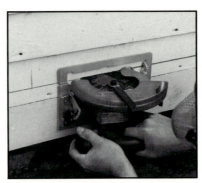

2 After striking chalkline ½ in. above floor level, remove clapboard with a circular saw set to cut only through siding.

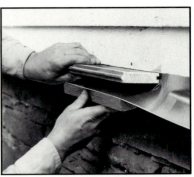

3 Slide flashing under siding, and bend so it will lie under flooring. The ¾-in.-thick spacer and 2×4 block shape bend.

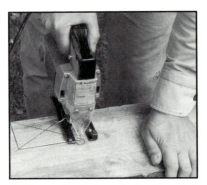

4 After cutting ledgers to length, use a sabre saw to cut the 2½×4½-in. ledger notches at crossbeam locations.

5 After tack-nailing ledgers in place, check that they're level and bore holes for installing the ⅜×4-in. lagscrews.

6 Temporarily nail or clamp single crossbeams at correct height to 6×6 posts. Mark post notch line with square.

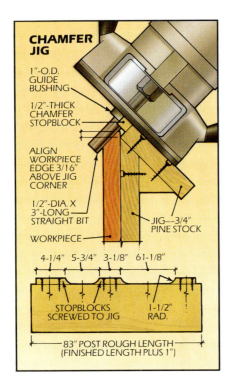

CHAMFER JIG

1"-O.D. GUIDE BUSHING

1/2"-THICK CHAMFER STOPBLOCK

ALIGN WORKPIECE EDGE 3/16" ABOVE JIG CORNER

1/2"-DIA. X 3"-LONG STRAIGHT BIT

WORKPIECE

JIG—3/4" PINE STOCK

4-1/4" 5-3/4" 3-1/8" 61-1/8"

STOPBLOCKS SCREWED TO JIG

1-1/2" RAD.

83" POST ROUGH LENGTH (FINISHED LENGTH PLUS 1")

bled main beam with nails and construction adhesive. Cut the joist notches in the remaining crossbeam pieces by clamping them together, cutting several kerfs with a circular saw and removing the waste with a chisel (Fig. 8). Then assemble each crossbeam.

Assemble the main beam, cross-beams and posts (Fig. 9). Use carriage bolts, nuts and washers to secure the main beam to each post. Toenail the crossbeams to the rim joist and ledger. Double-check the spacing between crossbeams, and saw the joists to length. Cut the notches as shown, tap the joists in place, and toenail (Fig. 10). To protect the framing from moisture, you can staple a layer of roofing felt along all top edges (Fig. 11).

The porch shown uses 1×4 tongue-and-groove fir porching for the floor. Cut each piece oversize in length, and nail diagonally through the tongue with 6d galvanized finishing nails (Fig. 12). Apply a coat of oil-based primer to the underside and edges of each piece. Trim the floor edge with a circular saw so it overhangs the main beam 1½ inches. At the porch end, you'll need to install a temporary cleat to the end beam to support the last piece of flooring until the trim is installed. Then, prime the floor.

Posts and Roof

The porch roof is supported by tapered, box-type posts, positioned directly over the 6×6 floor posts. Begin post construction by cutting 1×6 stock about 2 in. oversize in length. Mark the narrower top width of each piece on one end, and the wider width on the other. Note that each post is made up of two wide and two narrow pieces, each cut to the same taper (see drawing on page 126). Tack-nail a straight 1×6 guide board to a post side, so the guide-board edge aligns with the top and bottom width marks. Set the table saw fence to the guide-board width, and rip the taper on the post side (Fig. 13).

After tapering all the sides, find the crosscut angle by first striking a centerline with a chalkline. Then, use a bevel gauge to mark the angled lines through the centerline that form an X. Adjust the bevel gauge across the bottom of the X (Fig. 14), and use this angle to crosscut all post stock 1 in. oversize in length.

Shape the stopped chamfers on the wide post blanks using a router with a guide bushing and ½-in.-dia. straight bit. Construct a jig to hold the router at 45° to the stock (see chamfer jig detail on page 128). Add small stopblocks as shown in the drawing to limit the length of the chamfers (Fig. 15). Rout the bevels on one edge of each wide piece first. Then, shift the stopblocks to the opposite end for routing the other edge of the pieces.

After the chamfers are cut, assemble each post with 6d galvanized finishing nails (Fig. 16). Apply a thin layer of construction adhesive or waterproof glue to the joints before nailing, and set all nails.

The post crown moldings are made by assembling simple moldings fabricated with a router mounted in a router table. You'll need ½- and ⅜-in.-rad. rounding-over bits, a ½-in.-rad. cove bit and a ⅜-in.-dia. half-round (or edge-beading) bit. The cove in the 1×3 stock is cut with a 1-in.-dia. core-box bit after rabbeting (Fig. 17). Miter the moldings to fit, and nail with a little construction adhesive at each joint (Fig. 18). Note that the mitered moldings are cut square even though the posts are tapered—the taper is not great enough to affect the joints significantly. With the molding in place around the posts, make the two square top pieces for each post. Use 5/4 stock for the lower component, and use a ¾-in.-rad. rounding-over bit on the edges of the upper ¾-in.-thick square stock. Nail these pieces together, and nail a centered 1½-in.-thick square to the bottom to fit inside the post top. When the posts are finished, apply a coat of oil-based primer and caulk the set nailheads. Then, cut the bottom of the posts to exact length and angle to match the slope of the porch floor.

Find the center of each post on the floor, and nail a 1½-in.-thick by 3⅞-in.-sq. block at these locations

7 Test fit inner main beam with single crossbeams and posts. Then, add outer main beam with nails and construction adhesive.

8 Cut notches in the crossbeam pieces by sandwiching them together, cutting saw kerfs and removing waste with a chisel.

9 Assemble main beam, crossbeams and posts. When all parts are aligned, bolt main beam to posts and toenail crossbeams.

10 Double-check joist lengths, cut to fit, and notch the ends to fit in crossbeams. Tap in place with hammer and toenail.

11 With framing complete, staple roofing felt strips over the upper edges to protect the wood from excess moisture.

12 Nail 1×4 tongue-and-groove flooring to framing. Priming bottom faces and edges increases the life of the floor.

(Fig. 19). Then, place a post over its block and temporarily secure it with braces tacked to cleats nailed to the porch floor. Check for plumb with centerlines drawn along the post faces.

Before the main roof beam is installed, rip 1×6 stock to 4½ in. wide for the beam bottom trim. Cut this trim to length so the pieces butt at the center of each post top, and nail in place (Fig. 20). Miter the trim at the corner post. Then construct the roof beam sections on the ground. Each section has two outer beams that butt at a post center, and inner spacers that overlap the joint by at least 2 feet. Secure the main beam by nailing through the trim from below (Fig. 21). Where the short end beam meets the house at the open end of the porch, remove siding and sheathing, and install support framing to the wall studs. You could also use a half post as shown at the opposite end.

With the beam in place, the temporary post bracing can be removed. Use a chalkline to lay out the roofline along the house wall. Cut a pattern rafter from 2×6 stock, and use it to lay out the angled roofline at the hip end of the roof. Then, mark the ceiling line with a chalkline and remove the siding that lies within the area where the roof and ceiling join the wall. Install flashing under the siding and fold it up so it's out of the way.

Cut the rafter notches in the rafter ledger and nail it to the studs in the wall with 16d nails (Fig. 22). Use the pattern rafter to lay out all the rafters and the hip ledger. After installing the hip ledger to the wall, cut and install the hip rafter as shown. Toenail all rafters to the ledger and main beam (Fig. 23), and fit jack rafters to the hip rafter as shown.

After the roof is framed, nail the ¾-in.-thick fascia to the rafter ends. Bevel the upper edge of this stock to match the roof slope—the lower edge extends below the rafters 1 in. Then, install the ⅝-in.-thick plywood roof deck with 4d galvanized nails. The crown molding goes on next. Install a 1½-in.-thick nailer to support the molding. Where the molding must be joined, miter the ends to help conceal the joint line (Fig. 24). After the crown is in place, install the roof beam fascia and the soffits.

You can use roofing over the plywood roof deck. Install this following the manufacturer's instructions. Use a notched trowel to apply the adhesive as each succeeding layer is nailed in place (Fig. 25). Install the roofing under the flashing. Apply roofing cement between the flashing and the roof.

13 Tack a 1×6 to a post side so it's aligned with post taper. Hold the guide strip against the table saw to saw taper.

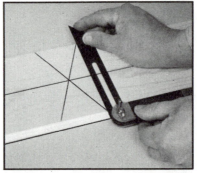

14 Find crosscut angle by first drawing centerline. Then lay out **X** with bevel gauge. Angle is found from edge to edge at **X**.

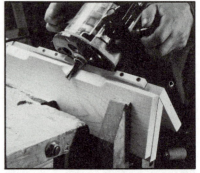

15 Cut chamfers with router and straight bit. Jig holds router at 45°, and small stopblocks shape chamfer ends.

16 Nail posts together with 6d galvanized finishing nails and waterproof glue. Set nailheads and cut posts 1 in. oversize.

17 Shape all post moldings with router table and simple bits. Corebox bit shapes hollow after rabbet is cut on table saw.

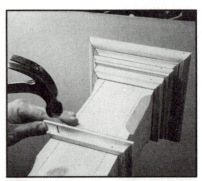

18 Assemble moldings with finishing nails and glue. Set nailheads, coat posts with oil-based primer and caulk nailheads.

19 Lay out 6×6 post centers on floor and nail 1½-in.-thick post block to floor. Then, install posts, plumb and brace.

20 Begin roof construction by nailing beam bottom trim to post tops. Butt trim at posts and miter at corner post.

21 Install triple-width beams in the sections. Middle 2×8 spans joint. Nail from underneath and toenail to posts.

22 Nail notched 2×6 rafter ledgers to house wall after removing siding. Note aluminum flashing bent up over ledger.

23 After cutting all rafters, toenail them to ledger and to main roof beam on 2-ft. centers with 10d galvanized nails.

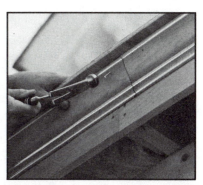

24 When roof decking is done, nail crown molding in corner between deck and fascia. Miter joints between pieces.

Notch and install the ceiling crosstie ledger as shown in the drawing. Cut and install the 2×4 crossties. Note that the upper edge of one crosstie must be notched to accommodate the hip framing. At the end of the porch, toenail nailers between the jack rafters. Install 1×3 furring strips on 16-in. centers across the crossties. Then, nail the 1×5 beaded tongue-and-groove pine ceiling to the furring (Fig. 26). Finish the inside by installing the inner beam fascia and ¾-in. cove around the ceiling perimeter.

Make a template of the ornamental bracket, as shown. Lay out the shape on 2×6 stock and cut each bracket on a band saw. Install a pair of brackets 3 in. apart over each post (Fig. 27). Then, evenly space the remaining pairs between the posts. Finally, make the beveled corner trim on the table saw, and install in the corner between the soffit and beam covering. Then, rout and install covering board trim as shown in the drawing.

Lattice, Steps and Rails

Build the lattice frame out of 1×4 stock. Notch the corners as shown in the drawing and join with 3-in.-long No.10 screws. Bore countersink holes for the screwheads about ¾ in. deep (Fig. 28) and plug the holes after assembly. Cut each lattice panel 2 in. longer and wider than the inside dimensions of the lattice frames. Then, nail the lattice panels to the frames.

Install the main beam trim with galvanized finishing nails, and temporarily nail the completed lattice frames in place. Then, secure the T hinges as shown in the drawing, and remove the nails. The lattice frames behind the steps and at the end are simply nailed in place. After the hinges are secured, install the post trim (Fig. 29).

Begin the steps by ripping the side boards and risers to width, and miter the boards to length as shown. Use 2×4 stock to cleat the side boards together (Fig. 30). After nailing from the 2×4 side, flip over the assembly and nail through the outside boards into the cleats. With each side complete, nail the mitered risers to the edges of the cleats (Fig. 31). Finish the steps by installing the stair treads and back bracing.

Select the clearest and straightest 2×4 stock available for the rails. Rout an ogee molding along two edges of each piece on both upper and lower rails. Then, set the table saw to 20° and rip the bevels on the upper rails (Fig. 32). Use a hand plane to smooth the rough-sawn faces.

Rip the underside component of the upper rail from ¾-in.-thick stock. Round the edges by taking successive beveled passes with a hand plane and sanding smooth. Use a dado blade in the table saw to cut the ¼-in.-deep baluster channel in the underside of the bottom piece (Fig. 33).

Screw a ¾-in.-sq. by 1⅝-in.-long rail-support block to each post and wall where a rail will be secured

(Fig. 34). Position the blocks 1½ in. below the height of the top rail. Then, after cutting the upper rail components to exact length, cut a notch at the ends of the ¾-in.-thick piece so that it fits around the support blocks. Nail the upper rail components together, slide in place over the support blocks and secure the assembly by toenailing.

The porch shown used standard, pressure-treated colonial-style balusters available at most building supply dealers. Cut all balusters to exact length. Then, determine the distance between each baluster by first estimating the number of balusters required between two porch columns. Multiply the baluster width (1⅝ in.) by the number of balusters and subtract this number from the distance between the columns. Then, divide the result by the number of balusters plus one. Cut a scrap spacer block to the length between the balusters.

To install the lower rail and balusters, cut the lower rail to a tight fit and tap in place. Position a baluster between the rails at each end. Then use a wedge to hold the lower rail against the baluster bottom while finishing nails are toenailed around the baluster. Toenail the bottom rail to the posts. As each baluster is added, move the wedge underneath for support and use the spacing block to locate the next baluster position (Fig. 35). After nailing to the bottom rail,

plumb each baluster and toenail to the top (Fig. 36).

You can make the newel posts at the bottom of the steps from solid 6×6 hardwood planed to 4⅝ in. square. If this size stock isn't available, you can laminate the blank from thinner lumber using waterproof glue. Mark the center of the square faceted section on each side of the blank. Clearly lay out a full-width circle on each face at this center, and install the blank in the lathe. Start the lathe at its slowest speed, and observe the layout circles as the blank rotates—the area inside the circle will not be turned. Turn the area outside the circle down to a cylinder. Use a roundnose scraper and skew to approach the circle line carefully. Once that area is finished, shape the remaining details (Fig. 37). At the ball end, turn the waste down to roughly 1½ in. diameter. When the post is finished, saw away the waste and shape the ball top with a sharp chisel and sandpaper (Fig. 38).

Cut the pieces for the hollow newel post base, and assemble three sides and the top with finishing nails and construction adhesive. Secure each base to a post with 2¼-in.-dia. by 3-in.-long lagscrews (Fig. 39). Secure the post assemblies to the steps by first nailing the post spacers in place as shown in the drawing. Then, lagscrew through the spacer and into the 2×4 cleat of the first step. Nail the remaining post base boards in place.

25 Apply appropriate roofing adhesive with a notched trowel to secure each course of roll roofing to the last.

26 After 2×4 crossties and 1×3 furring strips are in place, secure 1×5 beaded tongue-and-groove ceiling with finishing nails.

27 Install brackets in pairs over post centers. Then, space additional pairs evenly between posts. Secure with finishing nails.

28 Use a clamp to hold lattice frame together when boring counterbored screwholes. Install 3-in. No.10 screws.

29 Install lattice frames with T hinges (except behind steps). Finish porch floor trim by nailing post trim between frames.

30 Assemble mitered sides with 2×4s nailed in line with riser positions. Then tip over and nail through into 2×4.

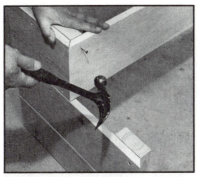

31 Nail mitered risers to 2×4 cleats with galvanized nails. Then, install back bracing and stair treads, and set all nailheads.

32 Make rails out of straight 2×4 stock. After routing ogee profile along two edges, bevel top rail tops on table saw.

33 Round edges of top-rail bottom section with hand plane. Use dado blade in table saw to form baluster channel.

34 Screw rail-support blocks where upper rail meets posts or house walls. Slide rail assembly in place and toenail.

35 Use tapered 2×4 wedge under lower rail for support when nailing balusters. Spacer block holds baluster at correct spot.

36 Plumb each baluster with a level and toenail baluster to top rail. Set all nails and fill with caulk after priming.

37 Newel post is turned on lathe from 4⅝-in.-sq. hardwood. Blank can be laminated from thinner stock.

38 After the post is removed from the lathe, saw off waste and rim top of post with sharp chisel. Then sand.

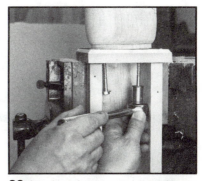

39 Attach each post to a base with two 3-in. lagscrews and washers. Leave off last side until assembly is attached to steps.

The upper newel post is a simple square box with stopped chamfers that match the main columns. Shape the beveled post top on a table saw, and mount a square 2×6 block to the lathe faceplate to turn the oval that's nailed on the post top. Then, toenail the rails and balusters in place.

Paint the unprimed portions of the porch with oil-based primer, and then finish with at least two coats of a quality satin-finish latex paint. Use oil-based porch and floor enamel for the floor.

A sphalt driveway maintenance

Asphalt Driveway Maintenance was written by Rosario Capotosto. Illustrations by George Retseck. Sears sells a variety of driveway maintenance products at its retail stores: driveway/ garage floor cleaner, 1-quart, item No.45504, about $4; patch compound, 1-gallon, item No.45465, about $6; crack filler, 10.5-ounce cartridge, item No. 38091, about $2; Sears' Best Easy-To-Stir sealer/filler, 5-gallon, item No.45477, about $12; squeegee/ brush applicator, item No.12778, about $6. Write to Sears, Dept. 703-PM, BSC 40–16, Sears Tower, Chicago, IL 60684. Sakrete cold patch comes in 66-pound bags, about $7 in hardware stores. For more information write to Sakrete, P.O. Box 17087, Cincinnati, OH 45217.

■ Your driveway, like your house, can easily become an eyesore if you neglect it. But it doesn't take much effort or money to keep an asphalt driveway in top shape and looking good. All a driveway needs is periodic attention, like filling cracks and potholes and applying a couple of coats of sealer.

If your driveway was installed by a good paving contractor, it's about 4 in. thick and was well-rolled on a substantial subbase. If so, it probably has stood up well and all it may need is occasional sealing for cosmetic purposes.

If, however, your driveway was installed by an unscrupulous paver, and is only an inch or so thick, then it's probably already falling apart. Sealing and patching will help its appearance, but they only postpone its inevitable deterioration.

Several forces act against even the best driveways. Temperature cycles, especially freezing and thawing, cause the driveway to expand and contract over time. Although flexible, a driveway has a limit to how many expansion/contraction cycles it can take. Eventually, small cracks open in its surface and water seeps through to the subbase. Periodic wettings compact and settle the soil, creating a sizable void under the pavement. Ultimately, the weight of an automobile will crush through that spot, causing a pothole.

Water trapped in cracks below the surface can also turn to ice during a freeze. Water expands when frozen and enlarges the cracks. Gas, grease and oil drippings act as solvents and damage the pavement by dissolving the asphalt, particularly during hot weather.

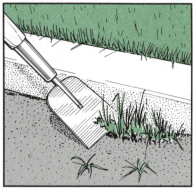

1 Remove clumps of grass and weeds with an ice scraper or a shovel. Scrape off hardened clumps of grease and dirt.

2 Clean oil and grease stains with driveway cleaner and scrub brush. Or use warm water and detergent.

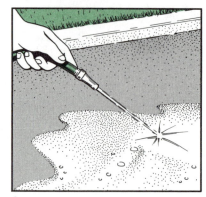

3 To remove cleaner and residue, thoroughly rinse off the scrubbed areas using a garden hose with a spray nozzle.

Surface Preparation

It's important to prepare your driveway's surface before sealing it. Like any coating, sealer bonds better when applied over a clean surface. Patches and repairs also last longer if they are made first, then protected by two coats of sealer.

Begin by using a shovel or ice scraper to scrape off lumps of grease and dirt. Pull grass or weeds out of cracks trying to remove their roots as well. Otherwise, scrape them off flush with the surface (Fig. 1). Use a knife or trowel to dig out the roots and dirt, and enlarge the hole to receive patching material.

Use a stiff broom to sweep clean the driveway and check for areas where grease, oil or gas drippings have marred and softened the surface. Clean these areas with a driveway cleaning solution or with warm water and household detergent using a stiff scrub brush (Fig. 3). Spray rinse the area with a garden hose (Fig. 4).

Patching

Small holes and depressions are repaired with asphalt driveway patching compound. This pastelike material contains small aggregate (gravel). For a small hole, chip out all broken blacktop material around the edges to about 2 in. deep. Brush out or vacuum loose

material (Figs. 4 and 5) and fill the hole with compound to about ½ in. higher than the surrounding pavement (Fig. 6). Use the end of a short length of 2×4 as a tamp to compact the compound until it's level with the pavement (Fig. 7).

If the hole is shallow and dish-shaped, complete the packing by placing a board facedown on the compound and hitting the board with a heavy hammer (Fig. 8). Finish the repair by tapering the compound to a feather edge with a trowel (Fig. 9).

The relatively fine consistency of the patching compound makes it easy to level, but since the feather edge is worked over the surrounding pavement, it's important that the pavement surrounding the hole be cleaned thoroughly to ensure the compound will adhere to it.

Cracks

Blacktop driveway crack filler comes in a cartridge and is used for cracks up to ¼-in. wide. Brush or vacuum loose material out of the crack, then lay in a continuous bead of filler (Fig. 10). Allow it to set for about 10 minutes, then stroke over it with a putty knife to level and firm the bead to the crack's edges (Fig. 11). If the crack is more than ½ in. deep, it should be packed first with sand to within ¼ in. of the surface.

4 To prepare small holes for filling with patching compound, clean out crumbling pavement and dirt using a stiff wire brush.

5 Loose debris can be removed from narrow holes and wide cracks using a crevice nozzle and a wet/dry shop vac.

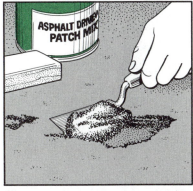
6 Mound patching compound in holes using a small trowel. Patch should be about ½ in. higher than the surrounding surface.

7 Tamp down patch even with rest of driveway using a small piece of 2×4. Pack down patch as tightly as possible.

8 Complete packing of dish-shaped potholes by placing a board facedown and pounding on it with a heavy hammer.

9 Smooth patching compound with a trowel and work it to a feather edge. This compound is ideal for repairs by curbs.

Potholes

A large pothole in the driveway is repaired with cold-mix, an asphalt-based filler that has larger aggregate than driveway patching compound. Typically, it comes in a 60- to 70-pound bag.

Use a cold chisel and hammer to chop out crumbling pavement until the pothole is rimmed with a clean, firm edge. If possible, undercut the hole slightly to lock the patch in place. Dig down until you get to a solid surface and remove loose debris from the hole's bottom. Shovel the mix into the hole, mounding it so it's about ½ in. higher than the surrounding surface (Fig. 12). Compact the mound by tamping with a block of 2×4.

You can also pack the cold-mix by placing a scrap piece of plywood over the mound and driving back and forth over it with the front wheel of your car (Fig. 13). Deep potholes should be filled and tamped in layers. Add some mix, tamp, then add more mix and tamp.

Sealing

A coat of waterproof blacktop sealer, applied every two or three years, will protect the driveway from the sun, rain and snow and will improve its appearance.

The sealer comes in 5-gallon cans and usually needs only to be stirred before use. Read the product label to determine how much area it will cover. Usually this ranges between 200 and 300 sq. ft., depending on the porosity of the surface. Apply the sealer with a long-handled applicator that has a squeegee blade on one side and a brush on the other. Roller applicators are also available.

First, pour enough sealer from the can to work a 3- or 4-ft.-wide strip across the driveway. Using the squeegee side of the applicator, spread sealer across driveway, working it into all tiny cracks and crevices (Fig. 14.) When the strip has been covered, flip over to the brush and use it to level the coating and smooth ridges left by the squeegee. Work the brush at right angles to the path worked by the squeegee (Fig. 15).

Don't leave puddles of sealer and don't spread it too thin. It's best to apply two coats. Read the label to determine how long to allow the sealer to dry before recoating.

10 Driveway crack filler is used on cracks up to ¼ in. wide. Fill deep cracks with sand before applying filler.

11 Let filler set for about 10 minutes, then smooth and compact it with a putty knife. Apply a second bead, if necessary.

12 Remove loose pavement around potholes by chopping it out with a cold chisel and hammer. Trowel in cold patch.

13 Cold patch must be thoroughly packed down. One method is to place plywood on patch and drive a car onto the plywood.

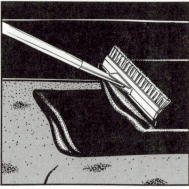

14 Apply two coats of sealer with squeegee/brush or a roller applicator. Spread the sealer first with the squeegee blade.

15 After sealer is evenly spread, brush at right angle to direction taken with squeegee. Work the sealer into the surface.

Lawnmower electronic ignition

Not every self-propelled power lawnmower, riding mower or snowthrower has a Briggs & Stratton engine, but most do—at least the ones made in the United States. Virtually all of the engines manufactured since 1963 with conventional breaker points can be retrofitted with a zero-maintenance electronic ignition. The electronic ignition unit, called Magnetron, is the same one B&S has put on engines at the factory since 1983.

The electronic ignition unit permanently eliminates the need for breaker-point adjustment or replacement, so more reliable starting can be expected. The ignition components are sealed in epoxy to protect them from moisture, oil and dirt. Unlike exposed breaker points, therefore, Magnetron parts are protected from con-taminating agents. The unit often outlasts the engine itself.

It's not absolutely necessary to remove the flywheel (as shown here) when installing the electronic ignition, though it does afford a good opportunity to check on the condition of the flywheel key. If the flywheel is removed, make certain to use the correct holder to prevent cooling fin breakage when loosening the crankshaft nut. When the nut is replaced, it should be torqued to the engine maker's spec. Don't attempt to pry the flywheel off either—it will likely be stuck in place and require a flywheel puller.

To install the Magnetron electronic ignition kit, just follow these 13 steps.

Lawnmower Electronic Ignition was written by Mort Schultz. Illustrations by Don Mannes. The Magnetron kit (part No.394970), which fits any horsepower Briggs and Stratton engine, is available from outdoor power equipment dealers.

1 Disconnect and ground the sparkplug cable, drain the fuel tank, and unbolt the housing which covers the flywheel. Remove the housing and the filter screen beneath it.

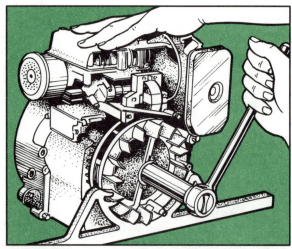

2 Turn the engine on its side and engage the flywheel fins with the holding tool. Unthread the nut from the crankshaft end and use a puller to remove the flywheel.

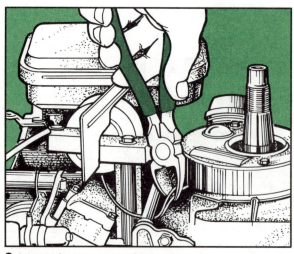

3 Locate the armature primary wire and stop-switch wire coming from the ignition coil. Cut both as close to the breaker points dust cover as possible.

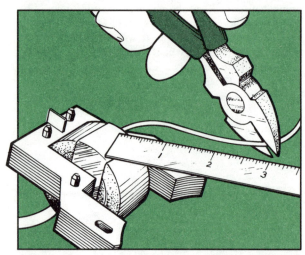

4 Unbolt and remove the coil assembly from the engine. Cut the stop-switch wire flush with the coil. Measure the primary wire 3 in. from the coil and cut it.

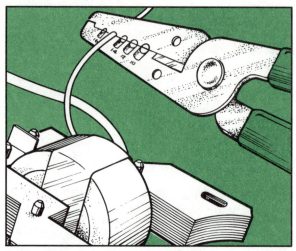

5 Carefully strip the primary wire insulation back ⅝ in. from the end. Use a knife to scrape the varnish from the wire, taking care not to nick or cut it.

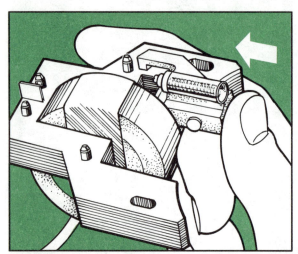

6 Push the Magnetron module into place on the armature leg until the retaining arm engages the angled portion of the leg and locks securely in place.

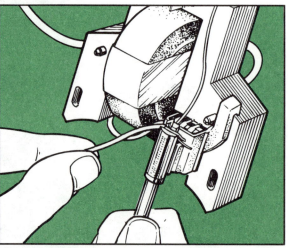

7 Open module wire connector using a drill bit to compress the spring in the barrel section. Insert armature primary and two module wires, then release.

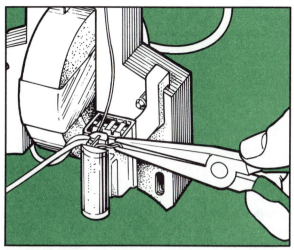

8 Twist the three wires together. Do the same for armature ground and module ground wires. Module ground is identified by a round terminal at its end.

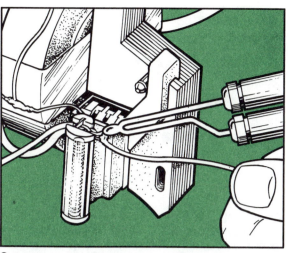

9 Solder the two ground wires together using a 60/40 resin core solder. Then solder the three wires at the module connector, taking care not to melt the plastic.

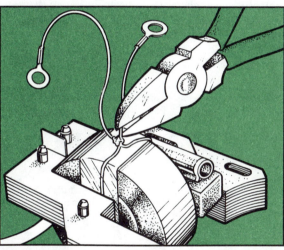

10 Cut the shorter of the two ground wires as close to the soldered connection as possible. Only one of the ground wires will be needed for this installation.

11 Position the coil assembly back on the engine. Slip one of the attaching bolts through the ground wire terminal end before starting the threads.

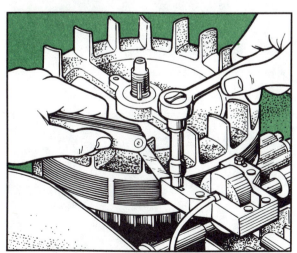

12 Replace the flywheel and nut. Set the coil-to-flywheel distance to the manufacturer's spec with a feeler gauge. Tighten the bolts which fasten the coil.

13 Discard the old stop-switch wire. Route the new wire through the same path and connect to the switch terminal. Bolt flywheel housing back in place.

Gas grill tuneup

■ Late summer may be the perfect time to tune up your gas barbecue grill. The barbecue season is well underway by then, and your grill has probably seen lots of use. Plus, some of the best barbecue days are still ahead in the Fall. If you use your grill year-round, it's easier to tune it up in the summer when you can do the necessary painting and cleaning outside, in nice weather.

Whether you have natural gas, stationary post model, or an LP (propane gas) model, the procedures you will use are the same. As a safety precaution, make sure you shut off the gas supply before doing any maintenance or repairs.

With natural gas-fired grills, you need to pay particularly close attention to the condition of the post. Inspect the post where it goes into the ground and at the top where it attaches to the grill. Look for signs of corrosion or holes in the post. If the post appears weak, contact your local plumber to have the post replaced and to check the gas supply line to the grill.

If your grill has a flexible gas supply hose, check to be sure it's intact and that the connections are tight. Bend the hose carefully, and look for cracks, cuts or wear (Fig. 1). If you find any, replace the hose.

Gas Grill Tuneup was written by Steve Toth. Illustrations by Dyck Fledderus.

ELECTRONIC LIGHTING INSTRUCTIONS   FUEL

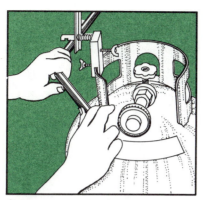

1 Check your grill's flexible supply line for a tight connection. Also, bend it carefully and check for cracks.

2 Scrape cooking residue and rust off the cooking grate. Then wash grate with warm water and soap, rinse and let dry.

3 Remove the grate and check whether it is sound by tapping it with a hammer. This also knocks off residue and rust.

Cleaning the Grates

Check inside the grill. Open the lid and examine the cooking grate. If you have metal grates, and they are rusted or have a lot of burned-on cooking residue, scrape them off with a flat knife or paint scraper (Fig. 2). Then, lift the cooking grate out of the grill and wash it with warm, soapy water and rinse it well. Dry it thoroughly and coat the grates with cooking oil or nonstick cooking spray. If the grate shows signs of weakening or a few welds have let go, replace it.

If you have porcelain-on-steel grates, remove them and lay them on a work surface covered with a plastic sheet. Clean off residue with a nylon scrubbing pad and a paste of baking soda and water, or use warm, soapy water and a steel wool pad. Rinse off the grate and let it dry.

Check the lava rocks and fire grate. Replace the rocks if they crumble in your hand or if they have gotten so small they slip through the fire grate. Some-

times these rocks become coated with cooking residue. Rather than replace the lava rocks, clean them by turning them over and exposing the soiled side to the burner flame. The rocks should be burned clean after 20 or 30 minutes. Another way to clean the rocks is to boil them in a pot of water with a little dish detergent added. Dry the rocks in the sun before putting them back in the grill.

The fire grate may also need attention. This grate can weaken from years of exposure to heat. Check whether the grate is intact by tapping it lightly with a hammer (Fig. 3). This also knocks off scale and rust. Further clean the grate with a combination wire brush and scraper (Fig. 4). If the grate has become very thin or is warped from the weight of the lava rocks, replace it with a new one. If the grate looks okay, but is just a little warped, turn it over so the curve is facing up.

4 Finish cleaning the fire grate with a stiff scrub brush. If cleaning reveals weakened areas, replace the grate.

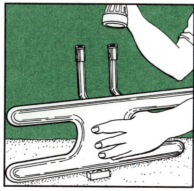

5 Shine flashlight down burner venturi tube to check if insects have built nests in it, obstructing the gas flow through it.

6 Push a narrow bottle brush into venturi tube to remove blockage. Withdraw the brush when it hits the end of the tube.

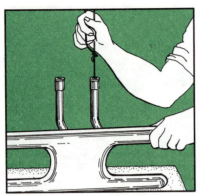

7 You can also use a hanger with a small hook formed on the end to pull obstructions out of the burner venturi.

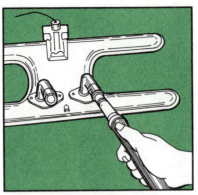

8 Use a garden hose nozzle to flush out burner. Water should flow out the burner ports evenly. If not, check for blockage.

9 Check the gas valve control knobs for free travel, both up and down and left to right. Replace valve if knob sticks.

Burner and Valve Check

With the grills removed, it's a good time to check the most important area, the burner. Spiders and insects like to build their nests inside the dark recesses of the burner's venturi tube and in the burner's orifice. These nests are so tough they can block the flow of gas to the burner, sometimes causing a fuel mixture to back up and catch fire at the front of the grill at the gas valve knob or orifice opening.

If the grill has not been used for a while, remove the burner and check for blockage. Shine a flashlight down the burner's venturi stem (Fig. 5). If you find blockage, there are several ways to remove it. Scrub the inside of the tube with a long, thin bottle brush (Fig. 6). Another way to remove it is to hook the blockage with a coat hanger—with a small hook bent into one end—and then pull it out of the tube (Fig. 7).

The third way is to flush out the venturi tube with a garden hose at high pressure for 3 to 5 minutes (Fig. 8). This is also an effective way to check whether any of the burner's ports are blocked. The water should come out of the port holes evenly. If it sprinkles out of some holes and none comes out of others, shut off the water and find the blockage. Remove any corrosion you find with a soft, brass wire brush. Open any clogged ports with a fine piece of wire. If, however, you notice cracks have burned through the burner body or even pinholes in the metal, replace the burner.

Check the gas valve to be sure it's operating properly. Push in on the valve knob and release it. The knob should snap back. Next, turn the knob from LOW to HIGH heat then back to OFF (Fig. 9). It should turn smoothly. If it binds or doesn't snap back as it should, replace the valve. If your grill has dual

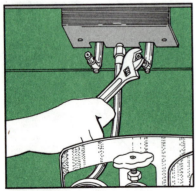

10 Unscrew the gas valve orifice with an adjustable wrench. Clean any dirt off the orifice with an old toothbrush.

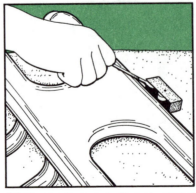

11 Use a cotton swab dipped in alcohol to clean grease off electrode's ceramic insulator. Inspect insulator for cracks.

12 Cover the gas valve and orifice with aluminum foil before scraping residue and debris out of the grill bottom.

13 Use a flat knife or paint scraper to remove as much residue as possible from grill's walls before washing it out.

14 Use a rag or paper towel to wipe up the cooking residue that has been scraped off the grill's walls.

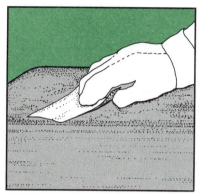

15 Prepare grill body for painting by brushing off loose paint. Scuff sand outside of grill with a fine-grit sandpaper.

burners, remember to check both valves and burner venturi tubes for blockage.

Sometimes, spiders or small insects can find their way into the small gas valve orifice at the top of the gas valve, or it can be clogged by dirt. Check this opening if the grill has not been used for an extended period, or check it at 6-month intervals if you use the grill year-round. To check the orifice, simply unthread it from the valve body with an adjustable wrench (Fig. 10). Clean away any residue on the orifice with an old toothbrush. Reinstall the orifice after it's cleaned and tighten it with a wrench.

Checking the Ignition

Most gas grills have some type of ignition system to light the burner. Some use a pushbutton ignitor, which creates a spark that jumps between an electrode and the burner.

The ignitor produces a click each time the button is pushed. If you cannot see a spark jump between the burner and electrode, then check the airspace between the two. The gap should be $\frac{1}{4}$ to $\frac{5}{32}$ in. wide. Check the manufacturer's instructions for proper gap and adjust the space with a pair of pliers. Check the wires going from the pushbutton to the electrode to make sure they are making good contact at all points.

Other gas grills use an electronic ignitor which requires a 9-volt battery. When you push the red button, a spark is produced at the burner, and it will continue to spark until you release the button. Both systems should be checked every two to three months.

If there is no spark, with either system, make sure the electrode inside the collector box near the burner is clean. Sometimes cooking grease or dirt can collect on the electrode's ceramic insulator, preventing it

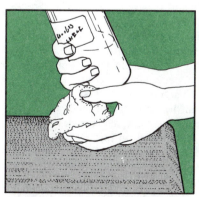

16 Degrease grill body by wiping it with a rag soaked with white vinegar. When the vinegar is dry, grill is ready to paint.

17 Spray paint grill body with automotive or high-temperature paint. Let paint dry completely before lighting grill.

18 Cover tank valve with aluminum foil and remove loose paint with wire brush. Scuff tank with fine-grit sandpaper.

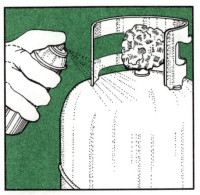

19 Wash off paint dust and spray tank with acrylic paint. Spray the primer on bare metal areas before painting them.

20 Check all the gas connections, hose fittings, valves and valve stems for leaks by brushing on a liquid soap solution.

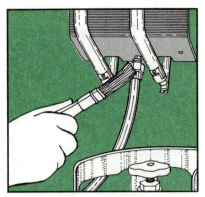

21 Bubbles forming in soap solution indicate there is a gas leak. Tighten the connection, such as at the gas hose.

from sparking properly. Clean the insulator with a cotton swab dipped in rubbing alcohol, then wipe it off with a soft cloth (Fig. 11). Check the ceramic insulator for cracks, and replace it if you find any.

If the electrode on your grill goes through the bottom of the aluminum-cast grill body, and it comes out next to the burner, check the insulator carefully. Hold the white end of the ceramic insulator with one hand. Reach under the casting and try turning the other end of the ceramic insulator. If the bottom turns and the top stays stationary, the insulator is cracked and needs to be replaced.

Cleaning and Painting

Before reassembling the grill, check whether the lower half of the grill body (the part you cook on) needs to be cleaned. If it does, move the grill to a work area and cover the ground with newspapers. Protect the gas valve and orifice by covering them with aluminum foil (Fig. 12). Also cover the electrode if it's attached to the casting, or remove it.

Scrape off cooking residue from inside the grill with either a putty knife or a scraper (Fig. 13). Then, wipe out the residue with a paper towel or rag (Fig. 14). Mix up a solution of strong detergent with warm water or use a grill cleaner and wash the inside of the casting with a scrub brush. Rinse it well and air dry. Remove the aluminum foil and replace the electrode and any wiring that was removed.

Inspect the paint on the outside of the grill to determine if the grill should be repainted. If the paint has deteriorated and if white spots show through it, repaint the casting with grill paint or high-temperature automotive paint.

Brush the outside of the casting with a wire brush or steel wool to remove loose paint. Sand the grill with a fine-grit sandpaper (Fig. 15). Wash the grill with soap and water to remove grease and dust, then let it dry.

Clean off any remaining residue or grease by using a lint-free rag that has some white vinegar soaked into it (Fig. 16). Once vinegar is dry, spray paint the grill (Fig. 17). Remove the aluminum foil around the gas valve and orifice.

Paint the grill's LP tank if it shows signs of light surface rust or if the paint is worn. Double-check that the gas is shut off, and disconnect the tank's gas regulator and hose. Cover the valve with aluminum foil and wire brush the tank to remove rust or loose paint (Fig. 18). Then, wash the tank with hot, soapy water, rinse it and let it dry. Spray the tank with an acrylic-base white paint. If the rusting is severe, prime the spots and let them dry before applying the white finish paint (Fig. 19).

If the tank is more than five years old (the date of manufacture is stamped on the protective metal collar around the tank valve), ask your local utility or gas supplier if they can pressure test it for leaks.

Once the grill is cleaned and painted, reassemble the burner, making sure that the venturi tube slips over the orifice on the gas valve. Connect all wires to the ignition system. Install the fire grate and lava rocks. You should have only one layer of rock covering the grate. Then, put the cooking grate on the grill.

Connect the gas tank to its fittings. Then, leave the grill's lid open and turn on the gas supply without lighting the grill. Check all gas connections, hose fittings, valves and valve stems for leaks by brushing on a solution of half liquid soap and half water (Fig. 20). If you have an LP gas tank, also check tank welds and the pressure relief valve on the back of the tank valve. Leaking gas will cause the solution to bubble up. Tighten leaking fittings, or replace them if tightening fails to stop the leak (Fig. 21).

Turn on the gas valve and light the burner. Close the lid and adjust the gas valve to a medium flame. Operate the grill for 15 to 20 minutes to bake on the paint.

Doorbell extension wiring

In many homes, the door chimes are located in the foyer, near the front door. That's a good central location, but if you spend much time in your kitchen, den or far end of the house, you may not hear the chimes when they ring. You can solve this by installing a chime in the room where you spend most of your time.

In the installation shown, a chime was installed in a recreation room above an unfinished basement. This is the easiest kind of installation since there is complete access to the wiring from the unfinished basement.

A new transformer was used (one capable of handling the existing chime plus the new chime) and wires were connected to the existing chime as they were before. The new chime was placed and bellwire run from it to the existing chime. The doorbell button wiring or the wiring from the transformer to the existing chime was not modified.

Map out a route for your wiring before you begin the job so you'll have an idea of the amount of wire you need and the scope of the job ahead.

Choosing a Chime

A trip to your electrical supply house will reveal a variety of chimes. Electronic chimes are very versatile. Some can be programmed to play up to 24 notes, so callers can be announced with a melody instead of the usual chime tones.

You should be able to hear the chime you're selecting before you buy it. After all, you're going to hear it every time someone's at the door. If you're looking for a bell sound, avoid the electronic units because they just don't sound the same as the real thing. Even the cheapest electro-mechanical chime produces its tones by striking a tone bar, making a distinctive sound.

Mechanical chimes have at least two notes. One will sound when the rear doorbell is pressed, and the other will sound for the main entry. It is possible to have as many as eight notes in a mechanical chime, but the 4- and 8-note units require a larger transformer than a 2-note unit.

If your home is very large and you want to avoid running wires, you might be interested in a wireless unit. These are powered by a battery and once you mount the sending unit on the door jamb, you're free to place the receiver anywhere in the house. You can also buy an extra receiver and leave one in a permanent location, while carrying the spare with you into the garden or workshop.

The other alternative is a plug-in unit, which can be powered from any standard outlet. You mount the sending unit on your chime, plug in the receiver and the plug-in remote unit will sound when the button is pressed.

Of course, the sound of these units will differ from the sound of your present door chime, and they cost more than typical 2-note chimes. If, however, your installation looks like it may be a difficult one, the extra cost will be outweighed by the amount of labor saved.

Transformers

Chimes require between 10 and 24 volts and between 5 and 30 watts. This is considerably less than the 120 or even 220 volts it takes to run appliances, lights or equipment in your home. A transformer is used to reduce the voltage. Transformers are available in different sizes, and because you are increasing the load on the doorbell system with an additional chime (and additional wire), you will probably need a transformer with more capacity.

To determine the size transformer you need, simply combine the wattage of the chimes. For instance, a standard 2-note chime uses 10 watts, so if you add a second 2-note chime, you need a 20-watt transformer.

Doorbell Extension Wiring was written by Paul Barrett. Illustrations by George Retseck.

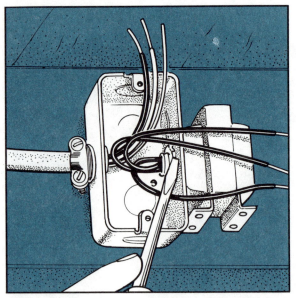

1 Mount new transformer to a junction box. Run transformer's power supply wires through knockout and tighten nut.

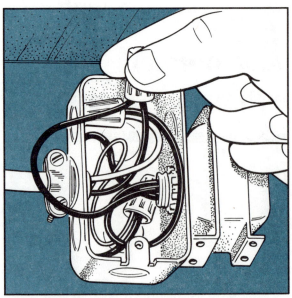

2 Make connections using wirenuts. Ground wires are hooked together, then to ground screw. Cover box with faceplate.

Buy a transformer equipped with overload protection. Check with your electrical supplier when you purchase the chime and the transformer, and read the literature supplied with the chime and transformer for this information.

Observe several precautions when connecting a transformer to its power supply. First, although the bell circuit is low voltage, the supply circuit is a full 120 volts, so disconnect power to the doorbell system at the circuit panel before beginning this job. Test the doorbell system to make sure that the power is off.

The National Electrical Code prohibits running low-voltage bellwire in the same electrical box with power conductors, unless there is a metal divider separating the two types of wiring. Attach the transformer to the outside of a junction box, and make the supply-side connections inside the box. Make the connections with wirenuts then attach a face cover to the box.

To connect the chimes to each other, you'll need bellwire which is rated to carry a maximum of 30 volts. It's available as individual insulated wire or in cables containing up to five color-coded wires.

The National Electrical Code has rules governing the installation of low-voltage cable to ensure that none of the low-voltage wires become charged with house current. Keep bellwire more than 2 in. away from light and power conductors. Do not install bellwire and power conductors in the same conduit or allow bellwire to become exposed to the power conductor.

Connecting the Transformer

With the power disconnected, remove the junction box cover and disconnect the power leads to the transformer. Next, remove the wires on the face of the transformer that run to the existing chime. Note which colored wire was connected to which terminal, so you can replace them in the same order on the new

3 Attach the chime wires to the new transformer. Use the wires' color code to position them as they were before.

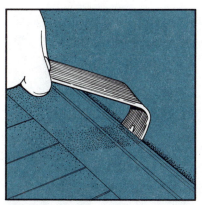

4 Remove baseboard under new chime. Pry with a flat bar and avoid denting the wall. Pull nails from behind baseboard.

5 In wall behind baseboard, cut a 2-in. square with a razor knife. Remove the drywall to gain access to the wall plate.

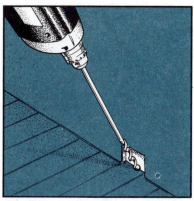

6 Using an extra-long ¼-in.-dia. auger bit, bore a hole through the plate to run bellwiire up from basement.

transformer. Loosen the nut that holds the transformer to the box and remove the transformer.

Mount the new transformer with its power supply side facing the junction box knockout. Run the transformer's wires through the knockout and tighten the nut on the inside of the box (Fig. 1).

Connect the power leads and ground wires with the appropriate size wirenuts (Fig. 2). The new transformer will probably have a ground wire where the old transformer probably did not have one. Hook the transformer's ground wire, the power source ground and a connecting ground wire together with a wirenut. Attach the connecting ground wire to the grounding screw in the side of the junction box. This applies to metal junction boxes only, not plastic boxes.

Replace the box cover and connect the two wires to the face of the transformer (Fig. 3).

Running the Wire

In general, plan the wiring route to be economical and to create the least disturbance in the wall and ceiling. The primary obstacles to overcome are the top and bottom wall plates and, of course, the floor.

Locate your new chime on an interior wall so you won't have to contend with insulation when you route the wiring. Examine the wall to determine if it is free of obstructions. Plumbing fixtures, heating and cooling registers, lights and electrical outlets on either side of the wall indicate that the wall contains mechanical services which may get in your way as you run the bellwire.

Remove a section of the baseboard directly below where you will locate the new chime. With a flat prybar, gently pull the baseboard away from the wall without piercing the wall surface (Fig. 4). Then, pull the nails through from behind the board with locking pliers.

Next, remove a 2-in. square of wall material at the floor to reveal the bottom plate of the wall framing (Fig. 5). Using a ½-in.-dia. auger bit, bore a hole through the bottom wall plate and the subfloor (Fig. 6).

Hold the new chime's mounting plate on the wall, directly above the hole in the floor. Use a plumb bob or level, if necessary, to position the plate above the hole in the floor. The chime must be mounted within the same stud cavity as the hole in the plate and subfloor. Trace the mounting plate on the wall with a pencil, including the location of the mounting holes and the larger hole for the bellwire (Fig. 7). Since the chime is located over a cavity and not a stud, you must drive screw anchors into the drywall and attach the plate by screwing into the anchors. Bore the holes for the screw anchors and a ⅜-in.-dia. hole for the bellwire (Fig. 8).

Run a fishtape through the hole for the wire and feed it through the wall cavity, the hole in the wall and into the basement. Attach the end of the fishtape to the bellwire and pull up the fishtape and bellwire through the hole for the chime (Fig. 9).

Next, insert the screw anchors in their holes. Remove the bellwire from the fishtape, and thread the bellwire through the mounting plate. Attach the plate to the wall with the mounting screws (Fig. 10).

Strip the insulation from the bellwire cable and from the individual wires, and attach the wires to the chime terminals (Fig. 11). Make note of the colors of the wires and the terminal screws to which they're attached. Then, route the wire to the primary chime.

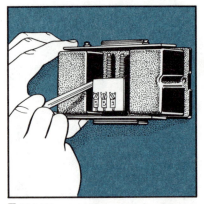

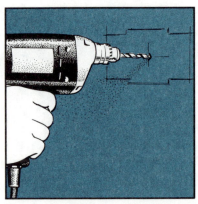

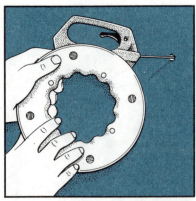

7 Hold the mounting plate for the new chime against the wall and mark the holes for the bellwire and screw anchors.

8 Bore a ⅜-in.-dia. hole for bellwire and bore a pair of holes for screw anchors to attach the chime mounting plate.

9 Insert the fishtape's end into the bellwire hole and run tape into basement. Connect the bellwire to the tape and retrieve it.

Running Wire Between Chimes

You should run the wire as directly as you can from one chime to the other. Fasten the wire to the underside of the floor framing with insulated staples, without piercing or crushing the wires.

Next, remove the cover from the existing chime (the old chime), unhook the bellwires—noting their position—and remove the unit from the wall. You should be able to use the holes in the wall for the original bellwire to fish the new line.

Remove the baseboard directly below the chime, and pull the nails through as before. Remove a section of the wall material and bore a hole down through the subfloor. Then, feed the fishtape into the hole at the chime and down through the hole in the floor.

Hook the wire from the new chime to the end of the fishtape, and pull it up to the old chime. Install the chime, replacing the old wires from where they came.

Attach the new wires on top of the existing wires. Both old and new wires should run between the same terminals on each chime. The screws are labeled on the chime as *front* (for the front doorbell), *rear* and *trans* (for transformer). The wire than runs from the *front* terminal on the new chime should connect to the *front* terminal on the old chime, and the same for the other wires.

Replace the baseboards, fastening them with 6d finishing nails and putty over the nail holes. Turn the power on and test the system. If the doorbell works, snap on the chime face covers. If not, check the chime and transformer connections.

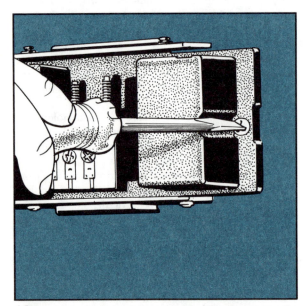

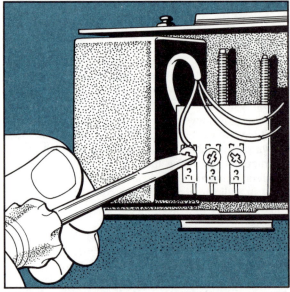

10 Feed the wire through the mounting plate, then screw the mounting plate to the wall. Avoid crimping the bellwire.

11 Strip the insulation from the bellwire cable, then from individual wires. Screw individual wires to chime terminals.

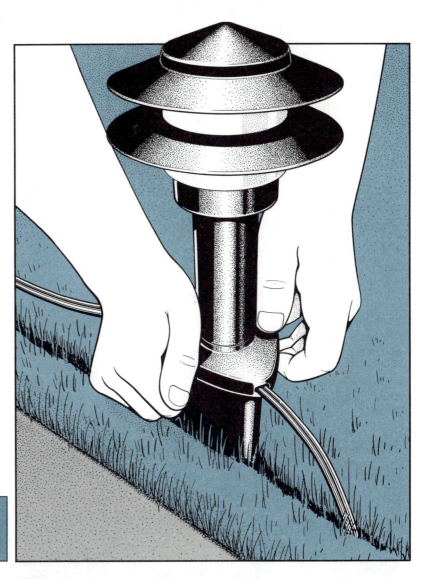

Low-Voltage Lighting Installation was written by Merle Henkenius. Illustrations by George Retseck. The low-voltage installation shown is an 8-lamp Malibu kit made by Intermatic, Inc., Spring Grove, IL 60081.

Low-voltage lighting installation

■ Low-voltage outdoor kits are safe and easy to install, so much so that little knowledge of electricity is required.

When shopping for a low-voltage landscape lighting kit, you'll quickly find there are two distinct price categories. Retail outlets catering to the do-it-yourselfer offer inexpensive kits ($50 to $80), featuring a limited variety of lamp heads, usually six to eight.

Specialty lighting outlets, by contrast, are likely to offer a better quality system that may or may not come in kit form. These systems offer greater creative flex-ibility when it comes to mixing and matching heads for specific effects, but are substantially more expensive. A single head might cost as much as an entire kit at your local hardware store.

If you're planning a more elaborate landscape lighting design, the high-end systems are clearly worth considering. If you're not planning such an elaborate design, and you are a little timid around electricity anyway, the more modest kits are simpler and easier to install. Because each landscape lighting kit is self-contained, there is no chance that you'll install more lights on a system that it was designed to support.

The Components

The model chosen to show here is an 8-lamp kit. It has four floodlamps and four 2-tier walk lamps. The kit also includes 100 ft. of buriable cable and a control box that houses a transformer (voltage reducer) and built-in timer. The timer automatically turns the lights on and off according to the times you set. The control box accesses house current with a standard 3-prong plug, so that no 120-volt wiring is required.

While the control box is weather-tight and can be installed outdoors, indoor installations are also worth considering. As most kits come with convenient 120-volt plugs, you'll be able to plug them directly into an outdoor receptacle. The problem, of course, is that an outdoor receptacle, having flip-up weather caps, is only water resistant when the caps are closed.

With a transformer plugged into the receptacle full-time, one cap will remain up, exposing the receptacle to driving rains. While most LV kits are installed this way, and are generally acceptable to local codes, an indoor receptacle would avoid the problem entirely. From a basement, utility room or garage, it's easy enough to bring the low-voltage end of the system outdoors, leaving the higher-voltage end sheltered indoors. Both methods are included here. As with any outdoor installation, the receptacle you tap should be ground-fault circuit interrupter (GFCI) protected.

Planning and Layout

Before purchasing a lighting kit, you'll want to consider factors of layout and design. Lamps to be positioned along a walk or drive are standard with each kit, as are floodlights. If you have a deck, you also might consider a kit that offers deck lights. Cable for the deck lights can be fed up through the deck and stapled along the underside, out of harm's way.

Some manufacturers offer a range of different heads that can be adjusted or focused in a number of different ways to yield more dramatic results. Plan your layout after you determine the best location for the control box. If sidewalks and other landscape obstructions will be a factor, position the box on the favorable side of the obstruction.

Measure from your control box location to each lamp location to determine how much cable and how many lamps and lamp styles you'll need. These factors will influence the type of kit you choose. Be sure to check your local codes to see if they have any specific requirements for low-voltage installations.

Installing Your Kit

Begin the project by mounting the control box on a wall within a foot or so of the chosen receptacle. If mounting the box outdoors, position it at least a foot above the ground. Then, to protect the cable from damage, encase it in conduit from the box to just below ground level.

The same is true if you're installing an indoor box. Bore through the rim joist or wall of your home and bring cable through the hole. Then, encase the exposed outdoor cable from the rim joist opening to

1 When using an outdoor receptacle, hang box at least 12 in. above ground. Protect cable to ground with conduit.

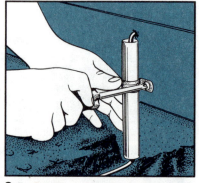

2 To bring cable from an indoor control box, bore a hole through rim joist or wall and feed the cable through the hole.

3 Protect the cable drop by running it through conduit. Be sure to secure conduit to building with conduit strap.

4 To fasten low-voltage cable to control box, turn box upside down and bind each cable wire under a screw terminal.

5 To mount control box, drive screw into wall (and stud behind) leaving 1/8 in. of shank exposed. Hang box on screwhead.

6 To set timer, adjust dial to current hour. Then, lift pegs from timer and reset them in desired ON/OFF indicator slots.

below ground. You'll also want to caulk the cable opening.

With low-voltage wiring, the conduit need not be joined to a line box or be weather-tight. The object here is to protect the cable from assault by garden tools or pests.

Assembling Lamp Heads

All kits will require some lamp assembly, but don't be intimidated. It'll be a simple step-by-step procedure. In the kit shown here, the walk lamps came in several pieces; a ground stake, extension riser, bulb socket and electrical leads (with self-piercing cable clip), and the globe.

Start feeding the electrical leads through the riser tube and into the stake. It's generally easier to make the cable connection before attaching the bulb and globe. Therefore, feed the cable through the opening in the stake platform and slide it through until it reaches the planned tap location on the cable.

The cable connections on most kits are incredibly easy. Each set of lap leads contains a channel with self-piercing cable taps built-in. Just lay the cable into the channel and slide a small plastic shunt over it. As the shunt forces the cable down into the channel, the taps pierce a wire in each side of the cable and make contact.

Then press the channel clip into a slot in the stake and tuck the cable neatly under the platform. With the electrical connection made, fold any excess lead wire into the riser and press the lamp socket onto the riser. Follow by inserting the bulb and twisting the globe onto the socket base.

When assembling a spotlight, you'll need to feed two leads through a bridge that spans the head and holds the bulb.

With the leads in place, press a bulb into the bridge and snap the bridge onto the head, with the bulb facing the back of the reflector. Then, snap the lens in place and fasten the head to its stake.

The electrical connections will resemble that of the walk lamps, but the cable will eventually be draped up one side of the stake and down the other when installed. If these cable loops are in a heavy traffic area, it's a good idea to tape them against each side.

Burying Cable and Setting Heads

When it comes to burying the cable and setting the lamp stakes in place, you'll have several choices, and may wish to combine methods.

You might choose to slice through the sod and lay the cable into the trench. In this case, you dig a small hole for each lamp stake. Then set the stake and replace the

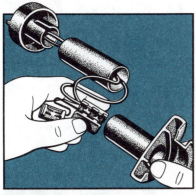

7 Begin lamp assembly by sliding connector leads (attached to clip) through riser tube and into platform of stake.

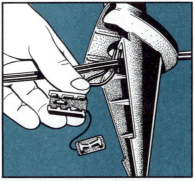

8 Feed cable through stake platform to the desired location. Then, remove cover from cable clip to expose contact points.

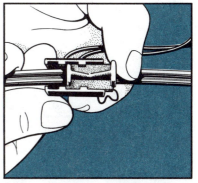

9 Lay cable into channel on cable clip and slide the plastic cover into place so cable is pierced by contact points.

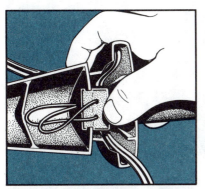

10 Press the cable clip into its slot under the stake position. Then, tuck the excess cable neatly into the platform recess.

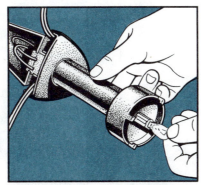

11 Once the cable is secured, insert the bulb into the socket until you feel it seat against its contacts.

12 After tucking excess leads into riser tube, slide the globe over the lamp socket tabs and twist until globe seats.

sod along the trench. In areas where frost heaving might push up the stake in winter, you can pack the stake hole with gravel and cover the gravel with sod.

If you use this method, keep in mind that newly laid sod requires special care. An easier and less destructive method is to slice into the sod with a flat-nose spade and pry the sod apart slightly. Then, use a paint stirring stick or dull putty knife to force the cable into the crevice so that it's well below sod level. To mount a stake in a similar fashion, slice a cross in the sod with your spade, then press the stake into the intersection of the two lines of the cross. When the stakes and cable are installed, tamp shut the gap in the sod.

A Deck Lamp Conversion

Special lamps are available to illuminate decks. The kit installed here offers a do-it-yourself conversion of a walk lamp into a deck-mounted lamp. The procedure is quite simple and is a reasonable alternative to buying a special deck kit.

To make this conversion, simply cut off a stake flush with its upper platform. Then, drill three small holes in the platform, attach the cable and screw the platform to the deck. The cable can be brought up through a space between deck planks, or you can drill a hole through the deck and feed the cable up through it. The cable should be buried until it passes under the perimeter of the deck. Once under the deck, staple it to the inner side of a support post and then to the underside of the deck timbers until you reach the lamp location.

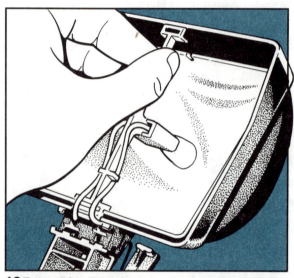

13 To install floodlights, feed wires through bridge and fasten bulb to center leg of bridge. Snap bridge onto lamp head.

14 Then, slide the lens into proper position over the floodlight's lamp head and snap in place. You should hear a click.

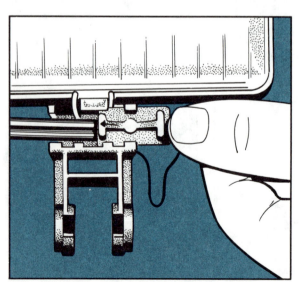

15 Again, lay the cable in the channel clip on the base of the floodlight and slide cover in place to make electrical contact.

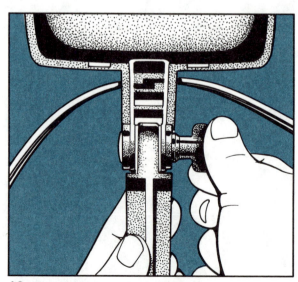

16 Mount floodlight head to stake with bolt and wingnut. Bolt and nut allow for on-site adjustment of light.

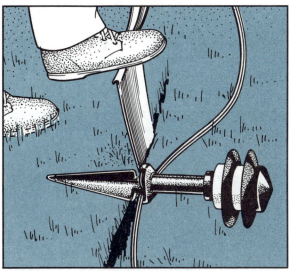

17 Lay cable, with lamps attached, along future path of lights. Slice through sod and pry seam open slightly.

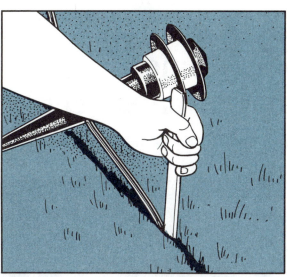

18 Force cable into spade opening with a paint stick or thin piece of scrap wood. Work gently to avoid damaging wire.

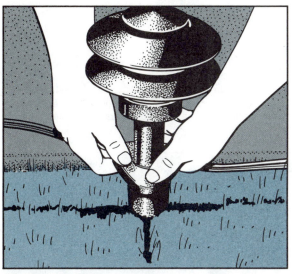

19 After making deep crosscut in sod, press stake into opening until its platform rests at ground level.

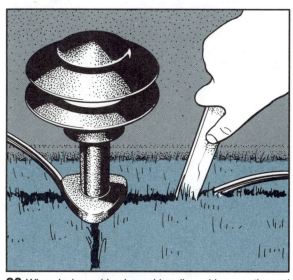

20 When laying cable along sidewalk or drive, pry the sod away from edge of asphalt or concrete. Then tuck cable into gap.

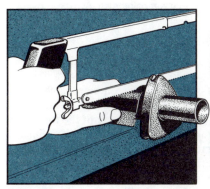

21 To convert a walk light into a deck light, cut off stake flush with bottom of unit's platform.

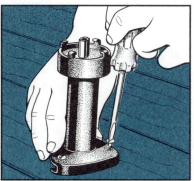

22 Make the electrical connection and slide excess cable into fixture tube. Then screw platform to deck out of harm's way.

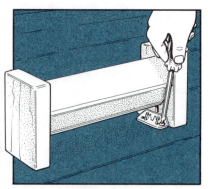

23 Dedicated deck lights are also available. To install, simply position where desired and attach brackets with screws.

Home improvement clinic

TECHNIQUES FOR FIVE COMMON PROJECTS

Home Improvement Clinic was written by Gary Branson. Illustrations by George Retseck and Don Mannes.

Clean away debris on damaged concrete with a wire brush. Concrete patch will bond poorly unless corner is prepared.

Use a paintbrush to apply concrete bonding adhesive to the damaged area. A synthetic bristle brush works best here.

Mix concrete patch in a disposable paint bucket, using a paint stirring stick. Apply patch with a flat knife.

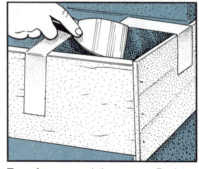

Tape form around the corner. Pack remaining patch into the form and leave the form in place until patch is dry.

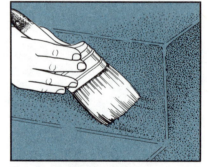

Remove form and smooth over patch with a wet paintbrush. Avoid patch until it is fully hardened in a few days.

REPAIRING CONCRETE STEPS

The corners on concrete steps tend to get cracked and damaged over the winter. This was once a tough repair, but today's concrete bonding products help make the job easier and increase the odds of a long-lasting patch.

Using a steel-wire brush, remove the loose concrete particles, working down to a firm surface. Next, apply a latex bonding liquid to the repair area (some concrete patch products contain this adhesive). In a cardboard mixing pail (available at your paint store), mix the concrete patch material. Use a paint scraper or trowel to apply the patch. Build up the patch until it's shaped roughly like the corner.

After the first application of concrete patch, place the wood form on the corner as shown, holding it in place with duct tape. Coat the inside of the form with oil to keep it from sticking to the concrete. Fill the form with concrete patch until you've built up a smooth, even corner.

While the concrete is still wet but firm, smooth the repair with a wet paintbrush. This also helps fill small voids in the concrete. Set up a ladder or other barrier to keep people off the step until the patch is dry.

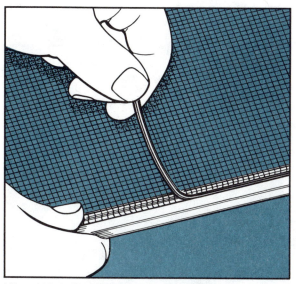

Lift up old vinyl spline using an awl or other sharp tool, then peel it out of the frame. Next, remove the screen.

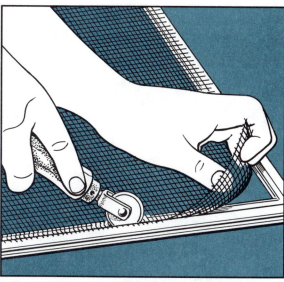

After slitting screen corners, place new screen over frame, and tape it down. Roll screen into frame with convex wheel.

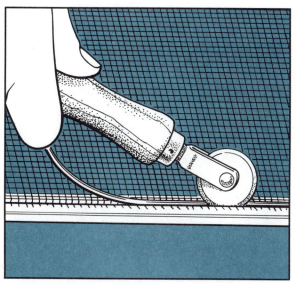

Cut new vinyl spline roughly to length. Then roll it into the frame with concave roller at opposite end of the spline tool.

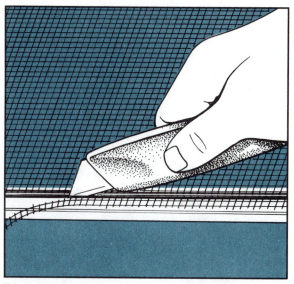

Trim off the excess screen using a razor knife. Press the knife's tip into the outside edge of the spline groove.

REPLACING A WINDOW SCREEN

Warm weather means it's time to throw open your windows, but it's also time to repair broken window screens. Start by buying a 2-wheeled spline roller, vinyl spline and screen at a hardware store.

Pry the vinyl spline and damaged screen from the frame groove using an awl or sharp knife tip. Discard the old spline, usually it is too dry and brittle to reuse (besides, new spline is inexpensive). Use a razor knife to cut a piece of screen slightly larger than the frame. Lay the frame on a table and the screen over it. Tape each edge of the screen to the table, and make a diagonal relief cut at the screen's corners, stopping at the frame groove. The relief cut prevents the screen from tearing at the corners or bunching up when it is rolled into the corner of the frame.

Press the screen into the frame groove on one side with the convex roller. This will cause the tape to pull loose from the table. Pull the screen tight from the opposite side and repeat the process. Do this on the other two sides. Press the spline into the groove with the concave wheel. Trim off excess spline and screen with a razor knife.

Water the damaged turf, or wait until after a rain when the ground is soft, to remove old grass from damaged spot.

Remove enough dead grass and soil so sod can be fitted into patch. Cut the sod to fit using an old kitchen knife.

Spread potting soil around patch to fill gaps and level the joint between old and new grass. Keep the sod watered.

REVIVING DAMAGED LAWNS

It's not unusual to find areas of dead grass on your lawn in the springtime. These dead spots are the result of snow being shoveled or plowed in deep piles along the driveway or street. Heavy, compacted snow, salt and other chemicals used to melt ice or snow kill small areas of grass. Fortunately, if these areas are attended to early in the growing season, they should be strong enough to withstand the withering weeks of late July and August.

To repair these damaged areas, wait until the ground is softer after a rain or watering. Then, scrape away the dead grass with a garden fork. Prepare the spot by loosening up the top layer of soil. Rake the soil smooth. Ask your lawn and garden dealer to recommend a gypsum soil conditioner, and apply it to the areas according to the product's label directions.

Reseed and fertilize the area, or cover it with sod. Sod is good to use on slopes, where seeds are liable to be washed away. Avoid walking on the grass and cutting it until you are sure it has firmly taken hold. Whether you sod or seed the area, water the patched area well to get the grass off to a good start.

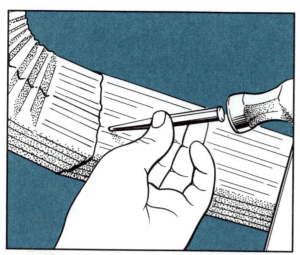

Use a metal punch to make a small dent over where you want to drill. Dent holds drill bit as it bites into metal.

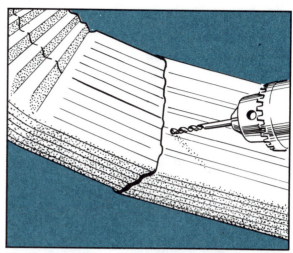

Run the drill at slow speed and don't force the cut. High-speed, high-pressure drilling can overheat the bit, dulling it.

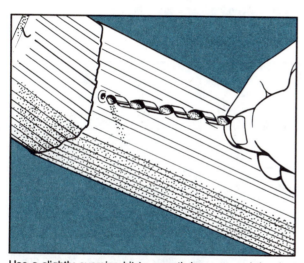

Use a slightly oversize bit to smooth burrs around the rivet hole. Lightly turn the bit with your fingers.

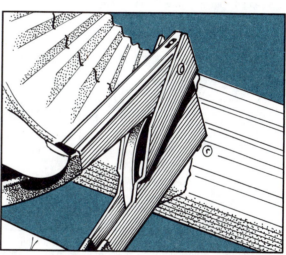

Fasten parts together with one or two aluminum rivets. On downspouts, top part always goes inside part below it.

REPAIRING RAIN GUTTERS

Here are a few tips to get gutters back in shape for the summer rains.

Variable-speed electric drills are great for gutter work because you can set them at low speeds. High drill speeds are fine for woodwork, but a fast-turning bit will spin on a gutter downspout or gutter bracket without cutting.

Mark where you want to drill with a metal punch. The dent left by the punch holds the bit while it bites into the metal.

Use pop rivets to joint gutter components together. Usually only one or two rivets are necessary to hold pieces together. To remove a rivet, just drill out its head with a ⅛-in.-dia bit. Run the drill slowly until you have drilled through the rivet head. Remove the head and punch out the rivet shank with a metal punch. Seal all repairs to the gutter with silicone or other suitable caulk.

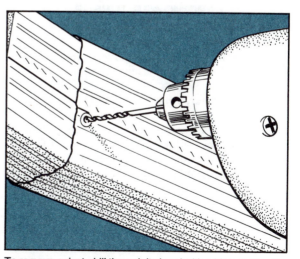

To remove a rivet, drill through its head with a bit matching the rivet's diameter (usually ⅛ in. dia.).

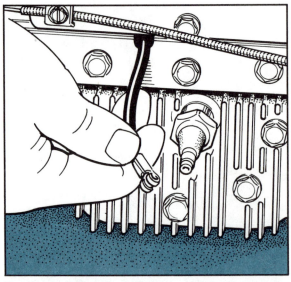

To prevent accidentally starting the mower, begin tuneup by removing the ignition wire from the spark plug.

Use a screwdriver to loosen the slotted bolt that holds the air cleaner. Clean the filter element or replace it.

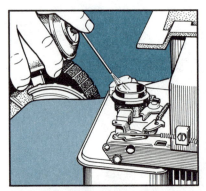

Spray aerosol cleaner such as Gum-Out into carburetor throat and on linkage. Lightly oil linkage after cleaning it.

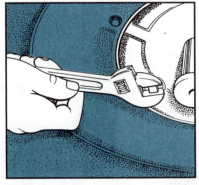

To drain oil from mower, remove the drain plug on the underside of the mower deck. Refill crankcase with fresh oil.

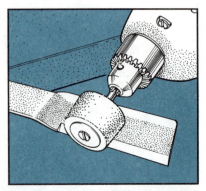

Sharpen the mower blade with an abrasive drum chucked in an electric drill. If blade is badly nicked, replace it.

LAWNMOWER TUNEUP

You don't have to be a professional mechanic to give your lawnmower a preseason tuneup. If your mower won't start, it's usually one of three things: The spark plug is fouled, the air filter is clogged, or the carburetor is dirty.

Unlike your car, which has multiple spark plugs, your lawnmower has only one. Because small-engine spark plugs work so hard, they frequently become fouled. Buy several spark plugs at once. Clean or replace the plug at the first sign of poor starting.

Remove the ignition wire from the plug, then use a socket wrench to remove the plug. Check the plug's electrode to be sure it is not burned or dirty. Clean the plug's electrode with fine sandpaper, or replace it. Leave the plug disconnected.

Unscrew the bolt that holds the air cleaner. Take the top off the cleaner, and remove the air filter element. Replace it or clean it in warm water and detergent. Squeeze it dry.

Spray a cleaner such as Gum-Out over the carburetor and its linkage. Lightly oil the control cables and linkage, and reinstall the air filter.

Remove the oil drain plug (near the shaft and mower blade) and change the oil. Drain the old oil into a pan and return it for recycling.

Index

METRIC CONVERSION

Conversion factors can be carried so far they become impractical. In cases below where an entry is exact it is followed by an asterisk (*). Where considerable rounding off has taken place, the entry is followed by a + or a – sign.

CUSTOMARY TO METRIC

Linear Measure

inches	millimeters
1/16	1.5875*
1/8	3.2
3/16	4.8
1/4	6.35*
5/16	7.9
3/8	9.5
7/16	11.1
1/2	12.7*
9/16	14.3
5/8	15.9
11/16	17.5
3/4	19.05*
13/16	20.6
7/8	22.2
15/16	23.8
1	25.4*

inches	centimeters
1	2.54*
2	5.1
3	7.6
4	10.2
5	12.7*
6	15.2
7	17.8
8	20.3
9	22.9
10	25.4*
11	27.9
12	30.5

feet	centimeters	meters
1	30.48*	.3048*
2	61	.61
3	91	.91
4	122	1.22
5	152	1.52
6	183	1.83
7	213	2.13
8	244	2.44
9	274	2.74
10	305	3.05
50	1524*	15.24*
100	3048*	30.48*

1 yard =
 .9144* meters
1 rod =
 5.0292* meters
1 mile =
 1.6 kilometers
1 nautical mile =
 1.852* kilometers

Fluid Measure

(Milliliters [ml] and cubic centimeters [cc or cu cm] are equivalent, but it is customary to use milliliters for liquids.)

1 cu in = 16.39 ml
1 fl oz = 29.6 ml
1 cup = 237 ml
1 pint = 473 ml
1 quart = 946 ml
 = .946 liters
1 gallon = 3785 ml
 = 3.785 liters
Formula (exact):
fluid ounces × 29.573 529 562 5*
 = milliliters

Weights

ounces	grams
1	28.3
2	56.7
3	85
4	113
5	142
6	170
7	198
8	227
9	255
10	283
11	312
12	340
13	369
14	397
15	425
16	454

Formula (exact):
 ounces × 28.349 523 125* = grams

pounds	kilograms
1	.45
2	.9
3	1.4
4	1.8
5	2.3
6	2.7
7	3.2
8	3.6
9	4.1
10	4.5

1 short ton (2000 lbs) =
 907 kilograms (kg)
Formula (exact):
 pounds × .453 592 37* = kilograms

Volume

1 cu in = 16.39 cubic centimeters (cc)
1 cu ft = 28 316.7 cc
1 bushel = 35 239.1 cc
1 peck = 8 809.8 cc

Area

1 sq in = 6.45 sq cm
1 sq ft = 929 sq cm
 = .093 sq meters
1 sq yd = .84 sq meters
1 acre = 4 046.9 sq meters
 = .404 7 hectares
1 sq mile = 2 589 988 sq meters
 = 259 hectares
 = 2.589 9 sq kilometers

Kitchen Measure

1 teaspoon = 4.93 milliliters (ml)
1 Tablespoon = 14.79 milliliters (ml)

Miscellaneous

1 British thermal unit (Btu) (mean)
 = 1 055.9 joules
1 calorie (mean) = 4.19 joules
1 horsepower = 745.7 watts
 = .75 kilowatts
caliber (diameter of a firearm's bore in hundredths of an inch)
 = .254 millimeters (mm)
1 atmosphere pressure = 101 325* pascals (newtons per sq meter)
1 pound per square inch (psi) = 6 895 pascals
1 pound per square foot = 47.9 pascals
1 knot = 1.85 kilometers per hour
25 miles per hour = 40.2 kilometers per hour
50 miles per hour = 80.5 kilometers per hour
75 miles per hour = 120.7 kilometers per hour